I0220324

Le Pastiche Tintin 2

222 'Lost' Tintins

*"As a fictional character, Tintin can never really die,
but did you wonder what would happen if he aged?"*

~Mick Sleeper

Hommagé

John C. Stringer

2020

Collector's Edition, Vol. 2

See Vol. 1 *Le Pastiche Tintin: 111 'Lost' Tintins* (2019),
Plates 1-111, pages 1-177.

© **Le Pastiche Tintin 2, 222 'Lost' Tintins**

Les Non-Aventures de Tintin; Collector's Edition, Vol. 2.

First edition, Vol. 2. 2020.

Text and layout © the author John © Stringer, except for brief quotations and referential illustrations credited in the text, under "criticism, review, and news reporting" and "fair dealing" with sufficient acknowledgement (United Kingdom, Commonwealth, America) New Zealand *Copyright Act 1994* (Public Act 1994 No. 143) and its amendments, especially s. 42.

First published, in New Zealand and USA, May 2020 by *Maiden New Zealand*. All rights reserved. Printed in Australia by *IngramSpark*.

Artwork: cover and p. 179, 180, 233 a, b © John Stringer. Back cover detail from Plate 170 author unknown and left, Plate 234 "Kachka." Frontispiece pencil sketch p. 178 © *Moulinsart*; p. 185; 186 © Bob de Moor; p. 187 © Dubus. All other artwork © as noted in the text and in specific credits page 456 including pastiche covers which are © the respective individual artists producing art of "Tintin" after Hergé, in his style; most unknown.

Library of New Zealand archive, acquisitions and legal deposit, Wellington 6011, POL-80431

ISBN 978-0-473-52166-0

Le Pastiche Tintin 2

222 'Lost' Tintins

Maiden New Zealand

Hommagé

John C. Stringer

2020

Collector's Edition Vol. 2

Contents

Below: *Tintin* magazine #43 and 112, 18 August 1949 and 14 December 1950 published by Raymond LeBlanc. A French book *Le Journal Tintin* by Dominique Maricq traces the history of the magazine (Moulinsart, 2012).

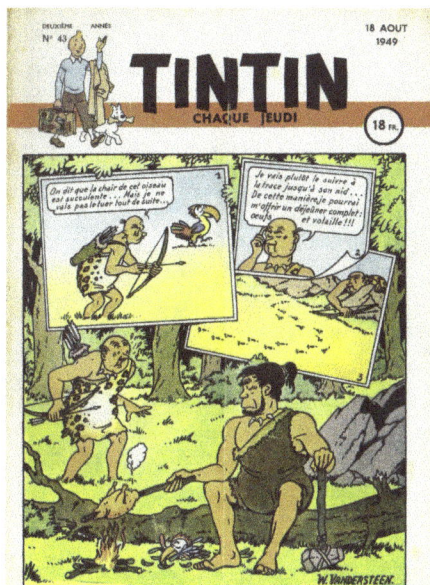

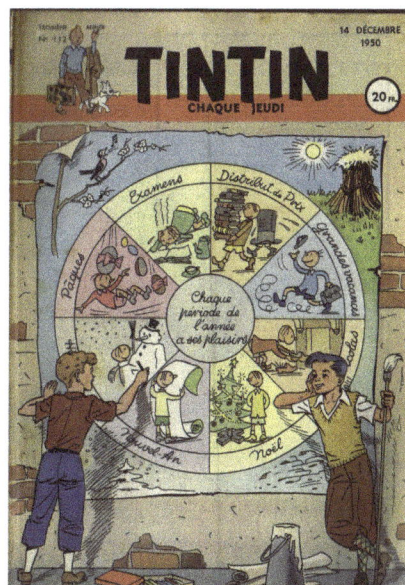

1. The Hergé Canon

The Hergé canon of 24 books in created order, 1930-1983:

1. **TINTIN IN THE LAND OF THE SOVIETS** (1930)
2. **TINTIN IN THE CONGO** (1931, redrawn 1946)
3. **TINTIN IN AMERICA** (1932, redrawn 1945)
4. **CIGARS OF THE PHARAOH** (1934, redrawn 1955)
5. **THE BLUE LOTUS** (1936, redrawn 1946)
6. **THE BROKEN EAR** (1937, redrawn 1943)
7. **THE BLACK ISLAND** (1938, redrawn 1943 and 1966)
8. **KING OTTOKAR'S SCEPTRE** (1939, redrawn 1947)
9. **THE CRAB WITH THE GOLDEN CLAWS** (1941, redrawn 1947)
10. **THE SHOOTING STAR** (1942)
11. **THE SECRET OF THE UNICORN** (1943)
12. **RED RACKHAM'S TREASURE** (1944)
13. **THE SEVEN CRYSTAL BALLS** (1948)
14. **PRISONERS OF THE SUN** (1949)
15. **LAND OF BLACK GOLD** (1951)
16. **DESTINATION MOON** (1953)
17. **EXPLORERS ON THE MOON** (1954)
18. **THE CALCULUS AFFAIR** (1956)
19. **THE RED SEA SHARKS** (1958)
20. **TINTIN IN TIBET** (1960)
21. **THE CASTAFIORE EMERALD** (1963)
22. **FLIGHT 714 [TO SYDNEY]** (1968; 1975)
23. **TINTIN AND THE PICAROS** (1976)
24. **TINTIN AND ALPH-ART** (1983 unfinished; notes and pencil sketches 1986).

Non-canonical animation books drawn like the other adventure editions.
25. **Tintin and the Blue Oranges** (1964)
26. **Tintin and the Lake of Sharks** (1973).

Musée Hergé, the Tintin museum in Louvain-la-Neuve, Belgium, funded by the Hergé estate.

2. Tintin Reverb, 222 'Lost' Tintins. Vol. 2.

In this second volume, I gather together 222 new Tintin tributes and pastiches from across the globe. This brings the collected works in Vol.s 1 and 2 to 333. A third volume (a fresh 333) will bring this to a final 666 pastiches.

There are now "*Thousands of Thundering Typhoons*" (pastiches) so a careful curation has been necessary. I have not, for example, filled this second volume with cheap 'cut-n-paste' *Photoshopped* covers (polyploids) whereby bits of Tintin art are simply gene-spliced on to something else, although inevitably that occurs. There are hundreds of those (at least 45 for *Shooting Star* alone; 40 for *Congo*; and many more for *Alph-Art*). Polyploids have little merit.

Instead I've selected pastiches with some sort of creative value. These are: either a reinterpretation of an existing adventure (such as *Tintin in America, Tintin in Tibet* or *Les 7 Boules de Cristal*); new art altogether (*Tintin in Quebec,* the *Spain series;* the *Lagoon* series; *Mission Antarctique*); a twist on an old idea (*Tintin in Stalingrad* or *Valley of the Cobras*); or the reworking of a fun idea (Tintin inserted in to *Star Wars* or the *Marvel* universe). Pastiche artwork needs to add value in some way to the genre of Tintin. Based on the fan response to Vol. 1, the international inter-generational love affair with Tintin living on in pastiches, remains undiminished. Look out for Vol. 3 in 2021.

Exposing Tintin to developments in the twenty-first century is also meritorious, such as Mars travel (**Plate 243**); transgenderism (**Plate 254, 319**); or the Middle-East as it is now (**Plates 227-236**). Inevitably Tintin and Haddock would have been the first to Mars and Snowy the first Martian dog. These are realities of our century Hergé would have engaged with, in his century, either directly or obliquely. It makes sense for pastiches to transpose Tintin here; similarly, in to locations he missed during the twentieth century.

As with Vol. 1, I've avoided sexualised Tintins, especially the pornographic ensembles best consigned to the dust bin. Alongside omissions there are welcome inclusions: an interview with pre-eminent pastiche artist Yves Rodier of Quebec; Harry Edwood's *Voice of the Lagoon* as well as *some recent Moulinsart/Casterman* collaborations, such as the colouring of *Land of the Soviets* and the tentative production of *Thermozéro*.

Vol. 1 began with *Alph-Art* the most parodied of all the adventures, so I do not return there (except for *Alf-Art*, **Plate 125** and *Omega Art* **Plate 254**). Instead I begin this volume with an additional 12 *Tintin in America* adventures, given Hergé wanted Tintin to visit America first in 1929 but Abbott Wallez packed him off to the Soviet Union first instead (for good Catholic propaganda purposes). As well as a generous bite of the Big Apple, Tintin visits: China, Chile, Switzerland and even Pluto. There is WWII Normandy (**Plate 252**) and a companion Bosnia (**Plate 146**). Tintin meets *Batman* (a relationship expanded in Vol. 3) and the American comic theme is expanded with Tintin communing with other comics, such as *DC* and *Marvel*. This culminates in a wedding at **Plate 224** of pop culture characters over which he officiates. that helped shape or were shaped by Tintin. (See also **Plates 121a,b** and **305**).

The geography in Vol. 2. widens. As well as 12 new *America* adventures, there are ten to the Middle-East; eight to England plus Ireland and Scotland. *Tibet* is revisited in seven pastiches; six in France; four adventures in Spain; and Asia gets a good look in, including Japan and Vietnam. Edgar P. Jacobs' duality with Hergé continues with various pastiches entwining Hergé and Jacobs characters and ideas. We go off-world too, even to Pluto, but also to *Star Wars*, tangle with robots, and explore UFOs and science fiction themes touched on in Vol. 1. This volume also revisits literary or movie allusions: *Harry Potter* [**Plate 260**], Tolkien [**Plate 279**], *The Time Machine* (*Back to the Future*) [**Plate 312**]. As the coronavirus Covid-19 deepens its grip on the world as I write, Tintin is even in Wuhan, China where the virus began in an animal market [**Plate 328**. See also **Plate 154**].

A note on how the 222 plates (Vol. 2) are arranged.

Plates are noted at top right and page numbers are at the bottom in the middle following on from Vol. 1 (2019). An **Index of the 222 Covers, Vol. 2** at the very back follows the index approach of Vol. 1 (see 1: p. 50). To help locate particular pastiches, they are arranged generally in alphabetical order by topic, title or theme (America, England, Mars, etc). Use the Index to locate artworks.

This is complex, as many of the covers are titled in different languages: English, French, Dutch, Danish. Translations are therefore provided in English as close as possible to a likely Tintin title rather than an absolute literal translation. Possible English translations are indicated at the bottom of each plate and in the index where necessary.

Alphabetical chronology is sometimes set aside to arrange some titles in obvious thematic clusters such as: the Mars adventures; America covers; the Middle East; France; ships; robots; *Star Wars*; etc, regardless of the main subject of each title. In other cases I have arranged similar pastiches side by side, such as the *'Coc en Toc'* roundels **[Plates 187-189]** which naturally sit together visually. This is done to equate the different pastiches with their natural visual companions rather than with the arbitrariness of translated titles, which are only organised in a general sense alphabetically to provide some structure. Some titles are gibberish anyway.

This Vol. 2 (2020) is twice the size of Vol. 1 (2019) and adds an additional 222 to the catalogue, bringing the combined pastiche, polyploids and parody covers to 333. Look for the final *Vol. 3, 333 'Lost' Tintins* in 2021 which will bring the entire collation to a final 666, a figure Edgar P. Jacobs would have been proud of (**Plates 109, 323**).

It's an eclectic romp of *"Jumping Jellyfish...Great Snakes,"* I hope you enjoy it.

John © Stringer, New Zealand, 2020.

Page 185 and left, working sketches by Bob de Moor.

3. New Tintins?

As discussed in *"Copyright Conundrums and Controversies,"* Vol. 1: p. 36, new adventures and copyright controversies have been vexed since Hergé died in 1983. There was *"fretting over the way his legacy is being managed...a long-running saga in Belgium."* Proposals to "complete" the unfinished 24th canonical adventure *Alph-Art,* by both Bob de Moor and Yves Rodier, were fraught. Both started and then stopped. Digital copies were bootlegged. There were some court cases involving Bob Garcia. Moulinsart was rather aggressive in attempting to freeze the brand and own all applications of the Tintin imagery, *"an abuse of powers as regards the cultural existence of the works* [with commercial rights]."

Above: a parody by Dubus in a Belgian newspaper shows Tintin pleading *'Let me go, Mr Rodwell, the children await me!'* who answers in front of his Moulinsart Inc Scrooge McDuck vault, *"No way, you belong to us!"* Reprinted in the *Sydney Morning Herald* 30 October 2015. The Hague courts later cast doubt on who owned copyright: Moulinsart or Casterman. The Tintin scene is transposed from *Crab with the Golden Claws,* p. 11.

That rigidity has softened in recent years, perhaps as resignation to the reality of the tsunami of international pastiches and the desire of fans for more with or without Moulinsart, or as a result of recent Hague court outcomes over ownership rights. Vlamynck, Rodwell and the estate trustees have loosened a rigid interpretation of Hergé's desire for no further adventures after his death. This affects three new possibilities at an official estate level: 1) a colouring of the first *Soviets* annual which was only ever published in black and white (unlike the other 23 volumes); 2) a new *Thermozéro* adventure, an unfinished storyline that Hergé at first developed for Tintin but shifted over to *Jo, Zette & Jocko;* and 3) a lavish book on the production of *Cigars of the Pharaoh.*

Colouring *The Land of Soviets*

After 1983, relations between Moulinsart and Tintin's long-standing publisher Casterman had even soured. In more recent years a new editorial director came to Casterman, 37-year-old Benoît Mouchart, former director of the Angoulême International Comic Festival. Mouchart worked on rebuilding bridges with Moulinsart. This culminated in Rodwell, Mouchart and other Tintin aficionados sharing a stage together at the Angoulême Festival, publicly discussing Hergé's legacy and possible future projects.

Mouchart achieved a sponsorship arrangement between Casterman and Musee Hergé. This led to a lavish co-production being agreed featuring the original black and white strip cartoons with the colourised annual art of *Cigars of the Pharaoh*. Then came a collaboration to colour the first adventure, the black and white *Tintin in the Land of Soviets*. Initially some test pages were done in sepia. Two copies were eventually produced in 2017, one by Casterman and one by Moulinsart (below; and see the two covers Vol.1: 29, top right and bottom).

Hergé had several projects over the years which, for one reason or another, never got off the ground: from *Tintin in the Far North*, an early tale of the Arctic ice floes (see **Plates 126-128**), to *One Day in an Airport*, in which his characters flow through an adventure in the confines of a terminal building. As well as the official republishing of *Soviets* and the *Cigars* feature, perhaps the most interesting developments are these unrealised Hergé's storylines. There exists a tentative agreement between Casterman and Moulinsart to publish an unfinished work by Hergé in the tradition of the *Alph-Art* posthumous project.

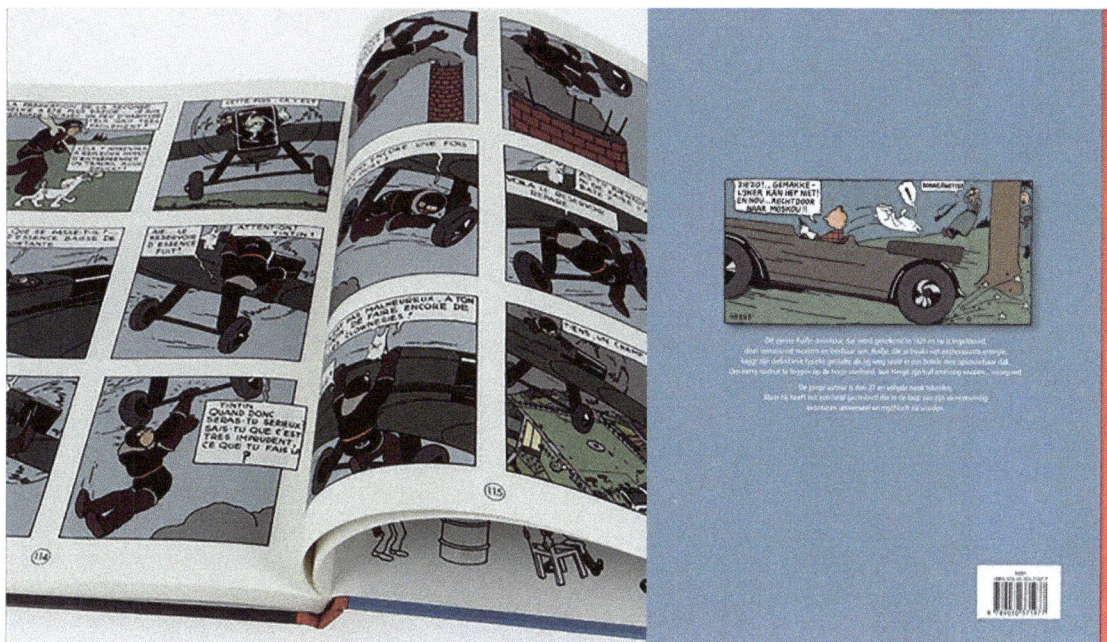

Thermozéro

Thermozéro was an unfinished story that sat contextually between *Tintin in Tibet* (1960) and *The Castafiore Emerald* (1963). After his labours on the very successful *Tibet,* Hergé was a bit burned out, and probably suffered another bout of depression that sapped motivation and inspiration. He'd read a 1957 article in *Marie-France* magazine (*La peur qui vient du futur,* "Fear from the Future") by Philippe Labro, about a mishap in a Texas laboratory that contaminated two families with radioactivity (themes developed at this time in the *Fantastic Four, The Hulk* and *Spiderman* by Stan Lee).

Hergé fleshed the idea out and set it in a Cold War context. He added British double-agents Burgess and Maclean (a nod to *Blake & Mortimer*) and the Bird Brother villains from *The Secret of The Unicorn.* He then threw in a Russian scientist for good measure. Half a dozen scripts were developed but, *"I felt trapped in a straitjacket that I couldn't get out of. I need to be constantly surprised by my own inventions."* [1]

Hergé was always strongly committed to story and knew the success of Tintin was due at first to story and only secondly to the art. Story always had precedence, which is why he made and kept such copious notes, and thoroughly researched ideas. He agonised over story ideas. Eventually he spoke with comics writer Michel Régnier [a.k.a "Greg"] the later editor of *Tintin* magazine, to see if he could massage the idea further. Greg initially came up with *Les Pilules* ("The Pills"). This evolved in to a Hitchcock type international crime cartel romp, with chases across Europe ending in Berlin, much like the *Bond* movies. Greg then replaced the radioactive pills with an ultra-cold chemical material below absolute zero (-273°C). He called this material "Zero Heater" which Hergé changed to "Thermozéro." It was a kind of elemental comic precursor to the fictional metal alloy *adamantium* of *Wolverine* fame.

In the script, Tintin sees a pedestrian knocked over by a car. As the man is dying, he slips a note into Tintin's jacket and a mystery unfolds. But Hergé felt the idea was too close to *The Calculus Affair,* and after he'd completed eight story-boards, he abandoned the idea. This may have been related to Hergé's inability to allow lieutenants creative responsibility, as with his refusal to credit Jacobs with co-production of the early books. The film *The Lake of Sharks* had also been written by Greg, and Hergé had not been entirely satisfied with *Sharks.* Along with his statement that Tintin absolutely cease unless he was involved, we perhaps see a glimpse of perfectionist control. Hergé was probably uncomfortable playing illustrative second fiddle to Greg's writing, Jacob's pencils, or anyone else, for that matter. Tintin was his, even if talented assistants did a lot of journeyman-draughting and 'fleshing-out.'

Yet, Hergé appears to have actually liked the story in part. Perhaps he was annoyed he hadn't thought of it and struggled to work within someone else's framework (which Jacobs did so faithfully for him, while working on his own

[1] Hergé on *Lemonde,* 17 July 2015, Frédéric Potet and Cédric Pietralunga, 'Tintin et le Thermozéro, l'œuvre inachevée d'Hergé" [archive].

ligne claire serialisations and annuals). This is understandable. A character like Tintin is very much a part of the DNA of a cartoonist and evolves as the artist works, growing in the telling and the drawing. Working under someone else's plotting may have diminished his interest in the character.

Hergé passed the idea on to studio lieutenant Bob de Moor to re-adapt as an idea for *Jo, Zette & Jocko*, Hergé's second-string series. De Moor re-sculpted *Thermozéro* past the eight Hergé storyboards but it was once again shelved. Instead *The Castafiore Emerald* emerged. It's been said, that without *Thermozéro*, *The Castafiore Emerald* would never have existed. Like '*Airport*,' which morphed into *Alph-Art*, *Thermozéro* morphed into *The Castafiore Emerald*.

Tintin in Tibet had pushed the books in a whole new direction and broken new ground. *Thermozéro* was a return to spies, secret messages and European car chases. Depressed as he was, maybe Hergé felt Tintin was going backwards. Ever the perfectionist, he was grasping for inspiration, trying to push Tintin forward on a creative upward trajectory (as if going to the Moon had not been enough!). This is perhaps why a UFO appears in the very next adventure, *Flight 714* and kidnaps Tintin, Haddock, Calculus and takes away some key second-tier characters (Allan and Rastapopoulos).

It was perhaps a feeling of repetition that got to him. *Thermozéro* might actually have been the best thing for him after all, as he began to work out his own non-Greg plot as an antithesis to *Thermozéro*, a book in which nothing happens, set entirely within the confines of Captain Haddock's mansion. *The Castafiore Emerald* was the result, one of the critics' most praised adventures.

Thermozéro remained on ice until after Hergé's death.

Three years later, in 1986, Bernard Tordeur published some of Bob de Moor's pencilled *Thermo.* artwork in a biography of de Moor by *Lombard*. Tordeur was the senior archivist at Studios Hergé before the shift over as "Moulinsart." In 2014 it was revealed the whole story had in fact been completed. Not as fully finished art, but fully plotted with lots more artwork by de Moor than was realised. Tordeur suggested there was sufficient art for it to be published, along the lines of *Alph-Art*. Apparently this had nearly been done after Hergé's death.

Thermozéro and *Alph-Art* had both stopped when the studio had dismantled, and staff were let go. The mindset never to allow any new work per Hergé's wishes became entrenched as gospel. Then in the mid 2010s, the new husband of Fanny Vlamynck, Nick Rodwell, intimated new adventures *could* be possible. Casterman immediately confirmed their interest. Another adventure in progress like *Alph-Art* emerged, rather than a finished pencilled and coloured adventure by another artist like Bob de Moor or Yves Rodier. This is eventually what happened, and an official *Thermozéro*, like the *Alph-Art*, was published.

Like de Moor pencilling *Thermozéro* as a *Jo, Zette & Jocko*, Rodier had also played with *Thermozéro*. He re-pencilled and inked several pages of Hergé/ de Moor *Thermozéro* drafts before abandoning the project. Others have then had a go at colouring Rodier's inks.

Following pages 192-195: original Hergé/de Moor sketches for *Thermozéro*. Yves Rodier re-drew and inked copies of these (see Rodier's full-page spread "29/150") which others such as Henri Blum later and independently coloured (**Plates 301-304**).

Below, a panel of Nami Rai's version of *Thermozéro* re-drawn and coloured from Hergé/de Moor and Rodier pencils and inks. See **Plate 301**.

ET LE THERMOZERO — Nami d'après Hergé

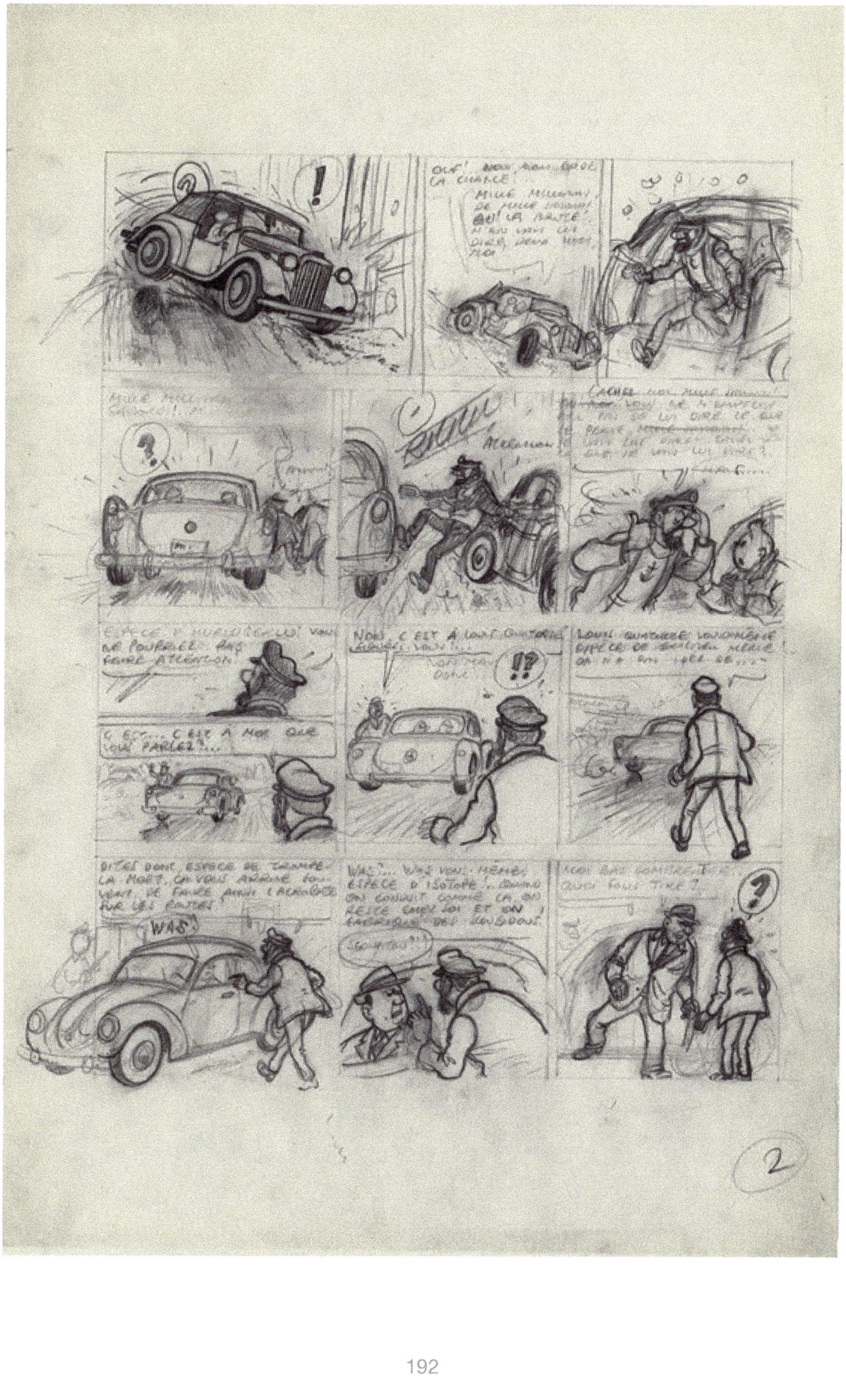
!
?
C'EST... C'EST À MOI QUE VOUS PARLEZ?...
!?
WAS
ESPÈCE D'ISOTOPE!..
?
2

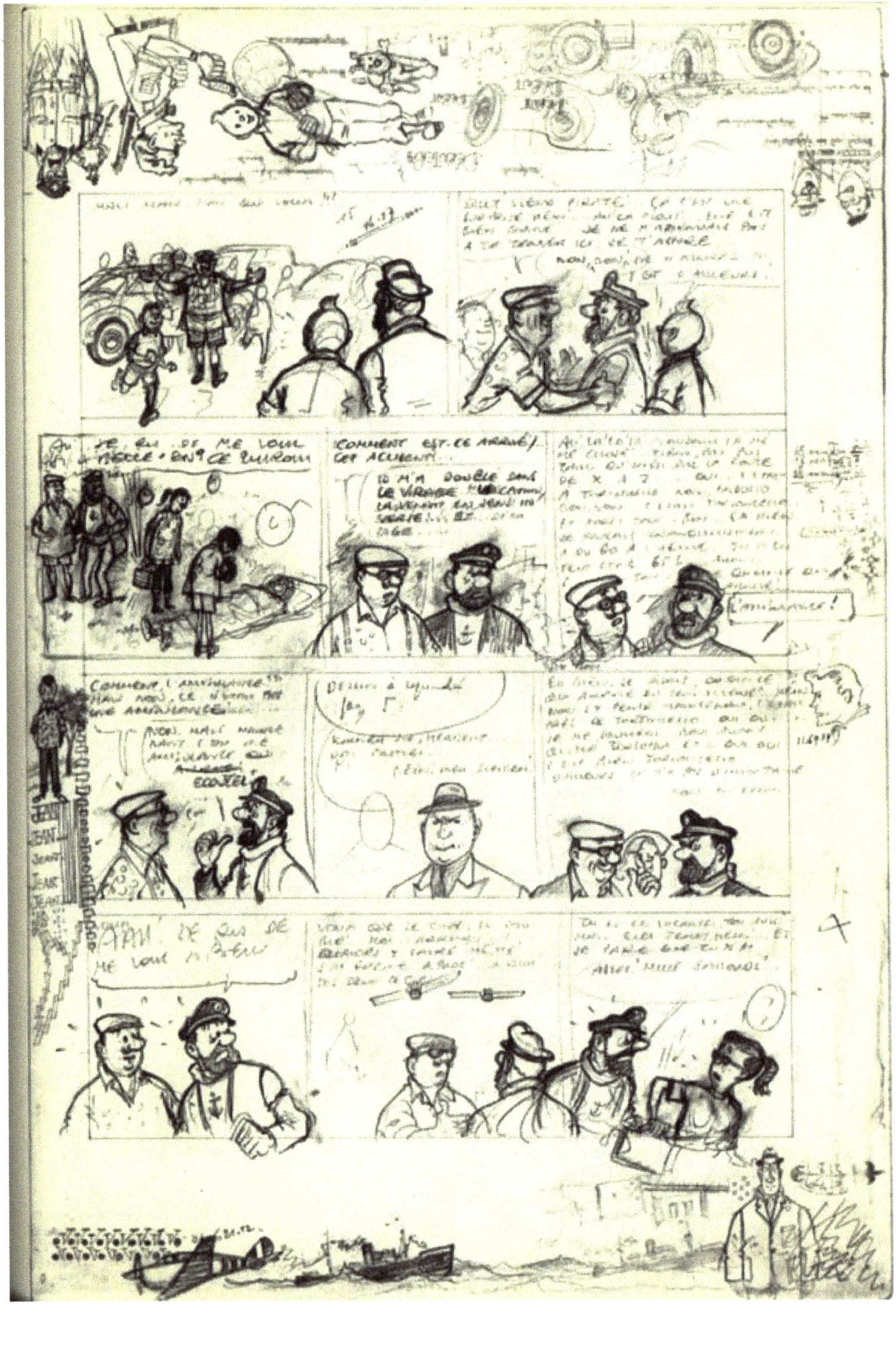

Hergé/de Moor *Thermozéro* sketches.

4. Tintin's Parents and Ancestry

Hergé was Belgian. Tintin exists within the French comics tradition but has American antecedence. Several commentators have noted Tintin's androgyny. There is also never any mention of his parents. He is therefore a kind of *Pippi-Longstocking* character. There is also a general absence of women or any romantic connections. Castafiore is perhaps the only real female connection for Tintin other than his early landlady before Marlinspike. Paternity is therefore of interest.

Plate 131 answers this intrigue. I suggested in Vol. 1 that Jacqueline Rivière and Joseph Pinchon's 1905 Breton handmaid *Bécassine* was a source for Tintin, certainly his pin-prick eyes as well as the idea of annuals. In Plate 131 *Bécassine* is depicted with Tintin in a pram holding a toy *Destination Moon* rocket 'neath the title *Mother of the Family (Mere de Famille)*.

The same applies in **Plate 136** where we have *Bécassine* again as mother and Haddock as father (or uncle?) at the birth of Tintin (*La Naissance de Tintin*). Snowy is also present so must be a very old wire-haired fox terrier. On the wall is Haddock's ancestor Red Rackham which may suggest Tintin's paternity.

In **Plate 265** an aged and overweight Tintin wheels his geriatric 'father' Haddock and an exhausted Snowy about in a retirement home wheelchair, *La Résidence du Soleil*.

In **Plate 226** we are actually shown his parents as well as puppy Snowy at their first meeting, *Tintin et Milou la Rencontre*. So those three pastiche artists all suggest a Tintin paternity of Haddock and *Bécassine*. **Plate 209** using Plate 227 shows Castafiore and Haddock watching home movies with Tintin.

However, I consider Tintin's *real* father to be the American rags-to-riches character *Jiggs* from *Bringing Up Father* drawn by American cartoonist George McManus and later assistants. It would explain why Hergé was so keen to export Tintin first to America, rather than the Soviet Union and then the Congo, as prescribed by Abbot Wallez. Hergé loved American comics and copied them.

Plate 306 (and see over) shows Jiggs as leader of a group of characters in a *Tintin in Tibet* tableau, with his cane, top hat and vest. Next to him is *Bécassine*. They are looking at a ligne claire in the snow instead of yeti tracks.

Below: *Bringing Up Father*, one of the longest running daily strips. Original art, "9-21" 1976, *Kings Features Syndicate* (artist Kavanagh Camp). 14 x 43cm.

Detail from **Plate 306**.

THE TINTIN FAMILY and COUSINS: 1) George McManus' *Jiggs* (*Bringing Up Father*). 2) *Bécassine*.
3) Edgar Jacob's *Mortimer*. 4) **Alix** drawn by Jacques Martin, one of Hergé's studio assistants.
5) *Monsieur Tric* drawn by Bob de Moor. 6) a Tintin-esque *Freddy Lombard* by Yves Chaland.
7) *Lambique* from Willy Vandersteen's *Bob & Bobette* (Dutch: *Suske en Wiske*, see 1: p. 49).
8) *Jojo de Pojo* by Joost Swart. 9) *Ray Banana* by Ted Benoit. 10) *Dick Hérisson* by Didier Savard. Next
to him is "**Chang**" the Pekinese dog from *Tibet* p. 6 (who also appears in Plates 53, 244, 306).
11) **Hergé** himself with his green arts folder (see *The Adventures of Hergé*, 1: p. 12). 12) *Alfred* the pet
penguin from *Zig et Puce* by Alain Saint-Ogan (below). 13) The hatted duck is **Gédón** by Bengamin
Rabier a true early source for Tintin, see 1: p. 9). 14) finally we have **Bicot** (Winnie Winkle) by Martin
Branner. Below: French progenitors and influences on Tintin, *Zig et Puce*.

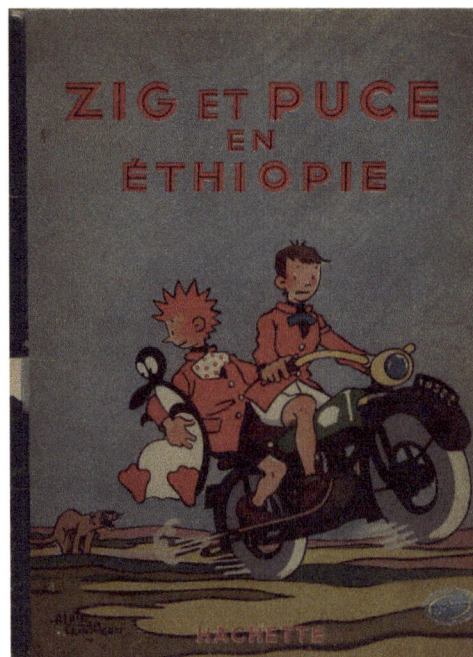

Jiggs (married to Maggie, the comic was also known as *Jiggs & Maggie*) was an immigrant Irish-Catholic American, a former hod carrier (or "hoddie"), the labourer who brought bricks to the bricklayer on site. Jiggs won the lottery and became rich. His cartoon antics revolve around attempts to reconnect with his former working class lifestyle away from the influence of his social climbing wife Maggie. The "Bringing Up Father" refers to Maggie's attempts to "lift" Jiggs up her aspirational social ladder.

In America, Jiggs represented Irish-Catholic 'low-brow' sensibilities set against Maggie's upper middle-class Irish-American desire for mainstream assimilation and acceptance. That dichotomy was quite pronounced in Irish Catholic ethics and vaudeville music of the times, as that ethnic group sought to establish an American identity alongside their Irish heritage (see *Gangs of New York*, 2002). Abbot Wallez and the young and impressionable Georges Remi would have been acutely aware of such themes as the leading Belgian Catholic newspaper of the time, concerned with such cultural aphorisms. It suggests a strong link and probably a direct influence between *Jiggs* and *Tintin*. George McManus also drew in a clean-cut cartooning style with solid composition inspired by Art Nouveau and Art Deco. I have already suggested the younger Georges Remi copied this style directly. *Bécassine* and *Jiggs* are strong prospects for Tintin's 'genetic parents' in terms of what formed him and how he looked. The other characters in Plate 306 are all ligne claire cousins of Tintin. We have here the 'family' with *Bécassine* as matriarch and, I suggest, *Jiggs*, as patriarch.

Bécassine is the true mother of French comics and the pioneer female character of the art form with a long publication legacy. She was created in 1905 by artist J. P. P. Pinchon (1871-1953) and writer-publisher Caumery alias Maurice Languereau (1867-1941). The beautifully coloured *Bécassine* stories were compiled into popular hardcover albums beginning in 1913. She is drawn in Breton peasant attire and clogs and originates from Finistère, a region strongly associated with traditional Breton culture. However, she also exhibits Picardy costuming, altogether a stereotypical un-Parisian provincial peasant. This was after all, the readership for the girls' magazine *La Semaine de Suzette* for which *Bécassine* was designed.

Carrying this caprice forward, we can suggest Tintin was born in Finistère, or Picardy, and was therefore provincial. His mother was *Bécassine* and his father an American traveller. We know Hergé copied *Bringing Up Father* to hone his art. *Bécassine and Bringing Up Father*, with other American strip comics such as *The Kinder Kids, The Katzenjammer Kids, Count Screwloose from Tooloose* and *Mutt & Jeff* were the creative progenitors of Tintin. Perhaps 'the jig is up' and we can suggest Jiggs is Tintin's dad.

5. Tintin's Cousins

Plate 47, Vol. 1: p. 108.

Blake & Mortimer (1946)

Edgar Jacobs who worked extensively on Tintin was discussed at length in Vol. 1. *Blake & Mortimer* was his parallel series from 1946 serialised in *Tintin* magazine and was also published in book form by *Lombard*.

Set in England and beautifully drawn, the main characters are somewhat bland, scientist Philip Mortimer and his friend Captain Francis Blake of MI5 who battle Colonel Olrik. It is a Conan Doyle *Sherlock Holmes* detective type series but is rich in science-fiction. There are 28 volumes, 26 of which have been translated in to English. It also had a television series.

Of interest is the frequent fusion of *Blake & Mortimer* imagery, ideas and titles within Tintin pastiches. See **Plates 141, 152, 181, 201 and Section 8: A, B, I, N.**

Lucky Luke (1946)

Above: *Tintin* ambles across Arizona in the attire he wore for *Tintin in America* with his Morris (and later Goscinny) American cousin *Lucky Luke* accompanied by the white *Snowy* and white *Jolly Jumper*.

Like *Asterix the Gaul*, *Lucky Luke*, "the man who shoots faster than his shadow," is another highly successful Belgian comic, but a western cousin to Tintin, written and drawn by Morris in a more free-flowing cartoon style more like *Asterix*.

Lucky Luke arrived sixteen years after Tintin, from 1946. In 1955 Lucky's creator Morris was joined by René Goscinny the writer of *Asterix* and they collaborated on text and art until 1977 when Goscinny died young. Morris died in 2001. It was drawn thereafter by French artist Achdé with the assistance of various writers.

Up to 2019 there have been 81 albums or special editions (*Dupuis, Dargaud* or in comic format by *Lucky Comics*). Like *Tintin, Lucky* was at first serialised as a comic strip in magazines (*Spirou* 1946-1967; *Pilote* 1967-1973; *Lucky Luke* 1974–75; as well as in the French edition of *Tintin* magazine 1975–76; and many others).

Lucky Luke has been translated into 23 languages; about half of the editions are in English and like *Tintin* and *Asterix,* has crossed over into other media such as live action or animated film.

Oumpah-pah the Redskin (1958)

Oumpah-pah, an onomatopoeia, was a serialised precursor to *Asterix* by creators Uderzo and Goscinny (*Oumpah* was something of an early *Obelix*). It appeared in *Tintin* magazine weekly 1958-1962. *Dargaud* and *Lombard* published books from 1961 and it was reissued by *Les Éditions Albert-René*. It is the Indian flip side to *Lucky Luke.*

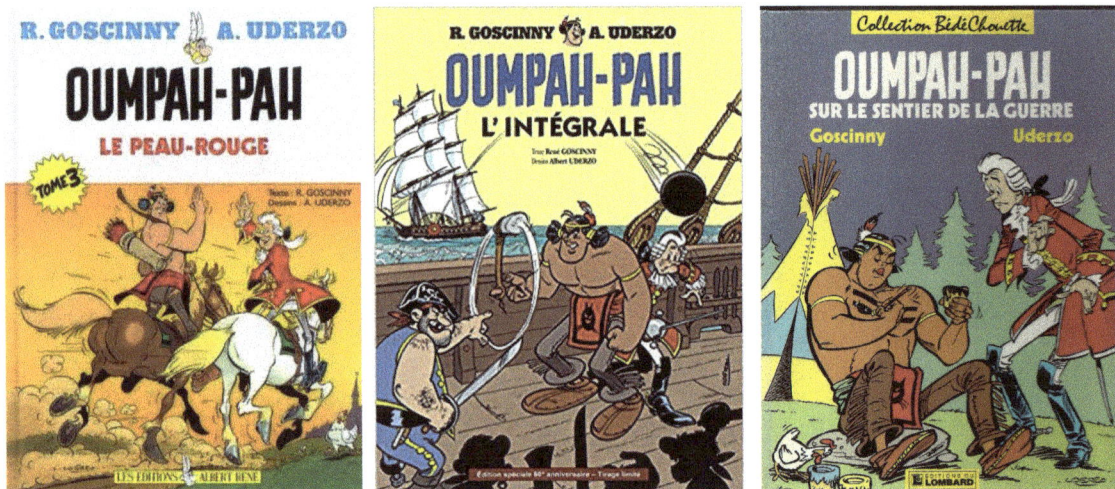

Asterix the Gaul (1959)

After *Tintin, Asterix* is easily the best known of the Franco-Belgian exports, and little needs to be said here. It began like its cousins as a serialised comic in *Pilote* among others, from 1959, so after *Lucky Luke* and *Oumpah* but before *Iznogoud.* It was written by Goscinny and illustrated by Uderzo, perhaps one of the finest of the Belgian cartoonists, who, like Tabary, continued writing as well as drawing the cartoon himself after the original writer died. It was serialised in Britain in *Valiant, Ranger* and *Look & Learn* magazines but Asterix was made into an ancient Briton called *"Beric the Bold"* or *"Little Fred and Big Ed"* and set in Roman-occupied Britain rather than Gaul. In 2020 American publisher *Papercutz* intends to publish all new American translations.

The comic survived the deaths of both writer and artist and continues to this day under other hands, such as Jean-Yves Ferri (script) and Didier Conrad (art). There are 38 volumes up to 2019, 14 more than *Tintin.*

Above: Serialised Asterix as *Beric the Bold* of ancient Briton (not Gaul) in British *Ranger* magazine 6 *November, 1965.*

Left, a Tintin-Asterix fusion series by Manga artist Kaka Nami Rai (see also p. 191).

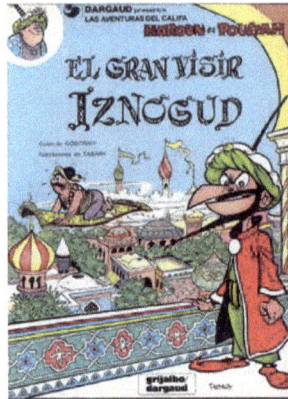

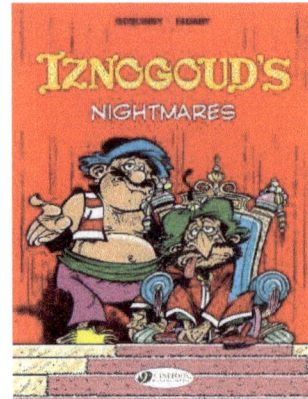

Iznogoud (1962)

Iznogoud ("Is No Good") is a lessor-known French cousin from across the border drawn in a more angular cartoon style by Jean Tabary but written by René Goscinny (*Asterix* and *Lucky Luke*, 1955-1977). The comic is based in Baghdad and like *Lucky Luke* rides the deserts, except *Iznogoud* has Aladdin type adventures in the East. His side kick in English is *Wa'at Alahf* ("What a Laugh").

Iznogoud followed *Lucky Luke* by 16 years, in 1962, the same number of years *Lucky* came after *Tintin*, so there were 32 years between *Tintin* and *Iznogoud* (1930, 1962). The Iago type character of *Iznogoud* was initially a secondary character, but was so strong, he took over *Les Aventures du Calife Haroun el Poussah* and was renamed "Iznogoud." Like the other Franco-Belgian comics, it began as a serialised cartoon in magazines like *Pilote*.

After Goscinny passed away, Tabary wrote as well as drew the cartoon. During Goscinny's era, *Iznogoud* was a series of shorter stories, but under Tabary it was written as a single thematic adventure book more like *Tintin*. It too has been adapted to film. There are 29 graphic annuals and 26 have been published in English.

The Bluecoats (1968)

In 1968 after *Lucky Luke* moved from *Spirou* magazine to *Pilote*, writer Raoul Cauvin invented a new western comic for *Spirou*, drawn by Louis Salvérius and later Willy Lambil.

Les Tuniques Bleues ("The Bluecoats") was set in the U.S. Civil War at Fort Bow, featuring principally cavalry Sergeant Chesterfield and Corporal Blutch. Much of the scenario was about the stupidity and cynicism of war, along the lines of the later *Catch 22*.

There are 63 books with 13 in English.

6. Tintin's Uncles

Bob de Moor

Bob de Moor was an assistant to Hergé from 1951 (*Destination Moon*) and a draughtsman working on research sketches, the books, and the animation of *Tintin*. De Moor's great skill was his ability to adapt seamlessly to Hergé's style and "draw Tintin." When Hergé died he pencilled up some pages for the unfinished *Alph-Art* initially with the support of Hergé's widow, Fanny. But she relented and the project was stopped. He then supported Yves Rodier in the same project, also without success.

De Moor drew many sketches for *Thermozéro* as discussed above. He worked alongside Jacobs in the *Hergé Studio*, and completed the unfinished Blake & Mortimer *Professor Sato's Three Formulas* (p. 209) after Edgar's death as he had tried to do for Hergé. Since de Moor's death, his friend Yves Rodier has drawn up and inked some of these sketches and paints the drawings as original coloured works for collectors.

De Moor drew many of the ships for Hergé because of an earlier professional interest in ship draughting. A year before Hergé's death he illustrated the Belgian band *The Machines*' album cover "A World of Machines" (1982).

STUDIOS
HERGÉ
S A

AVENUE LOUISE 162/ B\S 7 · 1050 BRUXELLES · TEL 649 20 42

NOTE D'ENVOI

Le 29 avril 1983.

A REDACTION DU JOURNAL TINTIN
EDITIONS DU LOMBARD
avenue P-H. Spaak, 1-11
1070   BRUXELLES

De - 11 coloriages de M. TRIC "Une course de
        ballons mouvementée" de 2 à 12

   - 2 coloriages de "QUICK ET FLUPKE"

   Veuillez avoir l'amabilité de nous retourner
   ce matériel après usage.

   Amicalement.

   BoB DE MooR.

                              Studios Hergé

Top right: early de Moor sketches. *Below*, a precious monogram from a 1991 luncheon between Bob de Moor and Yves Rodier. See here: http://www.bobdemoor.info/2014/05/14/yves-rodier-talks-about-bob-de-moor-his-death-filled-me-with-sadness.

CHOUETTE !
ENFIN L'ALPHART !!

A YVES,
EN SOUVENIR
D'UN ENTRETIEN
SYMPA.

BOB DE MOOR.

28-9-91

Yves Rodier

One of the best pastiche artists and one who tried his best to respect the Tintin heritage and work with the Hergé Foundation/Moulinsart, is in my opinion Yves Rodier. He stands out as following the spirit of Tintin himself, swimming in a *Lake of Sharks*.

Yves works in Quebec and has produced several 'official' Tintins, with the support of Hergé assistant Bob de Moor before his death. It was not to be. Yves pencilled a complete *Tintin and Alph-Art* and invented an ending (Hergé never got to one). After this was rejected alongside de Moor's previous efforts in pencil discontinued by Fanny Vlamynck, Rodier inked and coloured it and re-presented that. It too was rejected. So he committed them to a CD ROM and made his work available to select friends and a few collectors, promising Moulinsart he would never publish the 24th adventure, which he has not.

Unfortunately, his CD ROM was pirated and some unscrupulous entrepreneur published the artwork in book form and then translated it into English. These are sold online pretending to be official 24th adventures, which they are not. They are Rodier's coloured artwork based on Hergé's notes and sketches and republished without either's permission.

Those developments got Moulinsart offside with Rodier (who was not treated well) because he was suspected of surreptitiously publishing the adventure. But that was not the case. Disillusioned, Yves moved on, and created his own ligne claire adventures Simon Nian (see Vol. 1, p. 23) as well as *El Spectro* (below). He has drawn several pastiche Tintin covers (see **Plates 6a-8**, Vol. 1; **150, 222, 304, 327** Vol. 2).

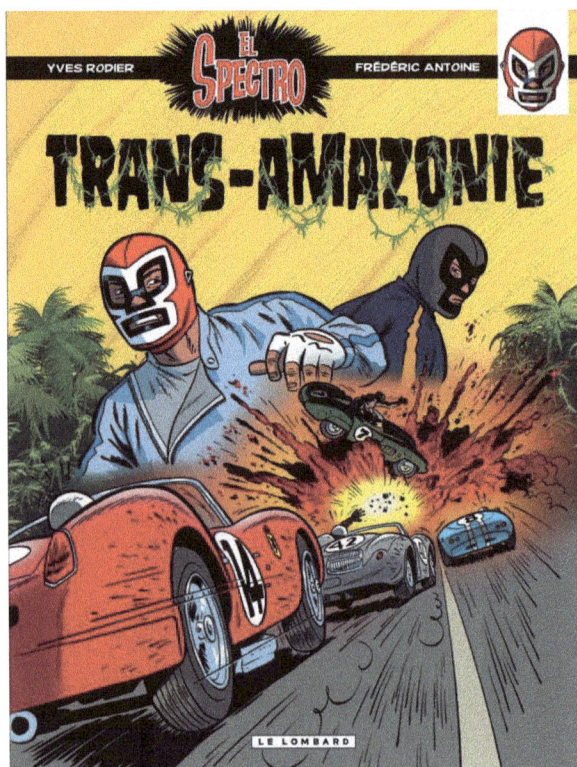

An interview with Yves Rodier, *"Tintin's spiritual son."*

1) What is your first memory of Tintin?

We had a lot of Tintin books in our home before I was born. My brothers are 13 and 12 years older than me so I always saw Tintin books around. A funny memory I have is, when I was around five, my oldest brother swam to an island that was, maybe, a couple of hundreds metres from the beach where we were. When he came back, I asked him how it was over there. He told me there was a giant spider that chased him around but got squashed by a giant apple that fell from a tree! Years later, when I read *The Shooting Star,* I realised he'd been telling me a story.

2) What was the appeal to you, and therefore what do you feel is Tintin's generic appeal as a comic character?

At the time, I loved to travel with him, to live amazing adventures in the four corners of the globe. I guess today that appeal is gone for the kids who can chat with *Facebook* friends they have everywhere in the world. But back then, it really was an open window on a world of adventures. I also liked his values and morals, which are rather socialist. He inspired me to stand up for my friends who were being bullied by people bigger than them, and to try to be kind and helpful to everyone.

3) What form did your interest and passion for Tintin take, after that first encounter?

Tintin did shape my way of thinking and acting. I also looked forward to watching the Tintin cartoons and movies on TV every year at Christmas time. But back then I never dreamed I would become recognised worldwide as Hergé's "spiritual son."

4) Did you first start drawing Tintin at school?

No, not at school... Not really... I think I started drawing him on the blank pages at the end of the *Tintin* books... I still have a couple of those drawings in my old books. It wasn't a passion back then, I would just draw anything I liked, *Tintin, Astérix, King Kong, Star Wars,* etc.

5) How did you meet Bob de Moor?

I wrote to him around 1988 to tell him I was working on finishing *Tintin and Alph-Art* and that I would like to have some guidance on the tools and material to use (what metal tip pens, what ink, what brand of paper, etc). He very kindly wrote me back and gave me tips I'd asked for. I think we may have corresponded a couple more times after that. And then, in 1991, just a couple of months after I'd finished the book, I saw in a Québec comics magazine that he was to be a guest at a comic book festival in Brossard, a suburb of Montreal. I found out who the event planner was and asked him if I could meet Bob. The guy, Réal Fillion, who became a close friend and a mentor, invited me to the festival. When he went to introduce me to Bob, Bob said *"Yves Rodier? The guy working to complete Tintin and Alph-Art ?! Is he here?!"* I was astounded to see that he remembered me! Bob and I went to lunch that day. I showed him my work, listened to his advice and comments, and we even talked about working together one day! It was a magical day for me, the little guy who had no professional experience and was 'coming out of the woods,' to be recognised by such an important artist. Unfortunately, Bob passed away a year later and I never got to work with him.

6) What is your favourite Tintin adventure and why?

It depends. I love *Prisoners of the Sun* for its mix of exoticism and adventure. It's also the one I think back to more fondly when I think of my childhood. But as an adult, I love *The Red Sea Sharks*. It's a very complex story, full of world politics, human tragedy as well as exoticism and adventure. I think it's the most beautifully illustrated Tintin adventure. Everything is perfect, the locations, the cars, the planes, the horses, the characters, and the colours are also stunning.

7) Could you talk about the Witches Beast? [Plate 328]. Is the creature you've drawn 'Nessie' of Scotland? And why did you select this idea especially. Loch Lomond whiskey, Loch Ness?

My story has nothing to do with the Loch Ness monster or even with Scotland. It takes place in France, near Switzerland, and the monster is not a real one. I think the inspiration for this story came to me from an adventure of *Pif the Dog*, which appeared in the French magazine *Pif Gadget,* when I was little. It was called *The Ghost of the Camping Ground*. In this story, *Pif* helped the owner of a camping ground who was about to go bankrupt because of a ghost who was scaring away his customers. In the end, we learn that it was actually a bandit who disguised himself as a ghost. I realised the connections between the two stories years after I finished mine.

Spike & Suzy have a Loch Ness encounter on one of their covers, I guess it's a pretty common subject. *Les 4 As* by François Craenhals also has a book about it.

The Author's Favourite Tintins.

If Yve Rodier's favourite adventures are *Prisoners of the Sun* and *The Red Sea Sharks*, I could nominate mine. They are *Cigars of the Pharaoh* and *Tintin In Tibet*.

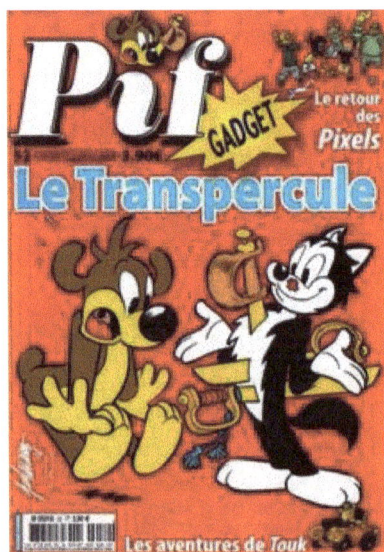

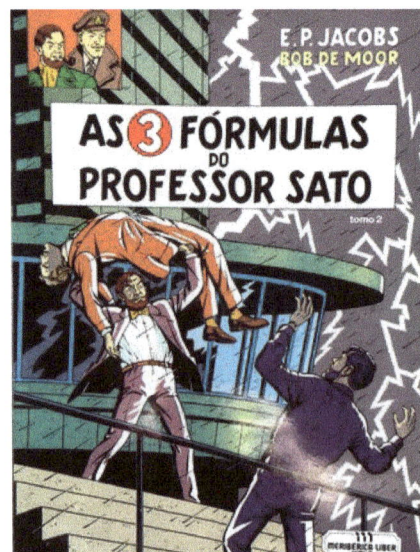

Cigars was one of the first adventures I came across as a child. I loved it for its exotic Egyptology and because it contains so many classic Tintin moments. The introduction of Calculus and Rastapopolous and the intrepid Thom(p)sons and Allan Thompson. There are all sorts of boat and ship escapades (eight different boats appear in *Cigars*, all beautifully drawn; in one scene Tintin escapes out a port hole and down a mast of a small boat alongside). There are also planes, racing cars, ambulances, a train, camel caravans and elephants. Edgar Jacobs is depicted as one of the strange mummies, and isn't that cover just so evocative of untold story? The characters adrift on the ocean in coffins is classic Hergé; the noble sheik with a copy of *Destination Moon* in his bedouin tent; armed Arabs on horseback in the desert ala Laurence of Arabia; the secret society in purple cassocks (see the Adesso version, **Plate 194**); the classic hypnotising fakir; the mental asylum; secret trapdoors in tombs and in tree trunks; the fake firing squad and burial that even fools Snowy. All these moments belong to *Cigars of the Pharaoh*.

Secondly, *Tintin in Tibet* for the sense of place, the paced journey through the rising Himalayas that takes Tintin out of his comfort zone; toying with the idea of a yeti (as Hergé does with a UFO in *Flight 714*, perhaps pushed by Jacobs); and the wonderful coloured 'cinematography' of the adventure itself. The loop with Chang paralleling Hergé's own life is a nice story arch where fiction meets non fiction; Haddock's heroism and character; and that evocative final panel of *Tibet* is one of the best in all of Tintin.

Harry Edwood *The Voice of the Lagoon*

After Rodier, my second favourite pastiche artist is the prolific Harry Edwood (Woodman). Edwood has produced dozens of pastiche covers, see Vol. 1, **Plates 14, 29, 48, 79-80, 94, 98, 103 ~**, and Vol. 2 **Plates 132, 182, 219~**.

Lagoon, originally "The O-Light Project" [**Plate 80**, Vol. 1] began many years ago when Edwood wanted to have Tintin scuba-diving, an obvious anomaly in Tintin except for the film *Tintin and the Golden Fleece*. Edwood worked the idea up as a Madagascar villains treasure romp, like Willard Price's 1968 *South Sea Adventure* with the Hunt boys. However, he felt it lacked sufficient drama.

Edwood wanted to try his hand at visual story-telling, something Hergé was very good at and worked at assiduously, refining and pruning till he had it just right. Many people can draw well, and mimic Hergé, but few are as good at story-telling. Narrative is important. Edwood sought for a simpler idea and one day it came to him – invent a talking fish! After many online fan title suggestions, "The Speaking Fish" settled as *The Voice of the Lagoon* which has more of a Tintin feel to it. In Peter Pan, Captain Hook and Mr Smee search the Mermaids Lagoon for the mysterious "voice of the lagoon."

Selecting the pretty Leopard Triggerfish as his subject was a good start. He drew an initial cover and realised it in colour (**Plates 219-220**). The book, beautifully drawn, is now finished and available as an ePub in pencils (**Plates 219a-c**).

Charles Burns

Charles Burns is an American writer and cartoonist known for his award-winning graphic book *Black Hole*. He illustrates fanzines and multi-media including the 2007 French-made anthology *Fear(s) of the Dark* in *ligne claire*. His trilogy: *X'ed Out, The Hive* and *Sugar Skull* is surrealist art with strong visual storytelling, covering themes such as mental illness, depression, hallucination and disturbed alternate states.

As well as drawing in *ligne claire* he uses a muted Hergé palette which makes his work appear much like Tintin. His comics are full of images of vivisection, aliens and altered creatures in the style of sculptor Patricia Piccinini with a fused Giger-Leunig sentiment.[2] The *X'ed* trilogy's main character closely resembles Tintin but with a black coiffure and a black cat, as well as a bandage on his right temple as sported by one of the *Plague Dogs* (1977) by Richard Adams (*Watership Down*) a morality novel about vivisection. The bandage suggests brain trauma, hospitalisation, neurological medical misadventures.

Herge is an obvious influence. The front and back covers of his *X'ed Out* volume feature *The Shooting Star* mushroom, a recurring visual motif in Burns that may invoke magic mushroom altered states. Burns references other Tintin iconography as well, such as *The Black Island* and his character has a black cat in the same pose as the Tintin & Snowy masthead (opposite). Burns created a Tintin pastiche *Le Voyage Fantastique* with Tintin riding a living Calculus submarine through a Burns surrealist underwater seascape, **Plate 192**.

Images below and over, from Charles Burn's trilogy: *X'ed Out, The Hive, Sugar Skull* including the back cover of *X'ed Out*. Note opposite, the black coiffure, black 'Snowy' cat, Black Island and his distinctive 'Alien' writing.

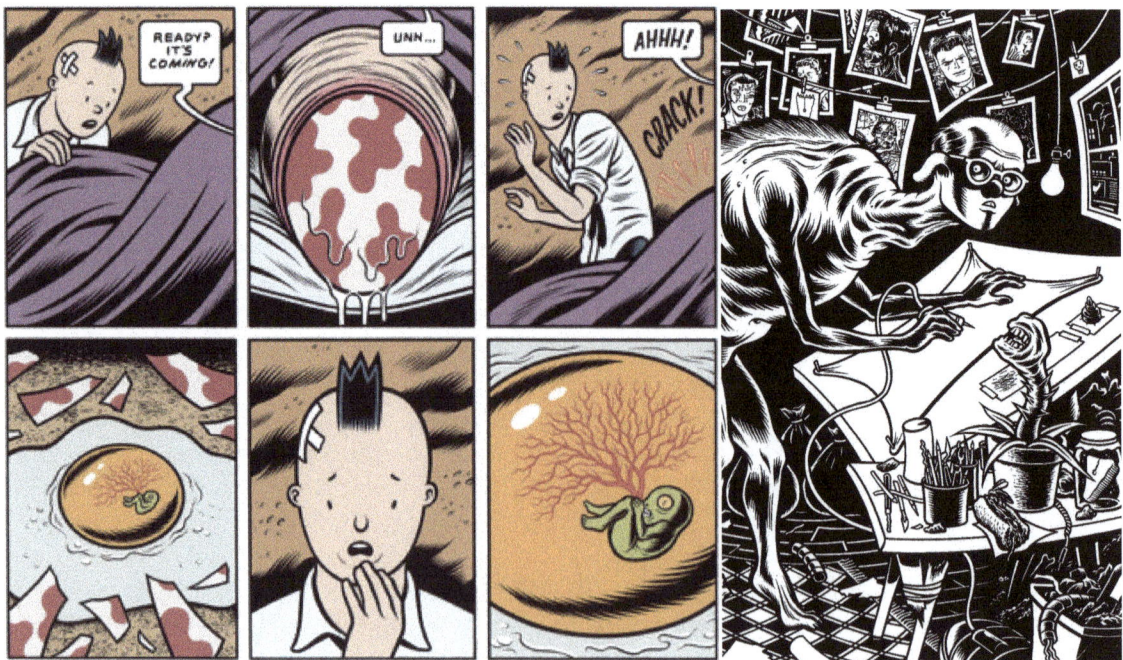

---

2 For example, Burns often titles his annuals with a Giger-esque alien script (opposite) and note the Giger-Bacon *Alien* parasite-as-pot-plant, in the self portrait immediately above right.

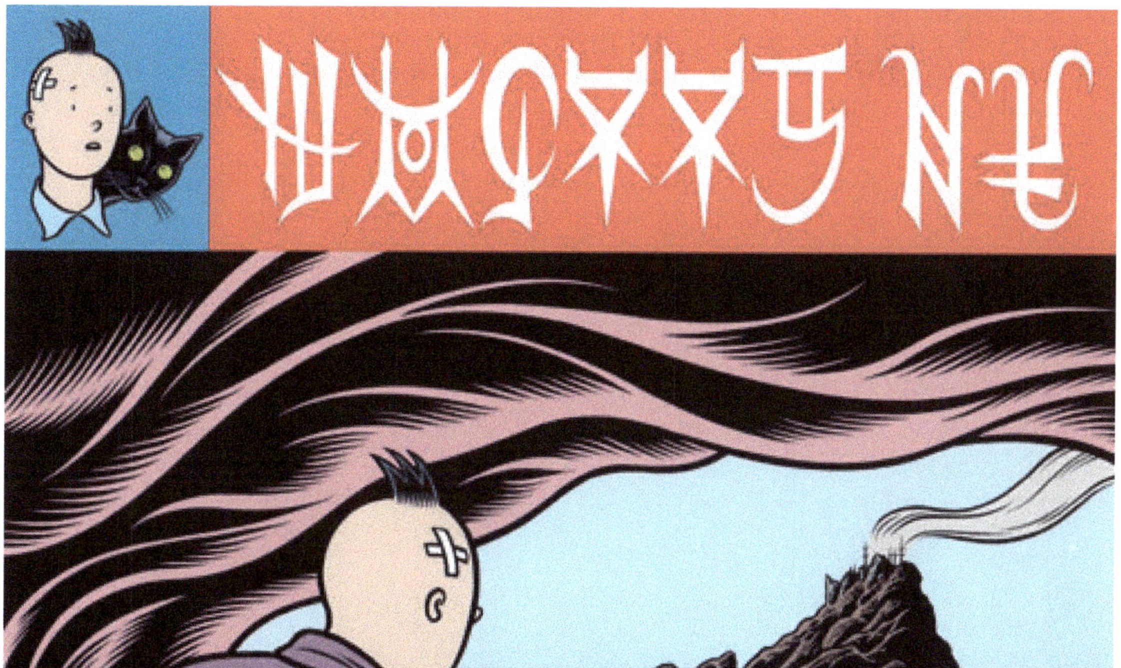

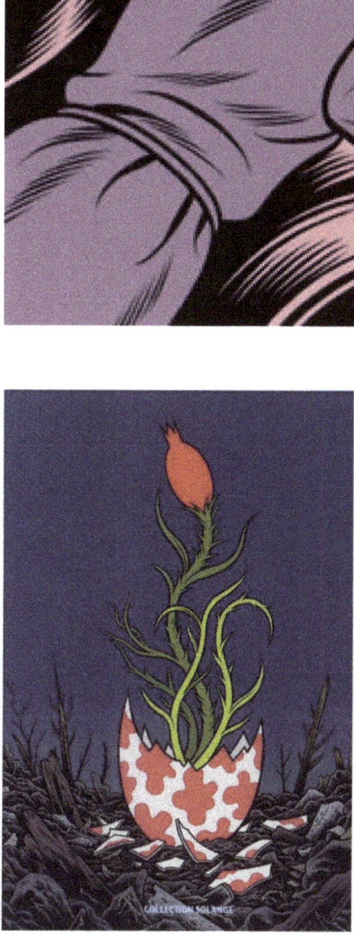
COLLECTION SOLANGE

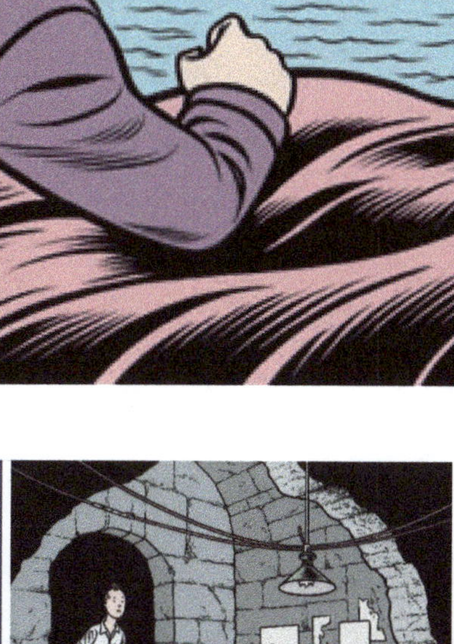

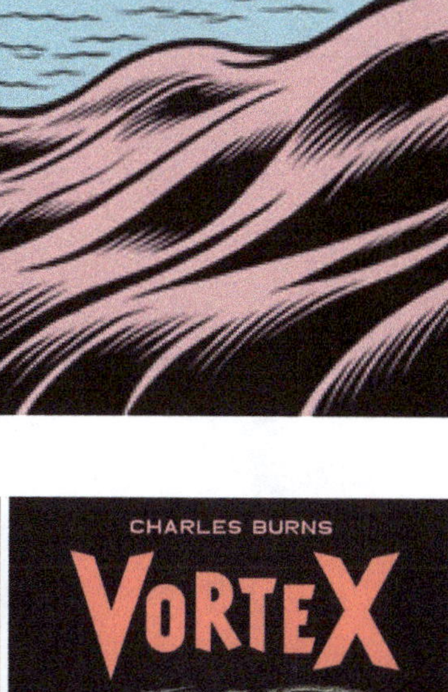
CHARLES BURNS
VORTEX

7. *Breaking Free; FlinFlins; Erasing Tintin*

Breaking Free by J. Daniels from 1989 is something of an anomaly in the Tintin panoply. It caused controversy in the English press for its transference of Belgian boy scout Tintin to British street yob. The book was described as "a "sad little publication," "naive and brutish." The story, set in England, features a number of Hergé characters, including Haddock as his uncle, but differs entirely from the Tintin synopsis. Tintin is simply appropriated as a disaffected petty criminal who works his way up to being a working class radical revolutionary in the Trades Union mould.

Panels are assiduously appropriated from Hergé art and refitted and re-contextualised to champion radical socialism of the stye now evoked by Bernie Sanders in America. Many see it as a clever post-modern parody.

Breaking Free was published in three instalments: 1989, 1999 and 2011 by *Attack International*. Because it appropriates and champions a world view anathema to Abbot Wallez and Georges Remi, it is curious the work has not been more vigorously attacked by Moulinsart on copyright grounds as other more respectful tributes have been.

Below: covers and the final panel escalating towards strike and social revolt copied from Tintin with new dialogue.

The FlinFlins are a real European family who diary world holiday adventures as Tintin pastiches, turning their lives in to a comic strip, which they publish to a blog site. They also sell books of their travel sketches which include Tintin covers. Their blog has some comic strips and drawings with comments about the Flinflins. The husband and wife replace Tintin and Snowy as the top left cover tag, see opposite and **Plates 118, 275.**

The problematic *Tintin in the Congo* and the bias against that album vs *Asterix* treatments of Africans, has been discussed elsewhere (Vol. 1, p. 28). There were the initial serialised strips and the black and white album up to 1931 followed by the coloured book in 1946 from which Hergé edited out various portrayals of Congolese nationals. One of these is the classroom scene in which Tintin teaches the Congolese children maths instead of the history of their 'fatherland,' Belgium (1931). But many vestiges of colonialism, imperialism and attitudes about the superiority of Western culture over Africans, remain. Given the severe human rights abuses in the 'French Congo,' this still sits awkwardly with Tintin who we have now cast in a more twenty-first century idiom. In 1975 a new version was published which was more humane to

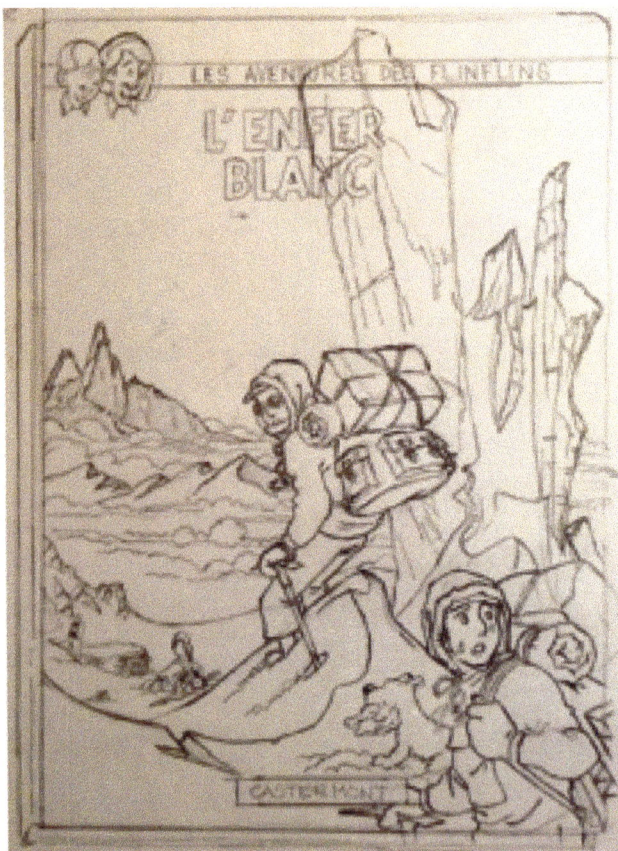

animals and in 2015 it received a new English translation. It was also the first of the adventures to be made available digitally. As much as we alter Tintin to fit our future, we are erasing him from his awkward past as well, so that he sits as an acceptable and laudable hero in whatever generation. Tintin pastiches work this social phenomenon, as social mores and fashions-of-thought change. To abide with us, Tintin has changed as well, not only from knickerbockers plus-fours to seventies flared slacks, but to Manga and Steam Punk.

Tintin, the eternal, but ever changing, Peter Pan.

Original page art from *King Ottokar's Sceptre* up for auction in late 2019 at Christie's, Paris.

The Pastiche "Publishers" in Vol. 2

Some of the variant names for Tintin, include: **Nitnit** (Tintin backwards), **TimTam, Dimdim, Dindin, Saint-Tin, Zinzin, Tintina, Pinpin, Quinquin, Tauntaun, Morintintin.**

The pastiche "publishers" (real, imagined or appropriated) usually derive their moniker as a pun from the Tintin world, i.e. "Casterboy," "Casterwoman," "Castorman" for *Casterman*; "Methane" for *Methuen*; or "Herpés" for *Hergé*, etc. They include here in Vol. 2 (plates):

Adesso 153, 171, 320; **Aimmesse** 240; **Alain** 309; **A-O** 329; **Avvd.net** 291; **Bilderberg** 254; **Boogaloo** (Bob de Moor) 323; **Bude Lemun** 273; **Burns,** Charles 192; **Bedestory** 120; **Caramba** 294; **Castherman** 287; **Castafiore** (Rodier, see also "Casterman," "Hommage," "Les Arumbayas") 222; **Casterboy** 253; **"Casterman"** appropriated throughout: 114, 115, 117, 119, 122, 124, 126, 129, 133, 137, 138, 140, 141, 147, 148, 152, 158-161, 163, 166, 167, 172, 175, 178, 180, 181, 190, 191, 193, 195-197, 199-201, 208, 210-212, 214, 217, 225, 245, 247-250, 256, 258, 261, 269-271, 277-278, 281, 295-297, 313-315, 325, 328, 331, 333; **Castermanhatten** 118; **Casterwoman** 274; **Castorman** 206; **Castorflot,** 207; **Chaque Jeudi** 241; **Consternan** (Consternation?) 128, 136, 310; **'DC'** 130 (see 'Marvel'); **D'Avril et Paolo** 224; **DeMeyer** 268; **Desclée de Brouwer** 172; **Dran** 177, 198; **Egmont** 282; **Erin Hunting** 143; **Ferrandez, J.** 145; **Fluide a Gratter** 332; **German** 298; **Goo5Ben5** 308; **Gordon Zola** 188; **Grand-Duc** 116; **Guin** 121; **Hallgren** 231; **Harmon** 242; **Harry** or **Harry Edwood** 219 a-c, 264 (also "Woodman"); **Harry Thompson** 134; **Heapinfrimp** 125; **Hergé De Silva** (Fernando) 286; **Herpés** 279; **Hergé** 292, 319; **Herrgé** 287; **Hessa** 243, 255; **Hommagé** (see also "Maiden New Zealand;" and separately "Rodier") 127, cover, 204, 223a,b, 209, 227, 257; **Jean C. Denis** 235; **Jicede** 118; **Juhis** 302; **Koghiman** 272; **Kolyma** 237; **Kukaracha,** 216; **L'Ceil du Pirate** 262, 266; **L'Ecailler du Cinema** 170; **L'Integrale** 218; **Lambeaux de Burns** 194; **Laotsumin** 144; **Le Passage** 238; **Les Arumbayas** (Rodier) 150; **Little, Brown** (a division of Hachette) 312; **Le Léopard Démasqué** (by Pauline Bonnifoi) 149 (by Gordon Zola) 154, 165, 188 (by Herve) 174; **Mammoth** 318; **Maiden New Zealand** (see "Hommage"); **'Marvel'** 307; **Masterman** 151, 155; **Memerman** 190; **MrWhaite** 289; **Muzki** 246; **Namiman** 301; **Oberon Bv-Haarlem** 176; **Pauline Bonnefoi** 113; **Pirotte** 184; **Rodier** 263, 304, 327 (see also "Castafiore" et al.); **Sterin** 162; **Souvenir** 254; **Swapmeetdave.com** 330; **Tintin Parodies** 276; **Tournare,** Alain-Jacques 244; **Tronchet** 239; **Woody & Hitch** 275; **Woodman** (Harry Edwood) 132, 182, 220, 293, 300; **XXIeme Siecle** 321.

Also in this series, Vol. 1 (2019)

Le Pastiche Tintin, 111 'Lost' Tintins

Plates 1-111.

Order from *Amazon* or *Info@ingramspark.com*

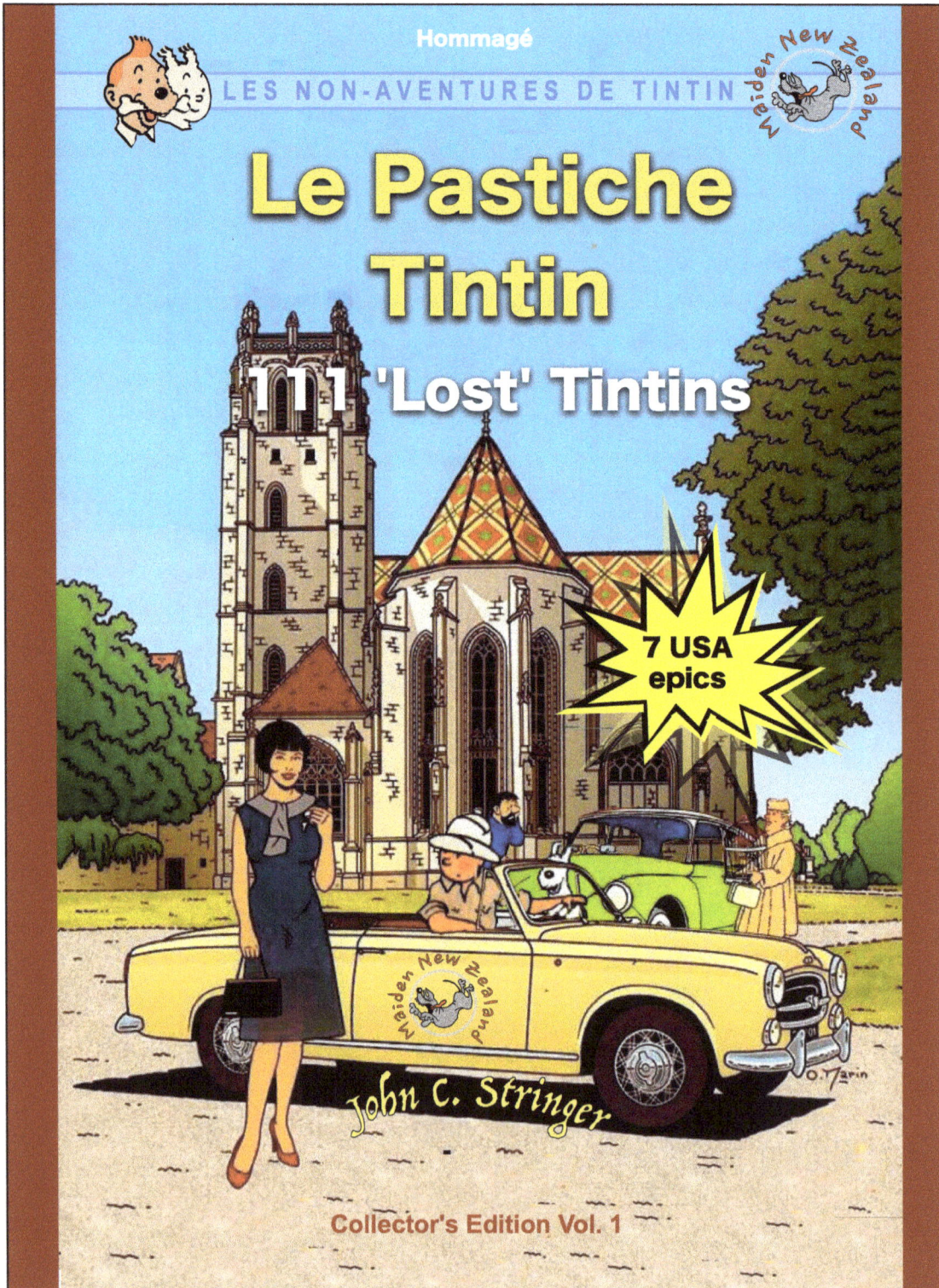

2019. *Le Pastiche Tintin, 111 'Lost' Tintins*
Plates 1-111

Le Pastiche Tintin 2, 222 'Lost' Tintins
Plates 112 -333

2021, *Le Pastiche Tintin 3, 333 'Lost' Tintins*
Plates 334-666.

d'après **HERGÉ**

LES AVENTURES DE TINTIN

TINTIN EN AMÉRIQUE II

Tintin, Snowy and Haddock are *Easy Riders* on Route 66. See also **Plate 123**
The Wild One.

-PAULINE BONNEFOI-
*
LES AVENTURES DE
SAINT-TIN ET SON AMI LOU
*
SAINT-TIN
EN
AMÈRES LOQUES

Haddock's parrot Iago from *Castafiore* attacks the Indian allowing Tintin to escape.

Plate 114

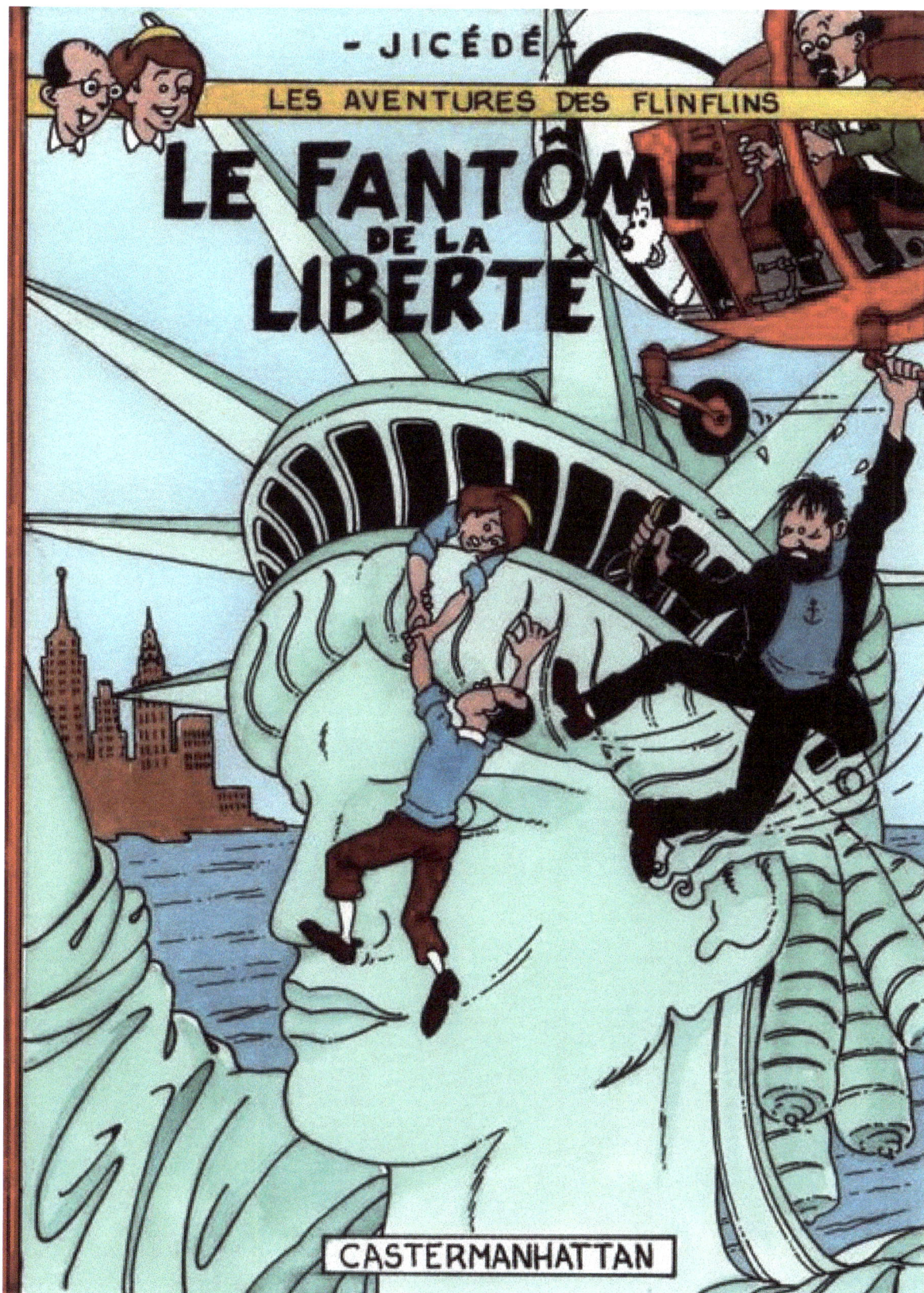

One of the Flinflin family holidays captured as a Tintin pastiche cover. See p. 215.

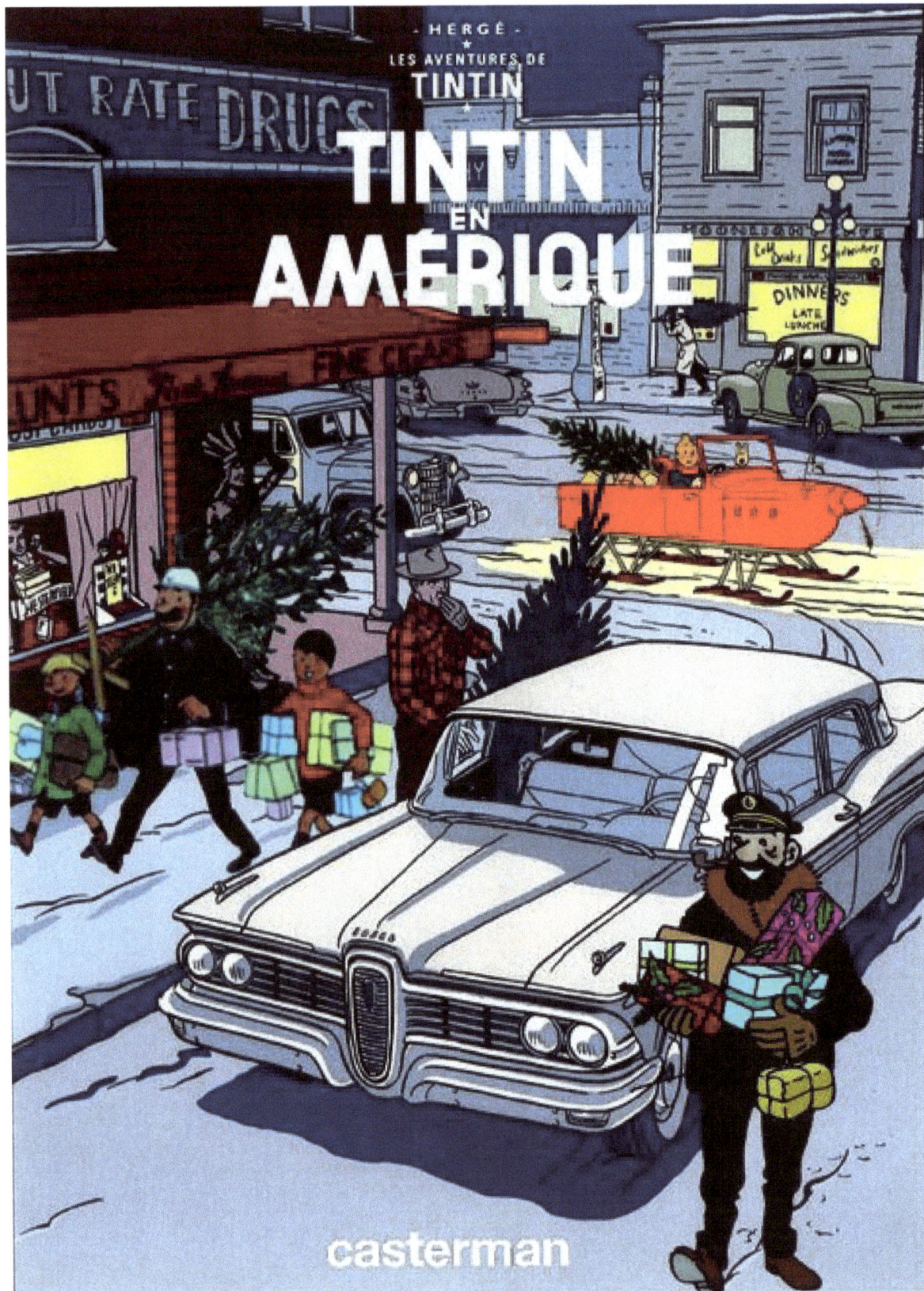

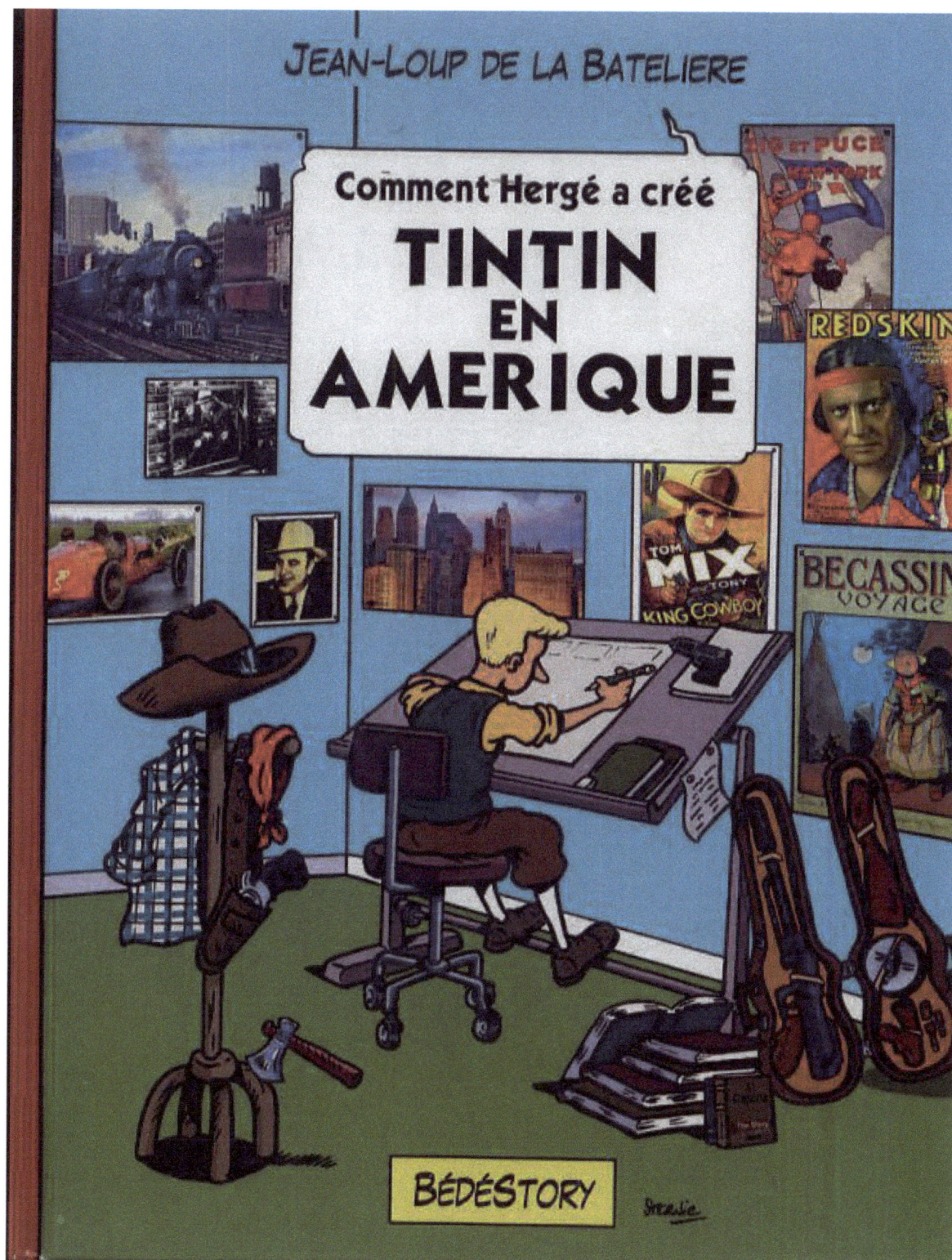

JEAN-LOUP DE LA BATELIERE

Comment Hergé a créé
TINTIN
EN
AMERIQUE

ZIG ET PUCE

REDSKIN

TOM MIX
TONY
KING COWBOY

BECASSIN
VOYAGE

BÉDÉSTORY

Tintin himself, or Hergé, with his cowboy outfit disrobed, sets about drawing his own America adventure at a drawing table. Note the influences: *Becassine*, *Zig & Puce*, Al Capone for the gangster scenes, cowboys and Indians.

"Tintin against Batman." A visit to America would not be complete without tangling with *Batman*. There are several Batman adventures traversed in Vol. 3.

"Flight for New York."

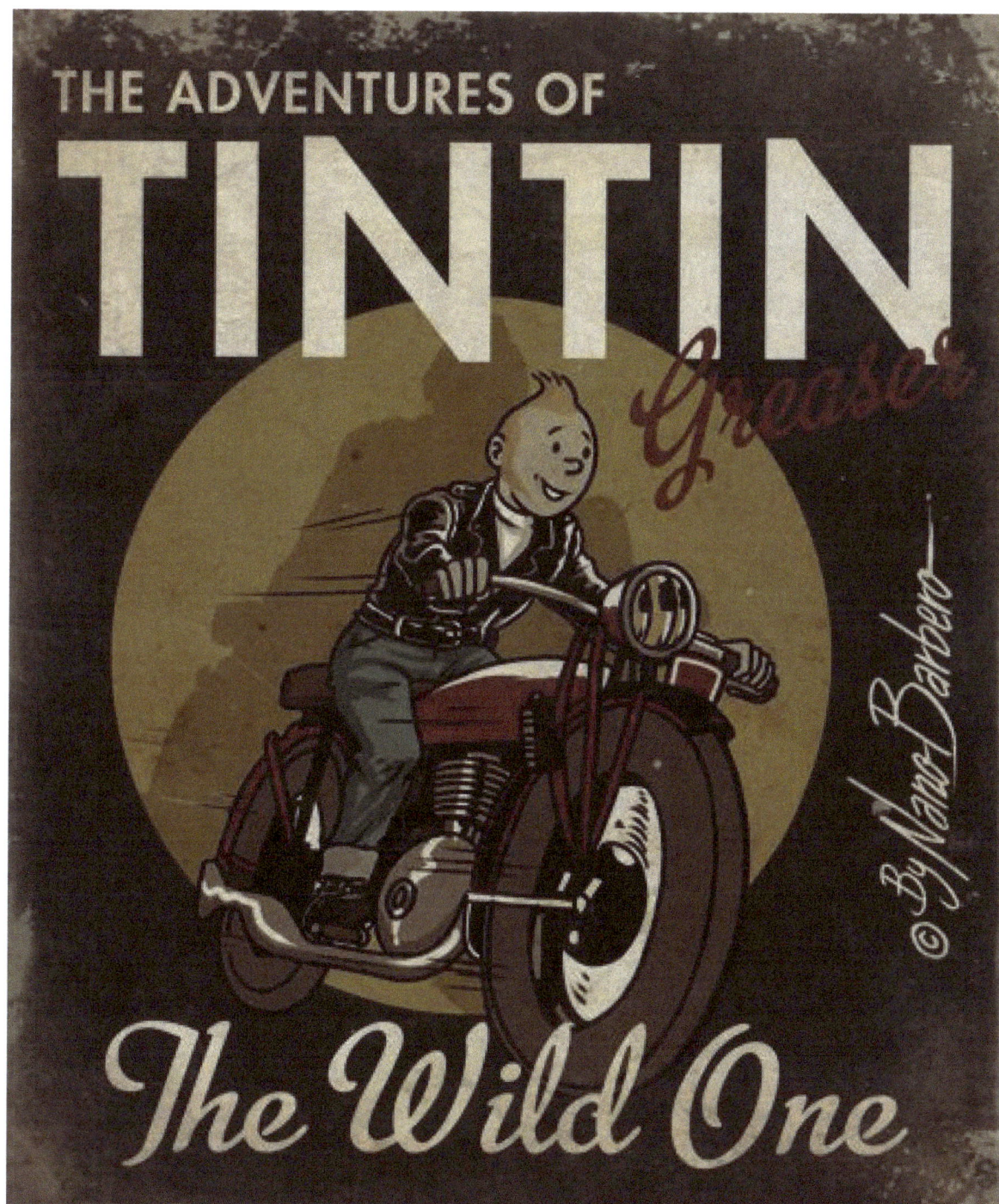

"The Adventures of Tintin Greaser." Tintin is the 1950s cult hero Johnny Strabler (Marlon Brando) *The Wild One*, 1953.

HERGÉ

LES AVENTURES DE TINTIN

UN JOUR DANS UN AEROPORT

CASTERMAN

"One day in an Airport." Another version of the airport terminal story arc that Hergé moved instead into the art world, resulting in *Alph-Art*. See **Plates 18, 19.** Some of this art is repeated in reverse on **Plate 195.**

Tintin meets Alf of American TV sitcom fame portrayed as Marat in Jacques-Louis David's 1793 painting *Death of Marat*. Thus "Alf-Art" a pun on *Alph-Art*.

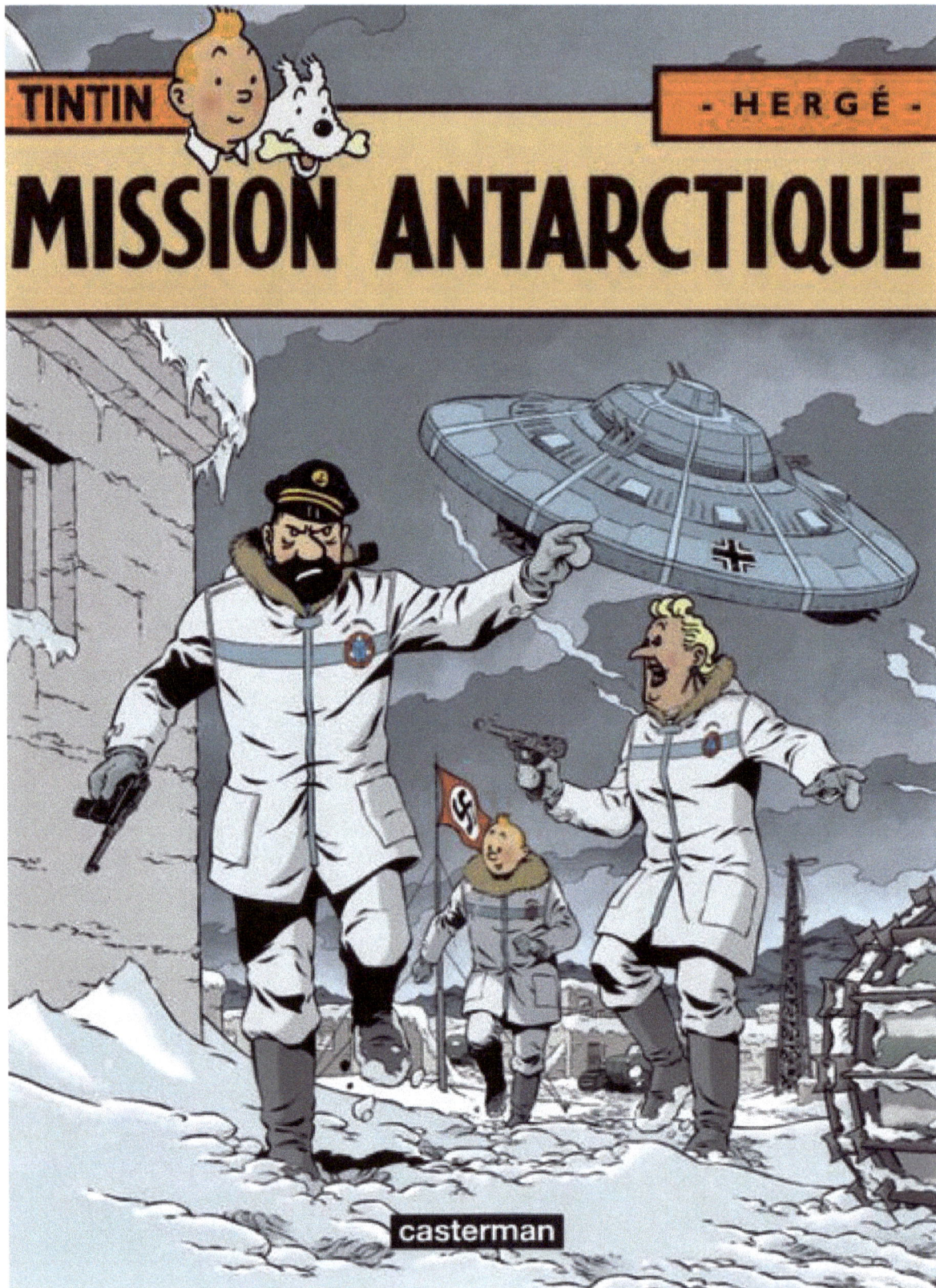

The Nazi UFO is not fanciful but a WWII design for a hovering aircraft among many experimental "special" weapons developed late in the war, such as the V1-2 rockets as well as successful jet propulsion. Nazi scientists' rocket technology got America to the moon ahead of the Russians. Hovering aircraft were trialed by the Americans, but were scrapped as unstable. They are probably the origin of some UFO reports. See Jacobs' fixed wing Nazi fighter, Section **8.D.**

- HOMMAGE A HERGE-

LES AVENTURES DE TINTIN

TINTIN AU FRIGO

"Chilled Tintin."

HERGÉ

LES AVENTURES DE TINTIN

TINTIN EN VALAIS

CONSTERNAN

"Tintin In Valais," one of the 26 cantons of Switzerland . It is grouped here with the other snow, ice themes.

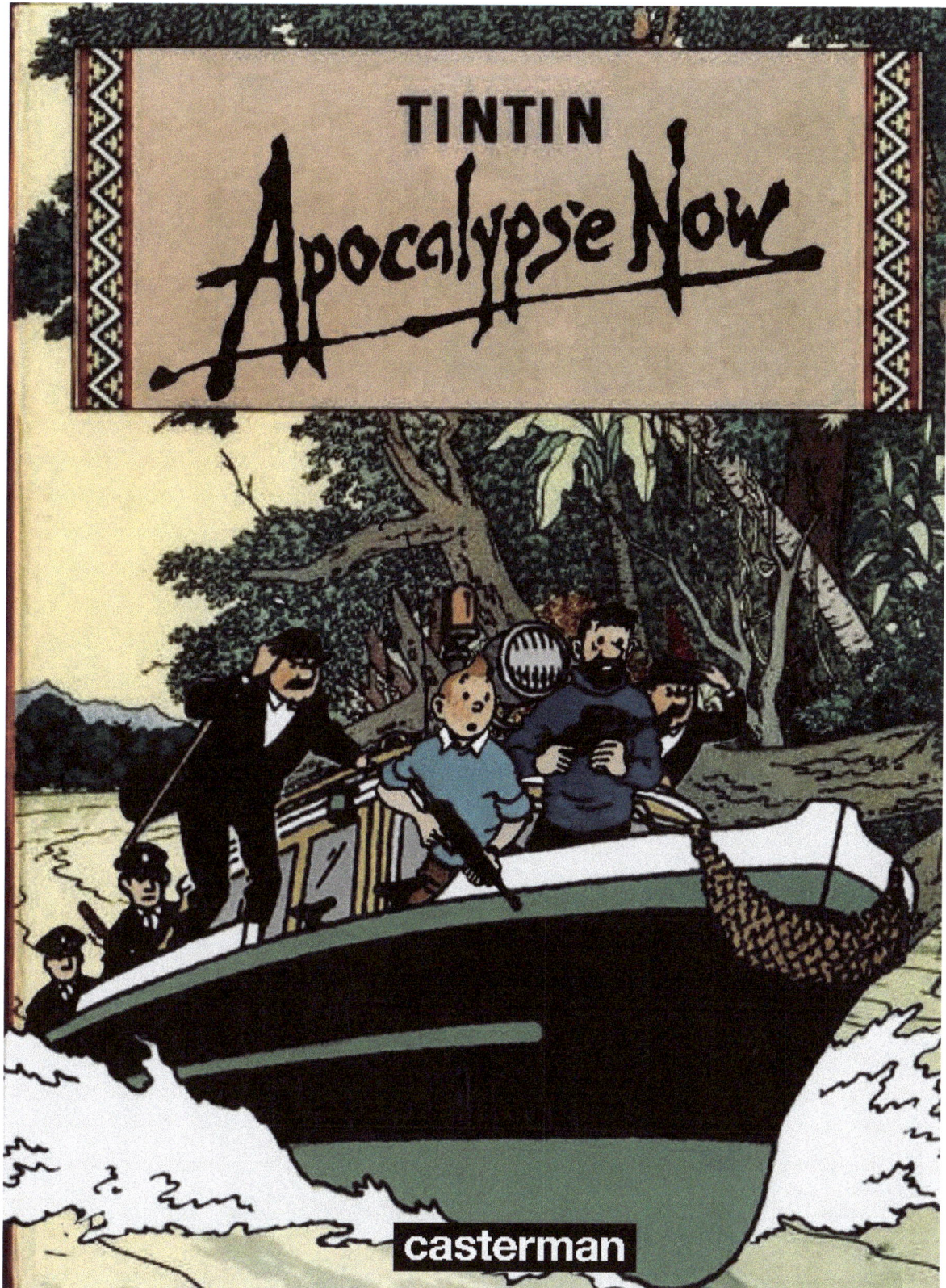

The background is from *The Broken Ear,* in which the motorboat replaces the dugout Arumbayan canoe. The motorboat resembles the motorboat in *Land of the Soviets* p. 55 but is actually photoshopped from p. 57 of *The Black Island*.

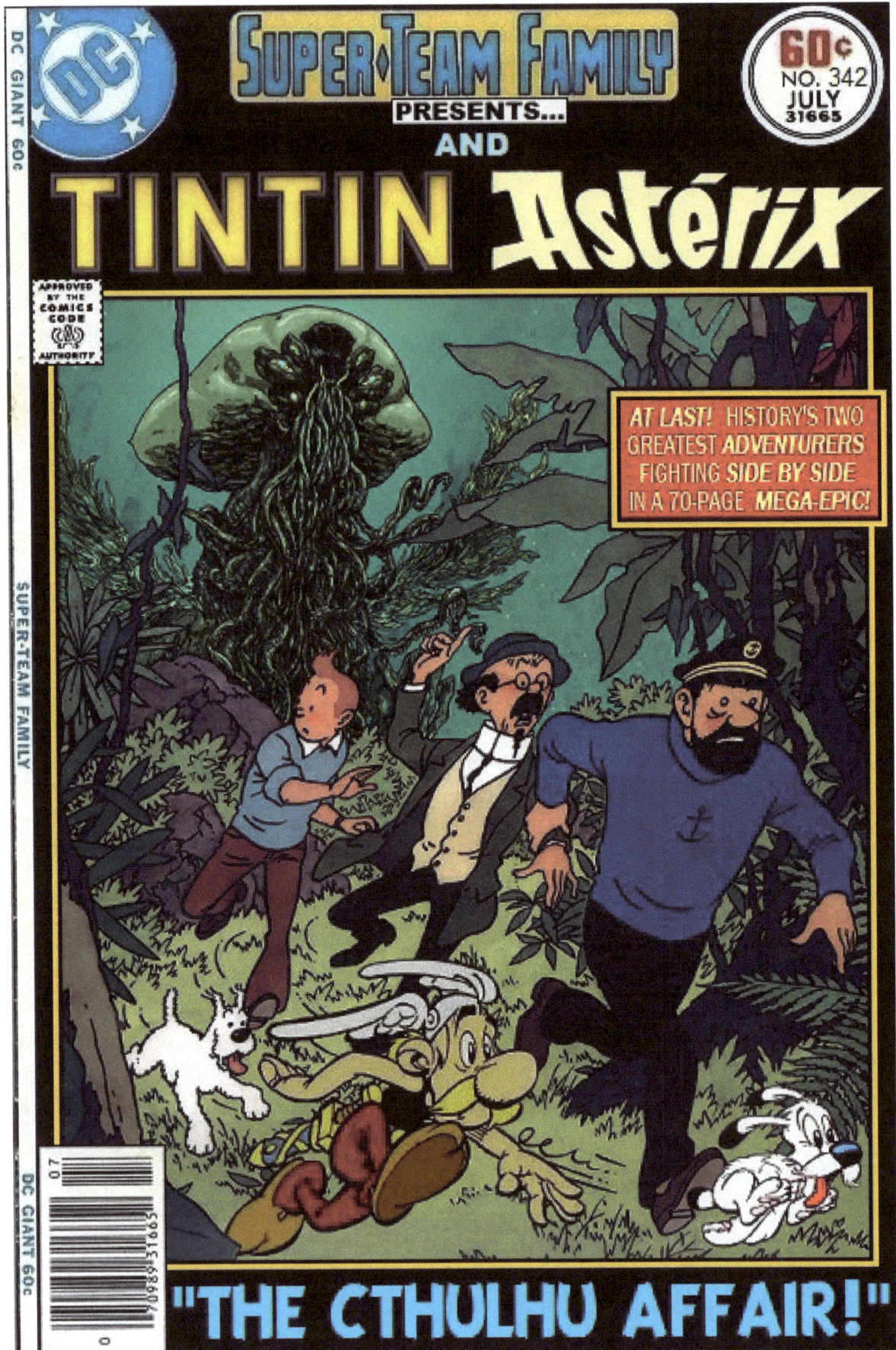

Picaros cover art with *Asterix* in a H.P. Lovecraft *Cthulhu* adventure. See **Plate 99.**

Mother of Tintin? See **Plate 136.**

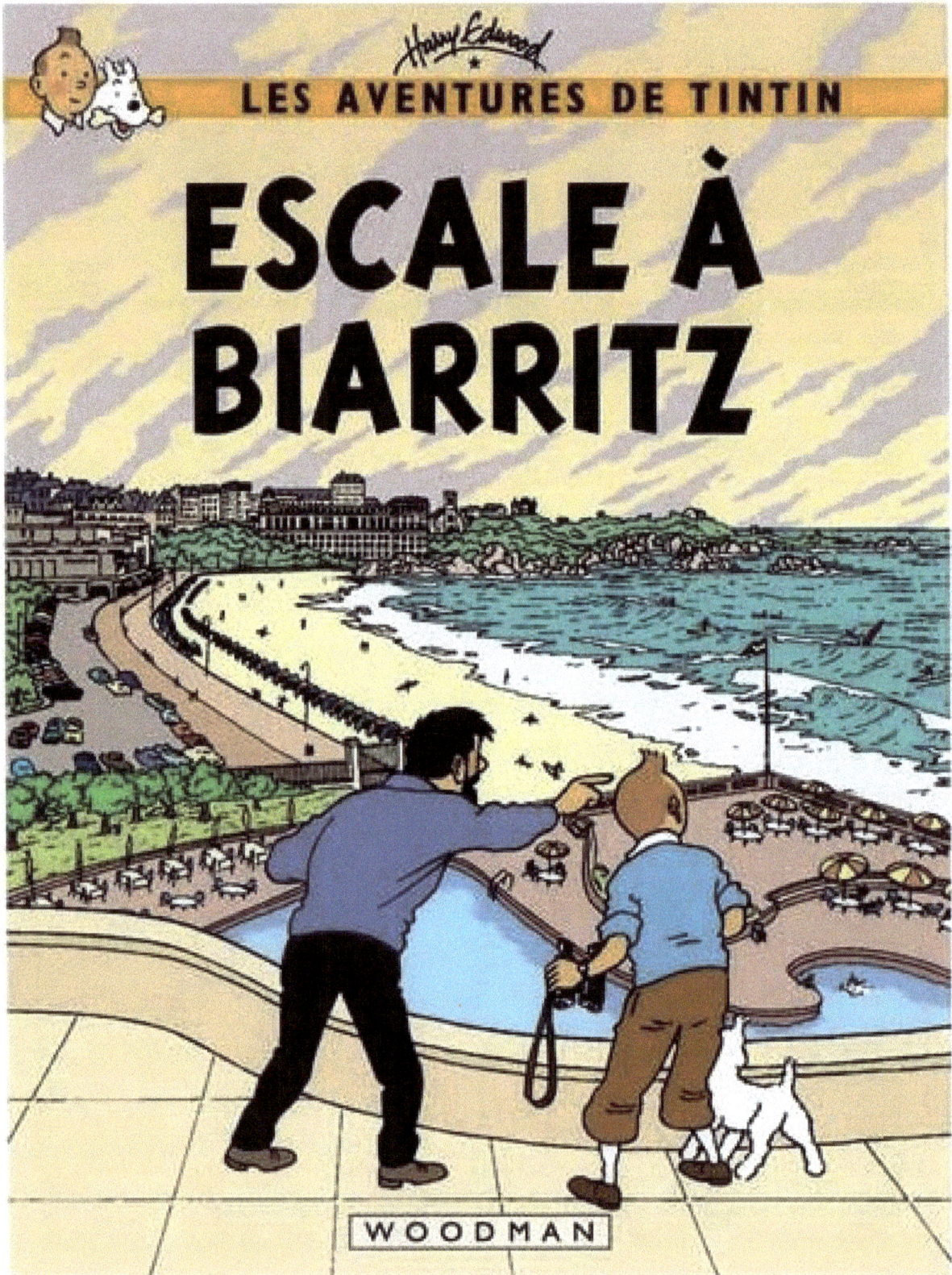

LES AVENTURES DE TINTIN

ESCALE À BIARRITZ

WOODMAN

"Stopover Biarritz" a French resort hotel, perhaps the one depicted center background.

LES AVENTURES DE TINTIN ET MILOU
D'APRES LES PERSONNAGES DE HERGE

TRAIN EXPRESS 4675
A DESTINATION DE BIARRITZ

CASTERMAN

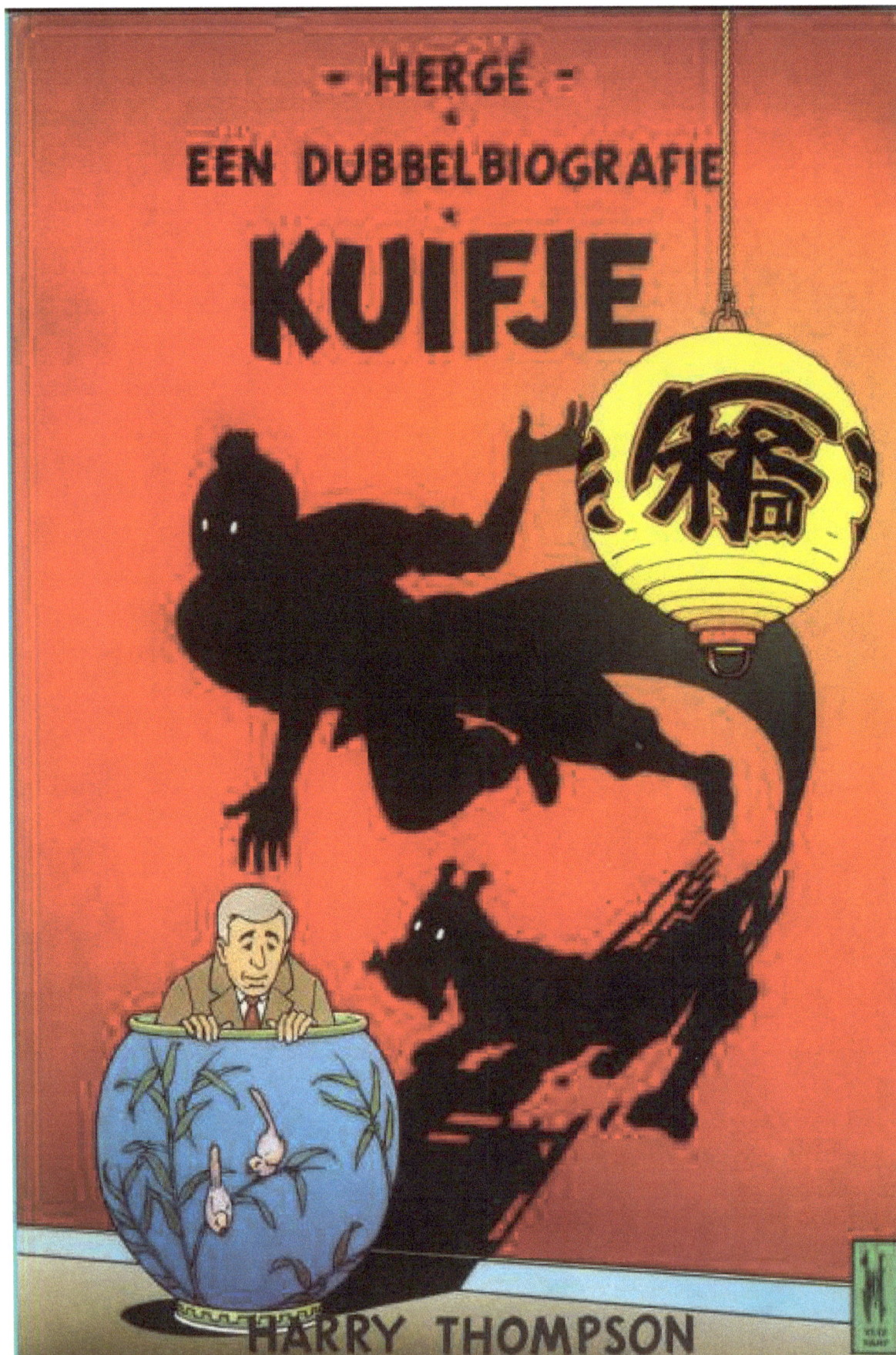

- HERGÉ -

EEN DUBBELBIOGRAFIE

KUIFJE

HARRY THOMPSON

Kuifje (Dutch for Tintin's coiffure). Hergé sits in a *Blue Lotus* porcelain vase. The double biography is perhaps Hergé and Tintin or Tintin and Snowy.

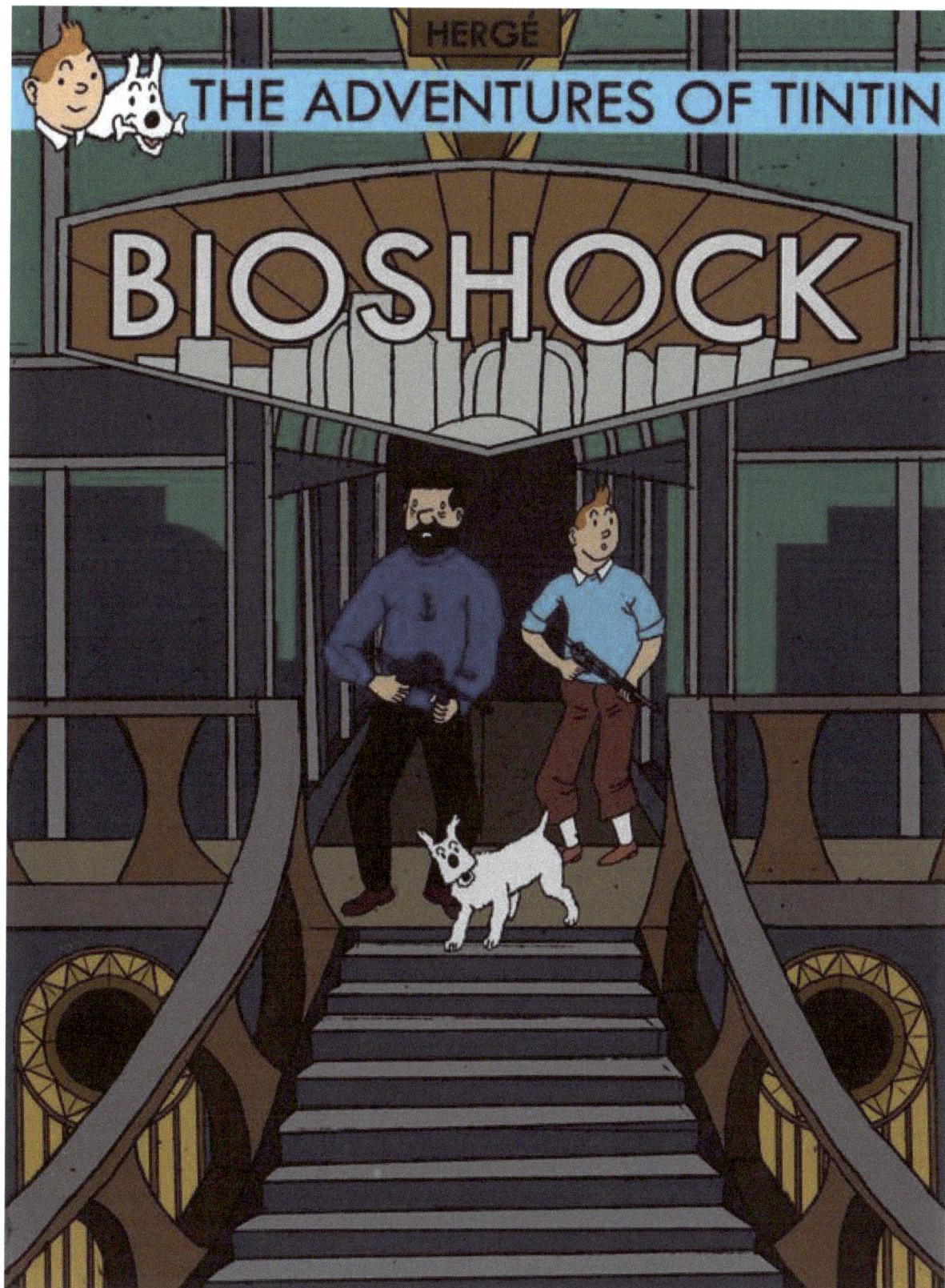

The pose is copied from *Flight 714*. Note the Art Deco influences, exemplars for Hergé's *ligne claire* style. See Vol. 1, p. 18. Plate 135: "Bioshock" is also a video game that revels in Art Deco, so this may be the visual reference.

d'après Hergé et Pinchon
★
LES AVENTURES DU
JEUNE TINTIN

LA NAISSANCE DE TINTIN

CONSTERNAN

"The Birth of Tintin." Father and mother of Tintin? See **Plate 131.**

"In the Land of Black Gold," Arabs are in pursuit of Tintin.

A good old fashioned Tintin car chase in black sedans in "The Black Valley."

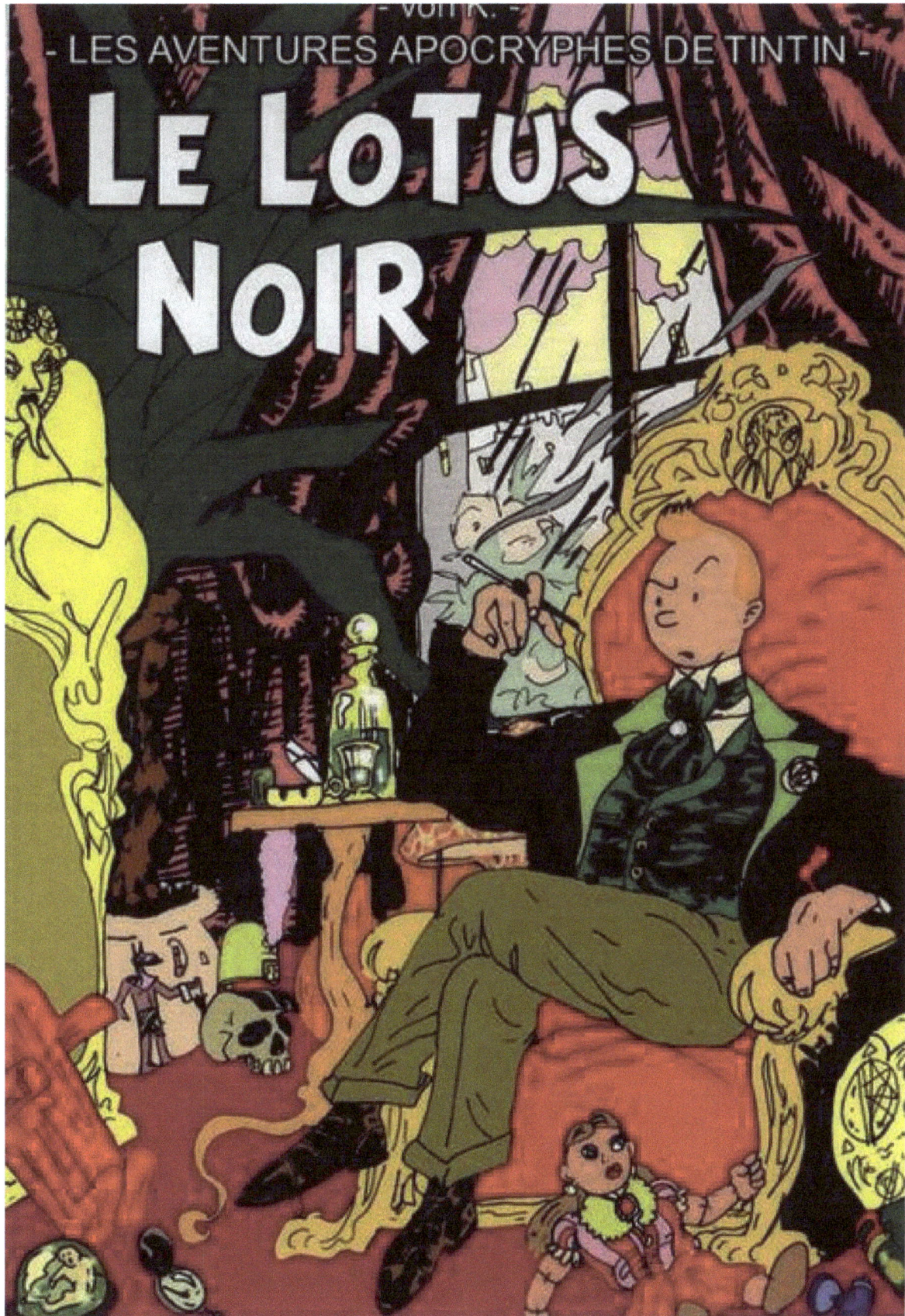

- VOIR K. -

- LES AVENTURES APOCRYPHES DE TINTIN -

LE LOTUS NOIR

"The Black Lotus." Tintin becomes a 'black' intrigue along the lines of a Scarlet Pimpernel.

- HERGÉ -

LES AVENTURES DE TINTIN

L'ILE NOIRE

casterman

A polyploid of Tintin characters photoshopped on to some *Valiant*-esque magazine art, perhaps *Tim Kelly*?

"The Curse of Francis Blake." Jacobs and Hergé characters cross over. The hat scene is from p. 2 of *The Calculus Affair*, Haddock's "very best hat!"

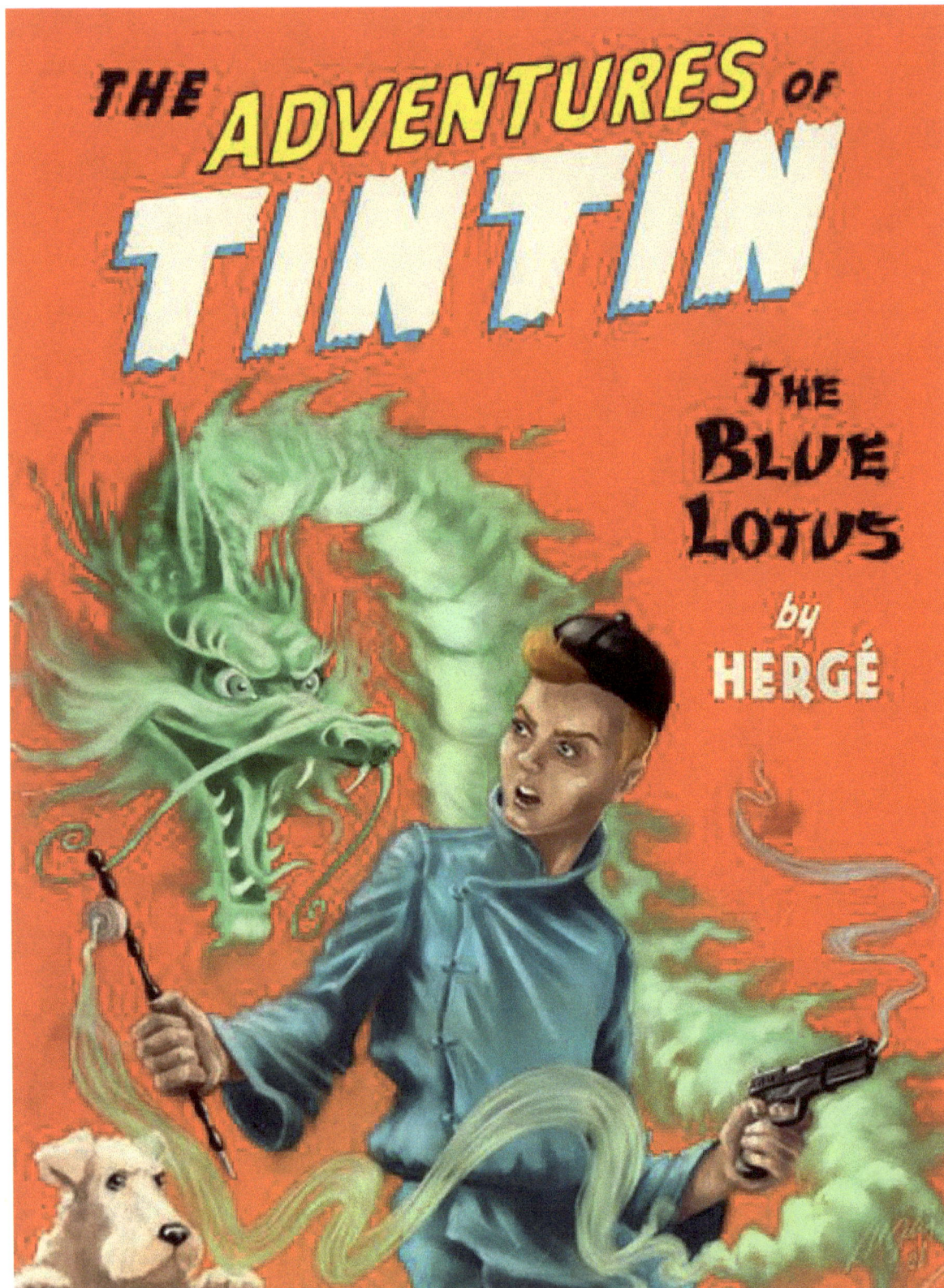

The Blue Lotus theme is carried over in colours and design synonymous with Chinese food packaging. Is this the "green perfume" (opium) of other pastiches?

The *Blue Lotus* in manga style.

A clever multi-layered pastiche in which a photoshoot is contrived of the 'film shooting' of the cover art of the original 1936 *The Blue Lotus* annual. But like the cover, the 'photoshoot' is itself drawn in *ligne claire* and is not a photo. Art contriving life, imitating art.

1936 in black and white, coloured 1946. This pastiche 1987, J. Ferrandez.

Tintin as a French peacekeeper in Bosnia.

There are several pastiches of fictional mis-adventures of Dupond & Dupont (Thomson & Thompson). The pool side figure is Ray Banana by Ted Benoit, a kind of French Johnny Bravo-Clark Gable character, see p. 197 (figure 9).

Art Deco and *Metropolis* influences are depicted, early exemplars for Hergé.

-PAULINE BONNEFOI-
*
LES AVENTURES DE
SAINT-TIN ET SON AMI LOU
*
LES PIES JOUENT DE LA CASTAGNETTE
ROMAN

Le Léopard Démasqué

"The Juicy (or Saucy?) Magpies of the Castagnette" a Spanish play on the Italian Castafiore 'nightingale.' The parrot she gifted to Haddock is silenced foreground.

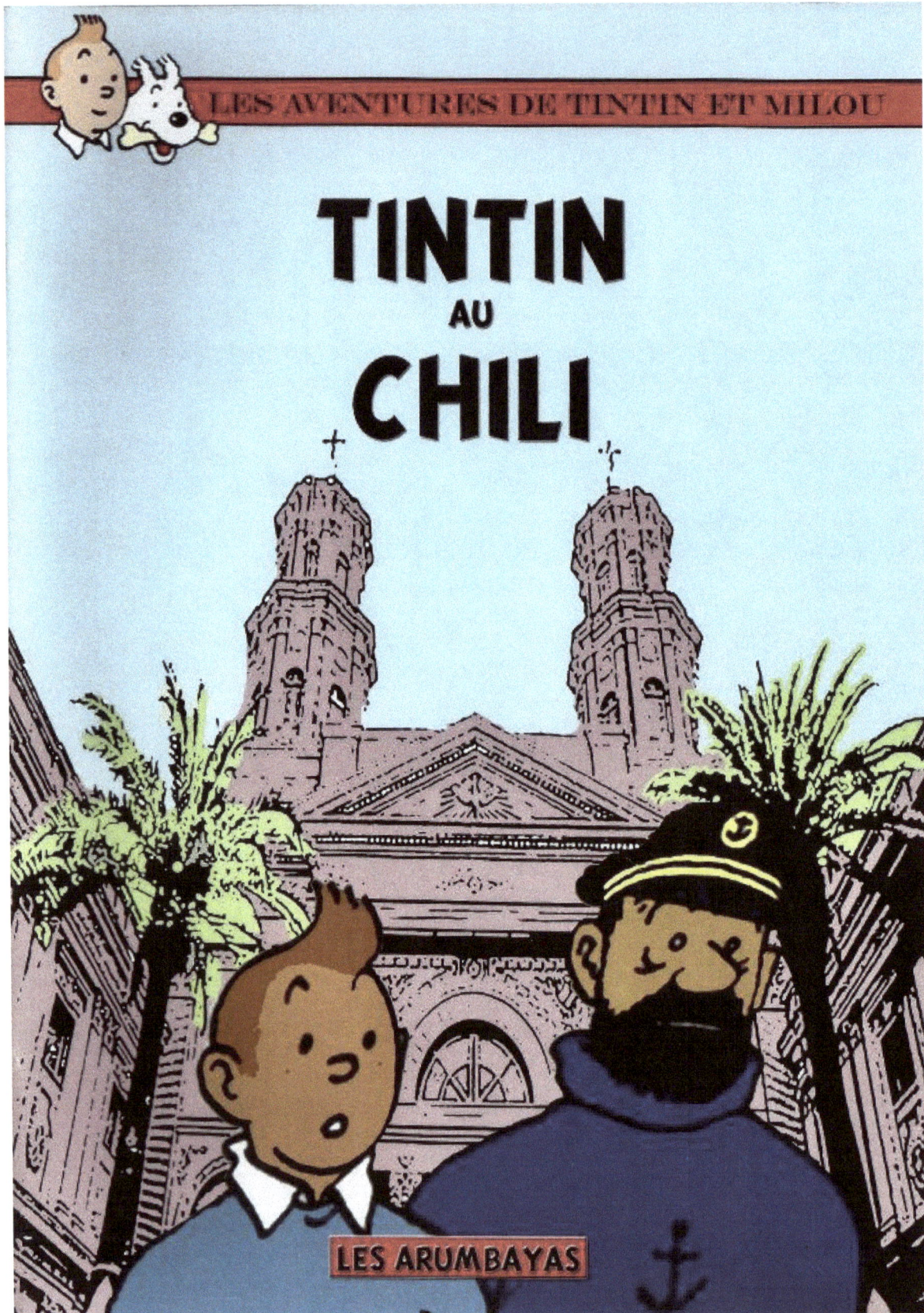

LES AVENTURES DE TINTIN ET MILOU

TINTIN AU CHILI

LES ARUMBAYAS

LES MÉSAVENTURES
DE TINTIN ET SURTOUT MILOU
D'APRÈS VARGÉ

TINTIN EN CHINE

MASTERMAN

SAFARIR, D'APRÈS L'ŒUVRE DE HERGÉ

A rather grotesque and unflattering contempt for the Chinese taste for eating dogs, in this case Snowy! And somewhat thematic in 2020 amidst the coronavirus outbreak from wild animal 'wet' meat markets in Wuhan, China. See **Plate 328**.

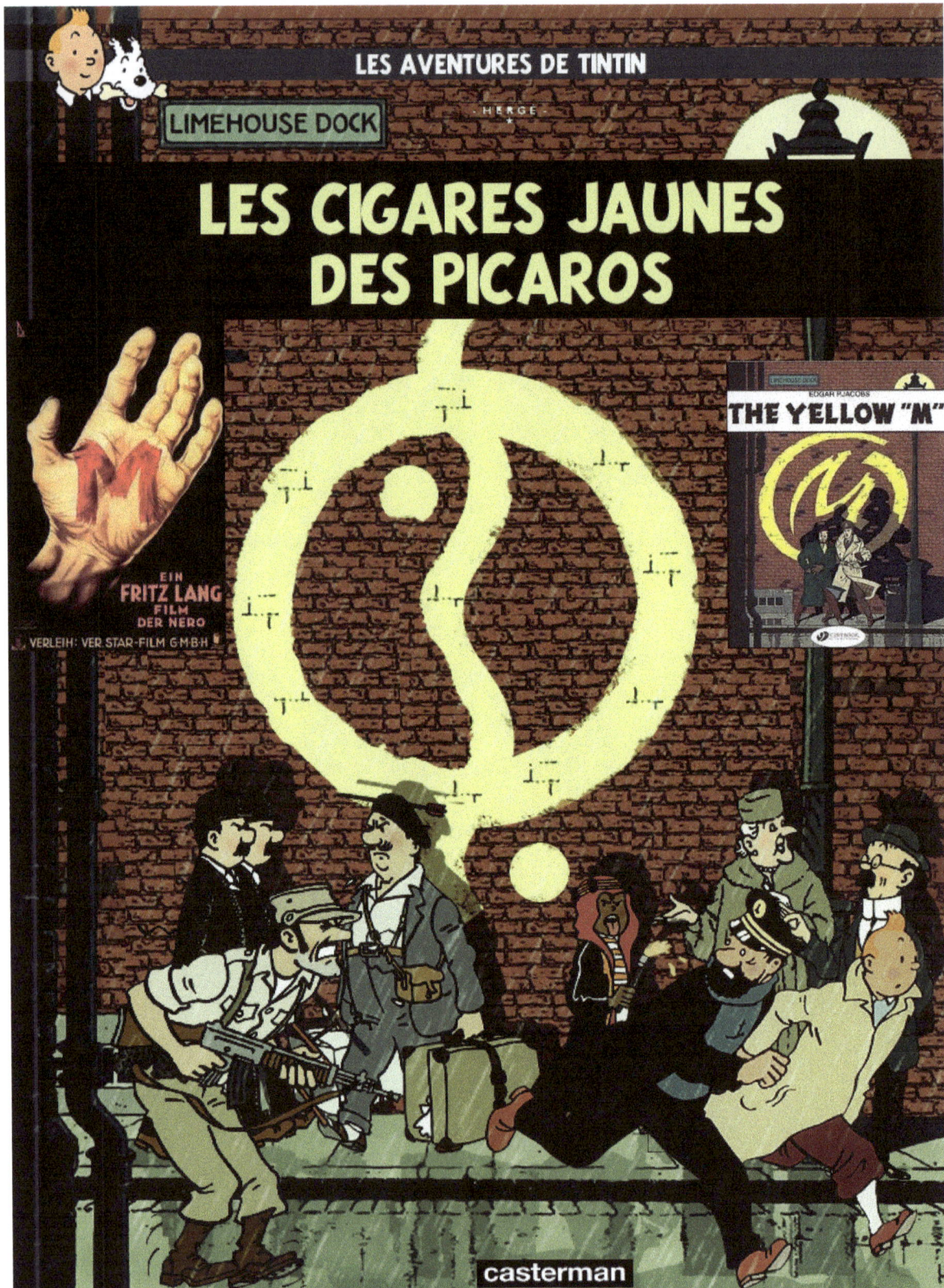

The *Cigars of the Pharaoh* logo replaces Jacobs' cover tableau of *The Yellow 'M'* as Tintin characters scurry across. In **Plate 332** Jacob's 'M' (inset right) becomes 'Z' but with Tintin. Jacob's Yellow 'M' was influenced by the 1931 German thriller "M" (*Mörder*) (inset left) by Fritz Lang now a classic and Lang's *magnum opus*. Both the Fritz and Jacob's thrillers chase down a psychopath.

GORDON ZOLA

LES AVENTURES DE
SAINT-TIN ET SON AMI LOU
★
LES SiX GARDES
DU PHARE AMON

Le Léopard Démasqué

"The Six Guards of the Amon Lighthouse." The seventh guard, a chain-smoking mummy, has squashed Tintin 'neath its coffin while it enjoys an aged cigar.

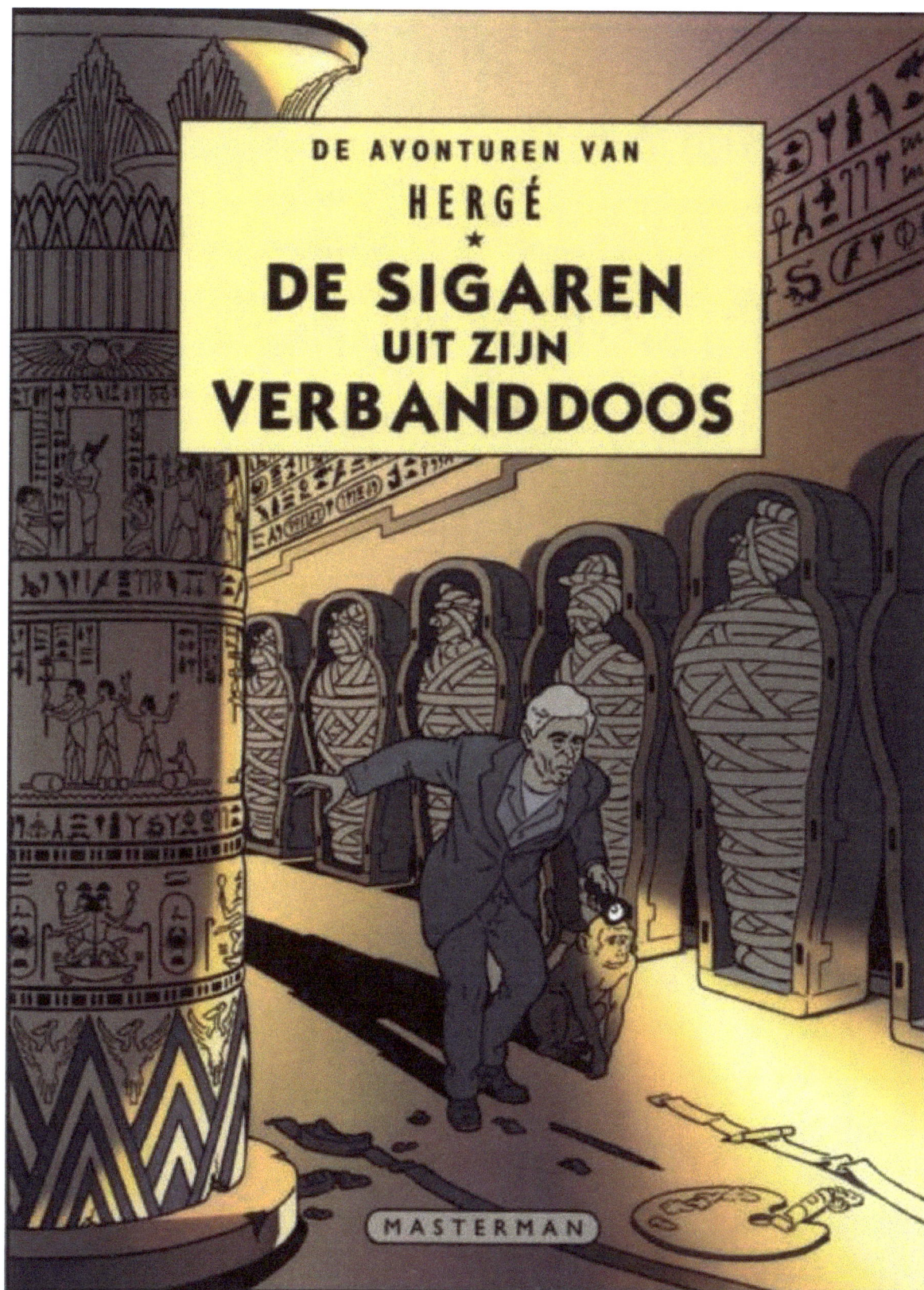

DE AVONTUREN VAN
HERGÉ
★
DE SIGAREN
UIT ZIJN
VERBANDDOOS

MASTERMAN

"Cigars from the (side) bandage box" (Dutch). Hergé explores the pyramid of the pharaoh. The mummies are, right to left: Castafiore, Calculus, Haddock, Thomson and Thompson. Looking closely at the column and the back wall, you'll see various Hergé motifs depicted as hieroglyphs, including the *Blue Lotus* dragon, the Thom(p)son's canes, Snowy, and the cigars logo as well as King Ottokar's sceptre, as well as the *Red Sea Sharks* tableau, etc.

外国漫画丛书

奇怪的雪茄

丁丁历险记

A Chinese pastiche of *Cigars of the Pharaoh*.

"The end of Black Line"? Tintin has lost his coiffure which is now a goatee. Snowy is a white cat like Charles Burn's 'Tintin' black cat, p. 212.

- HERGÉ -

LIGNE CLAIRE ET NOIRS DESSEINS

casterman

"Clear Lines and Black Designs." Instead of nails, the fakir reposes upon pencils with which Hergé drew clear lines.

- HERGE -

LES AVENTURES DE TINTIN

LA VALLÉE DES COBRAS

casterman

A Tintin-ised *Jo, Zette & Jocko* title. Is the woman an older Zette or perhaps Fanny Vlamynck? Note the hair in Vol. 1 cover art (**Plate 56**) and **Plates 296, 314.**

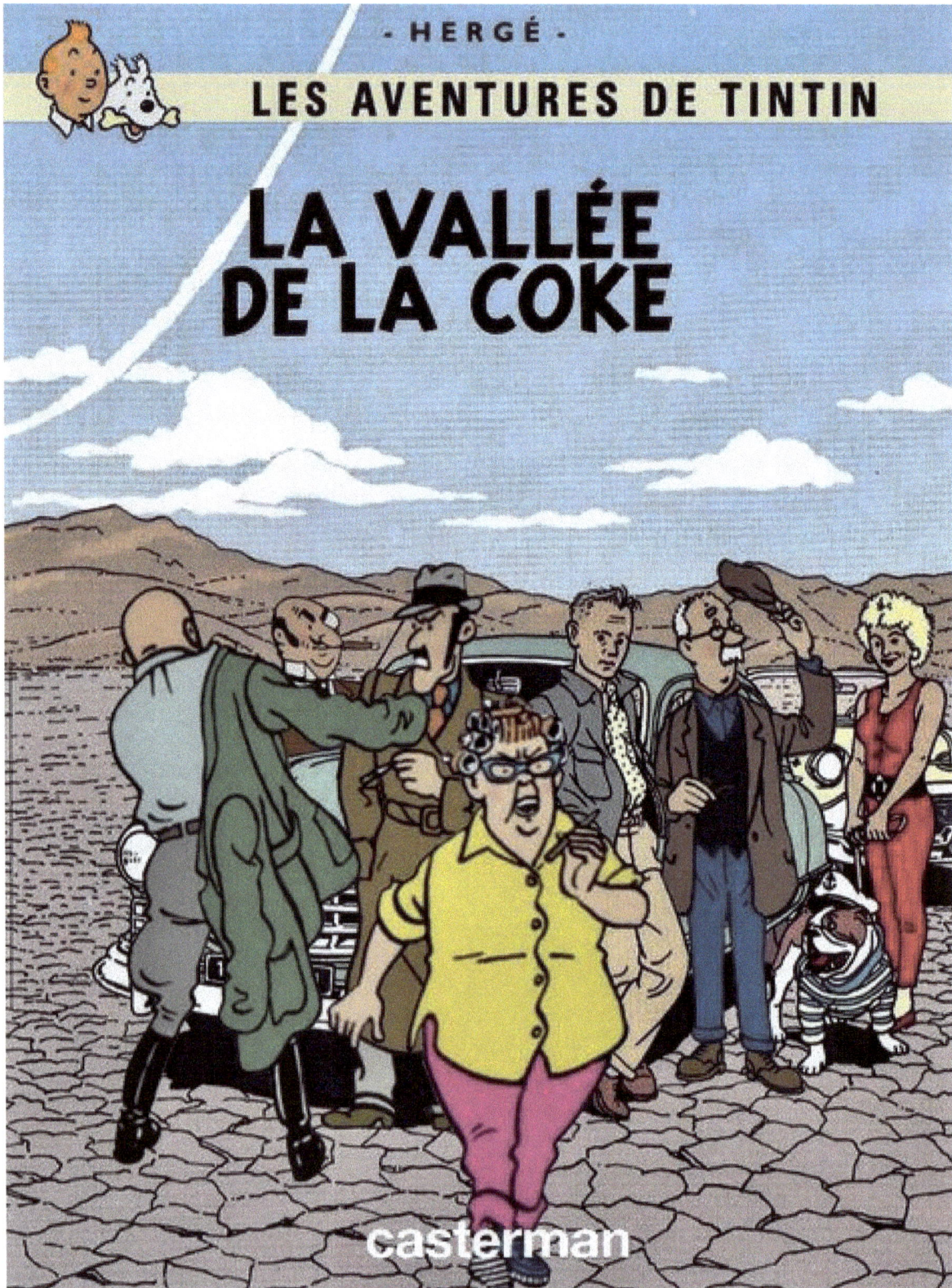

- HERGÉ -

LES AVENTURES DE TINTIN

LA VALLÉE DE LA COKE

casterman

"Coke (Cocaine) Valley." In the foreground of this coterie of criminals, is Peggy Alcazar who met and married General Alcazar when he was the knife thrower "Ramon Zarate." "Coke en Stock" ("Coke in Stock") is the original French title for "The Red Sea Sharks". Coke is synonymous in the French with criminals or "Sharks."

"Colonial Command in the Land of Black Gold." A reference to the controversial colonisation of the Congo by Belgium?

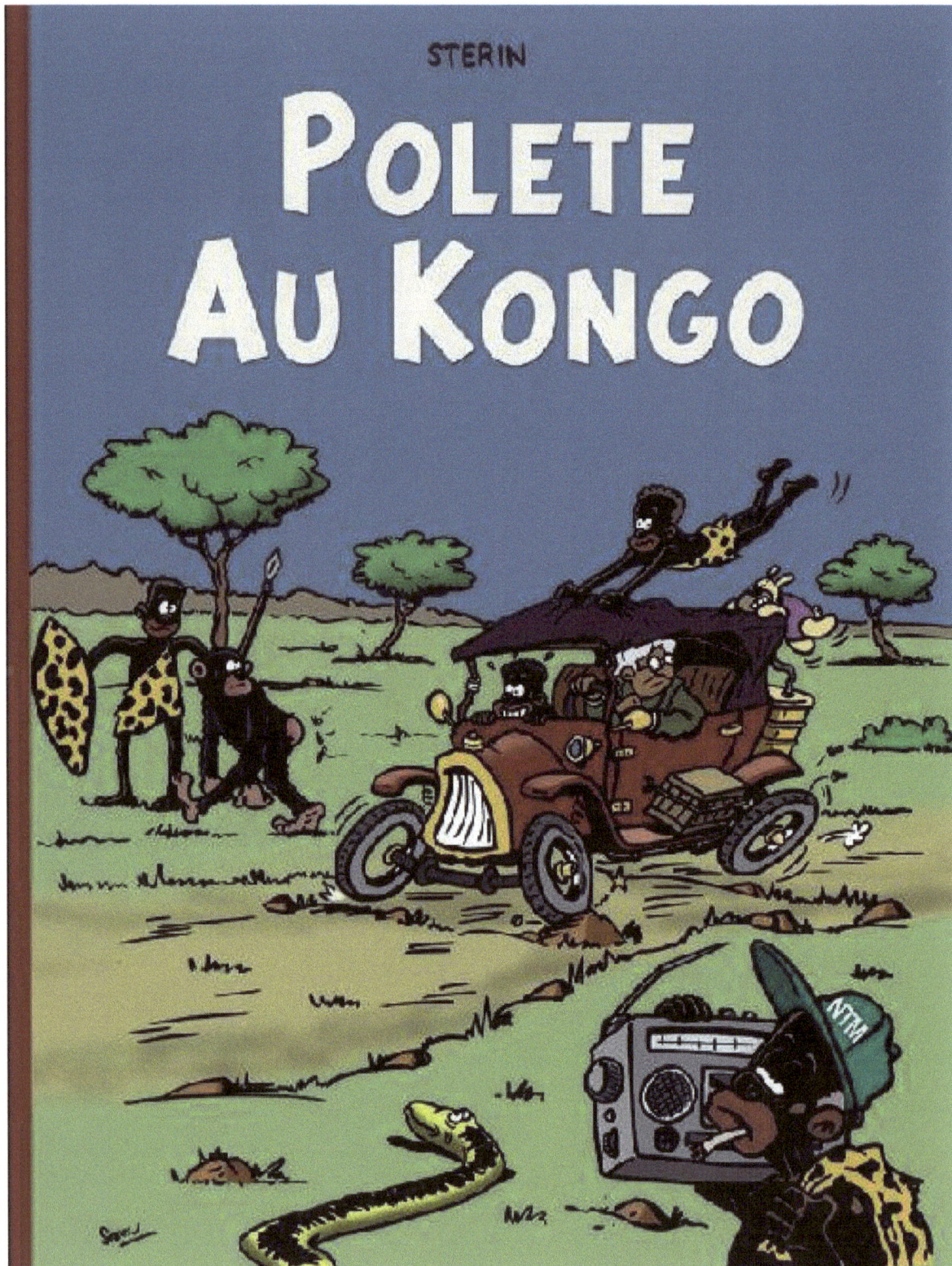

"Pole (survey) of the Congo"?

A pastiche evoking the various copyright controversies surrounding Tintin post-1983. Mikey Mouse is perhaps a reference to the Disney and Dan O'Neil (*Air Pirates/Odd Bodkins*) controversies. Mickey is on the wrong side of a dam of pastiches and copyright pressures, that will one day burst? Has Tintin just received a Garcia-like "cease and desist" letter from Moulinsart?

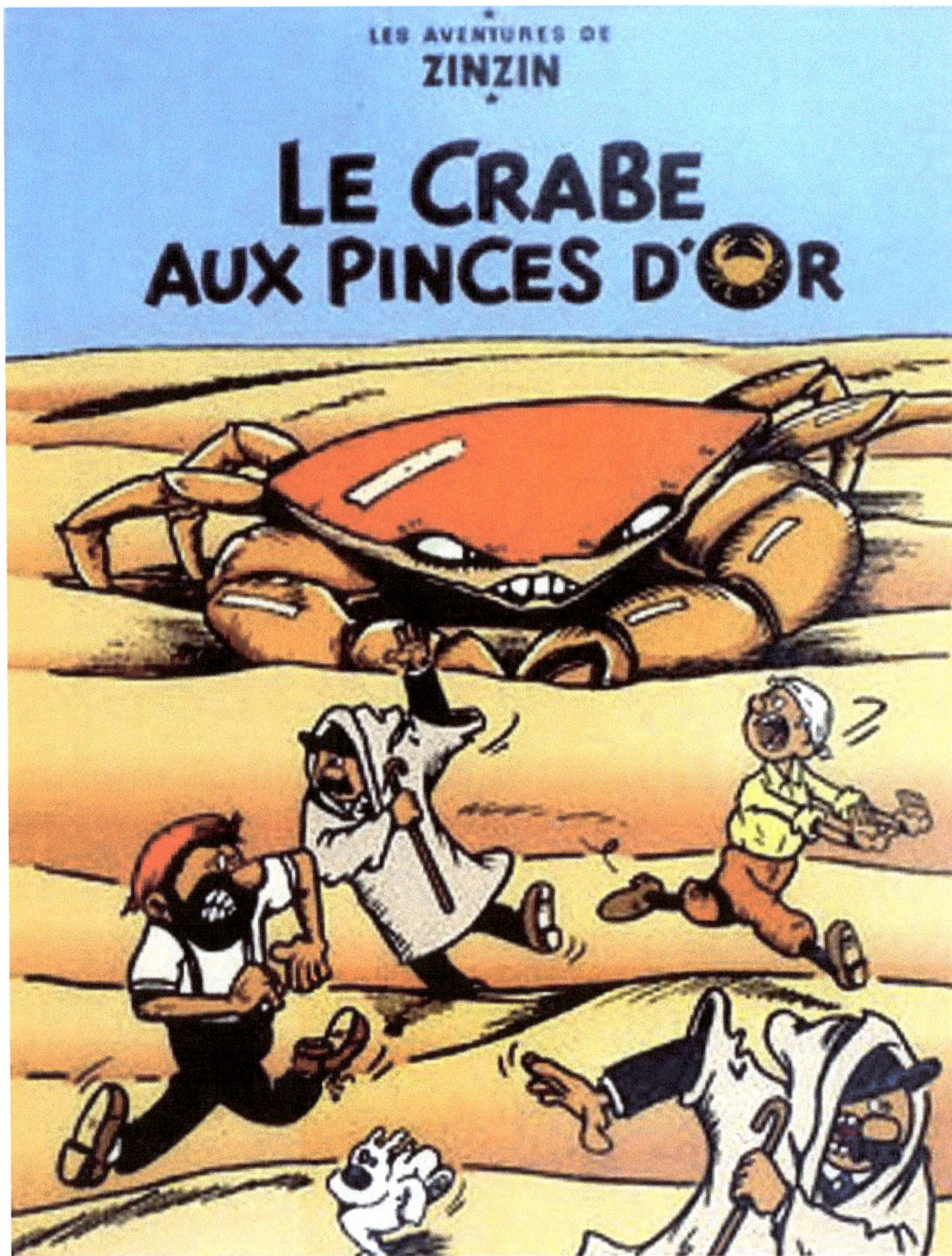

"The Crab with the Golden Claws."

-GORDON ZOLA-
★
LES AVENTURES DE
SAINT-TIN ET SON AMI LOU
★
L'ASCÈTE BOUDE
LE CRISTAL

Le Léopard Démasqué

"The Aesthete Sulks (rejects) Crystal." Once again we see Haddock's parrot Iago from *Castafiore*. See **Plate 113, 149.**

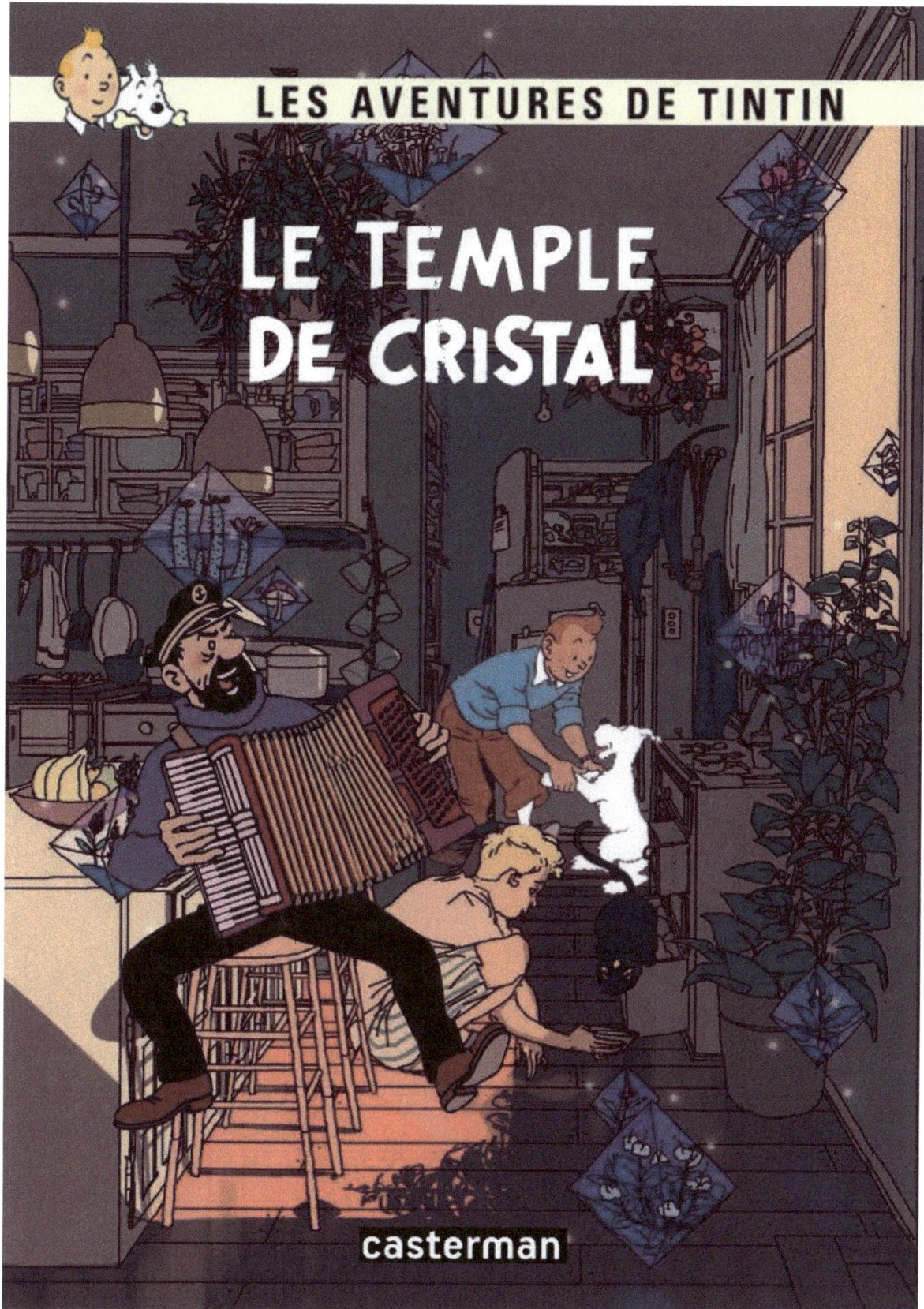

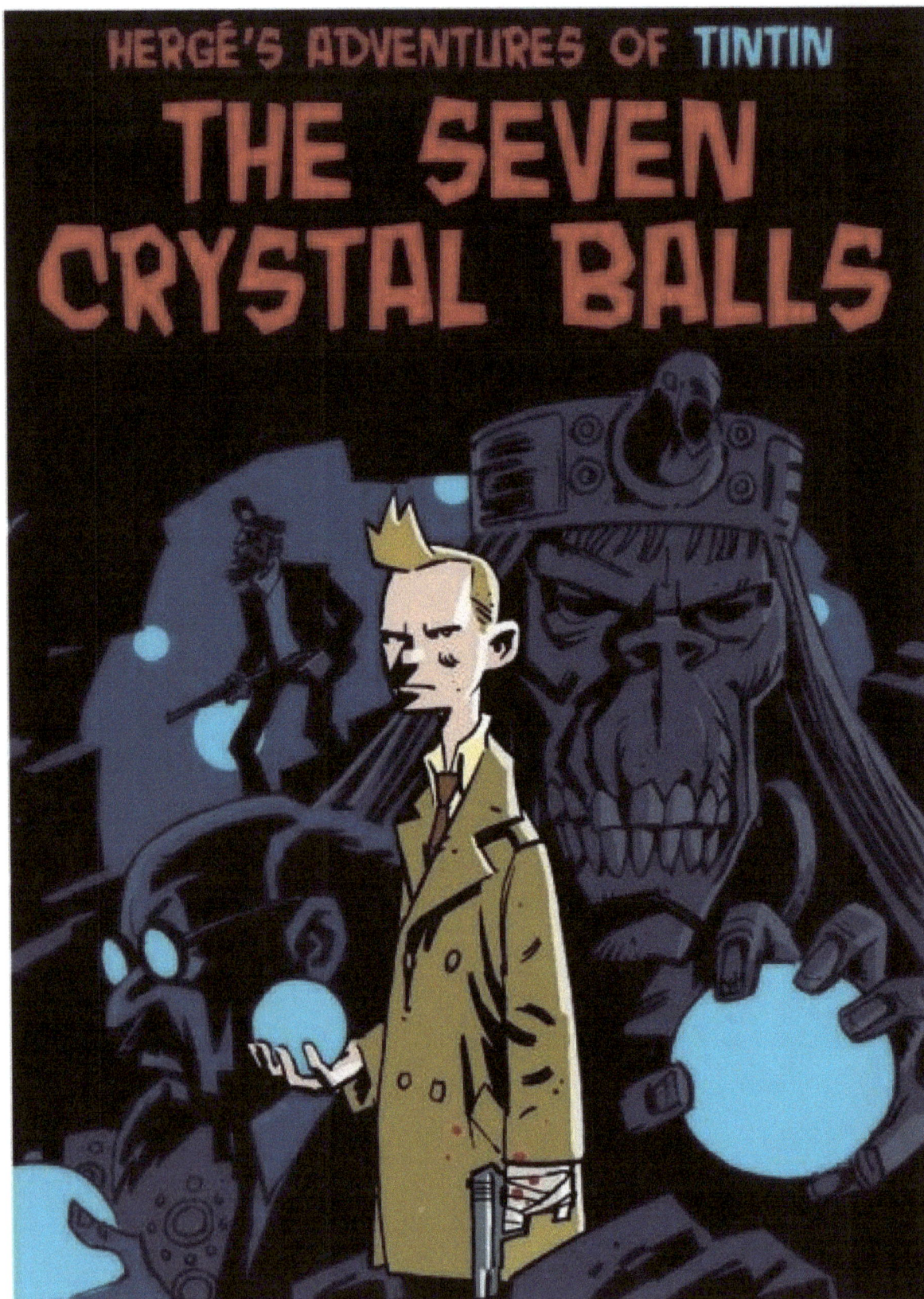

HERGÉ'S ADVENTURES OF TINTIN

THE SEVEN CRYSTAL BALLS

ALFRED HITCHCOCK

LA MORT AUX TROUSSES

L'ECAILLER DU CINEMA

"The Death Hunt." A pastiche of the 1959 Hitchcock movie *North by Northwest* and the famous plane scene. The detail is from p. 37 of *The Black Island*.

"The Ice Demon." Jacobs' cover art from *The Sarcophagi of the Sixth Continent* interposed with the Calculus shark submarine. See Section **8.G** p. 449.

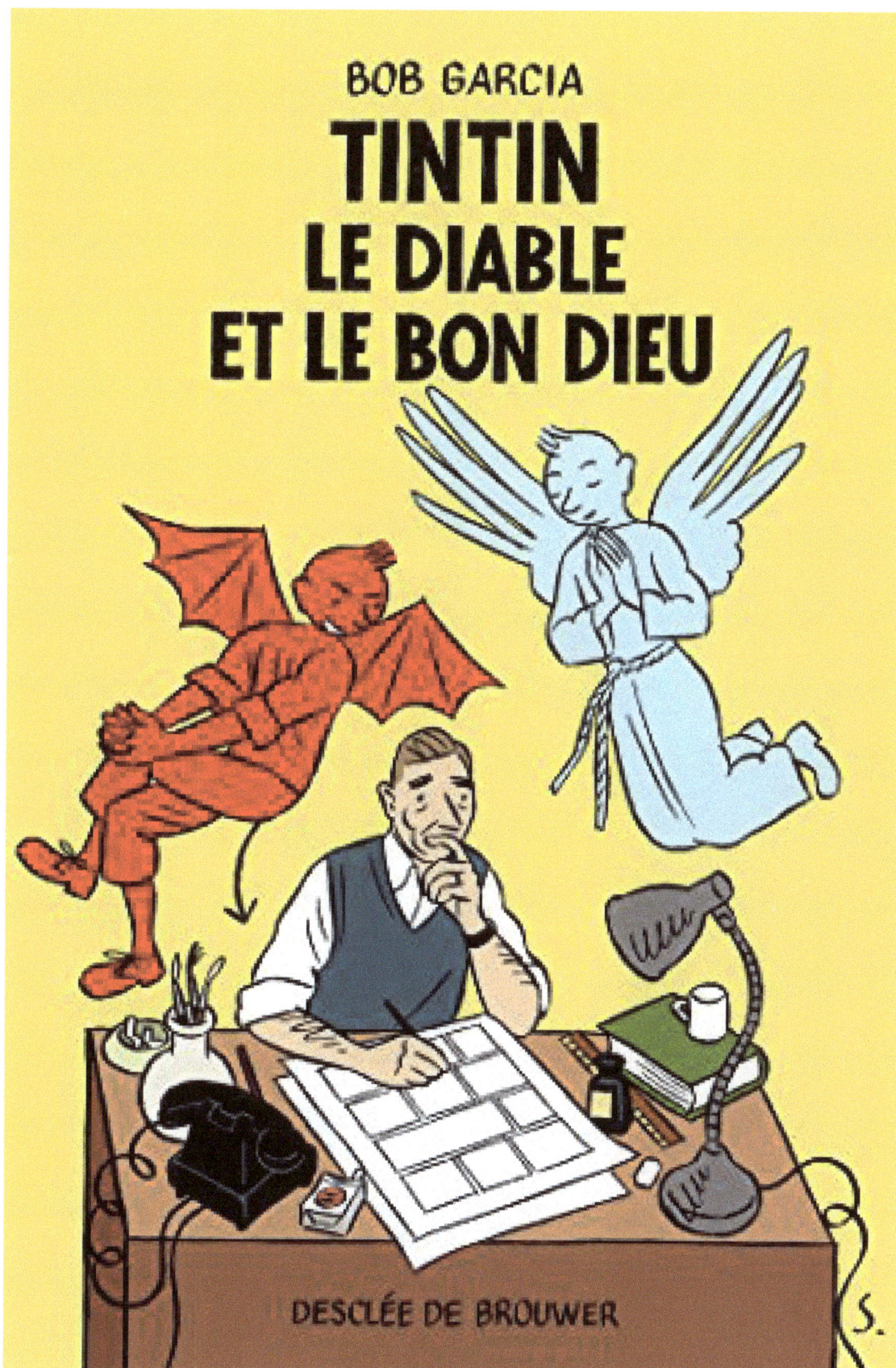

BOB GARCIA

TINTIN
LE DIABLE
ET LE BON DIEU

DESCLÉE DE BROUWER

"The Devil & the Good God." Is Hergé an angel or a demon? A reference to that scene in *Tibet* in which Snowy wrestles with his conscience over a note or a huge yak bone. A Garcia publication about his legal wrangles with Moulinsart and the Hergé estate.

"We Stepped (marched) on the Dune." A graphic scene utilising a *Black Island* Tintin and Snowy. Like *Marvel*, Hergé did not generally depict blood or killing. It was inferred.

There are several Dupond/t adventures. In this pastiche they utilise Calculus' pendulum to hunt down the treasure. See **Plate 67.**

-HERVÉ-

LES AVENTURES DE
SAINT-TIN ET SON AMI LOU
★
L'OREILLE
QUI SAIT

Le Léopard Démasqué

"The Ear that Knows."

Plate 175

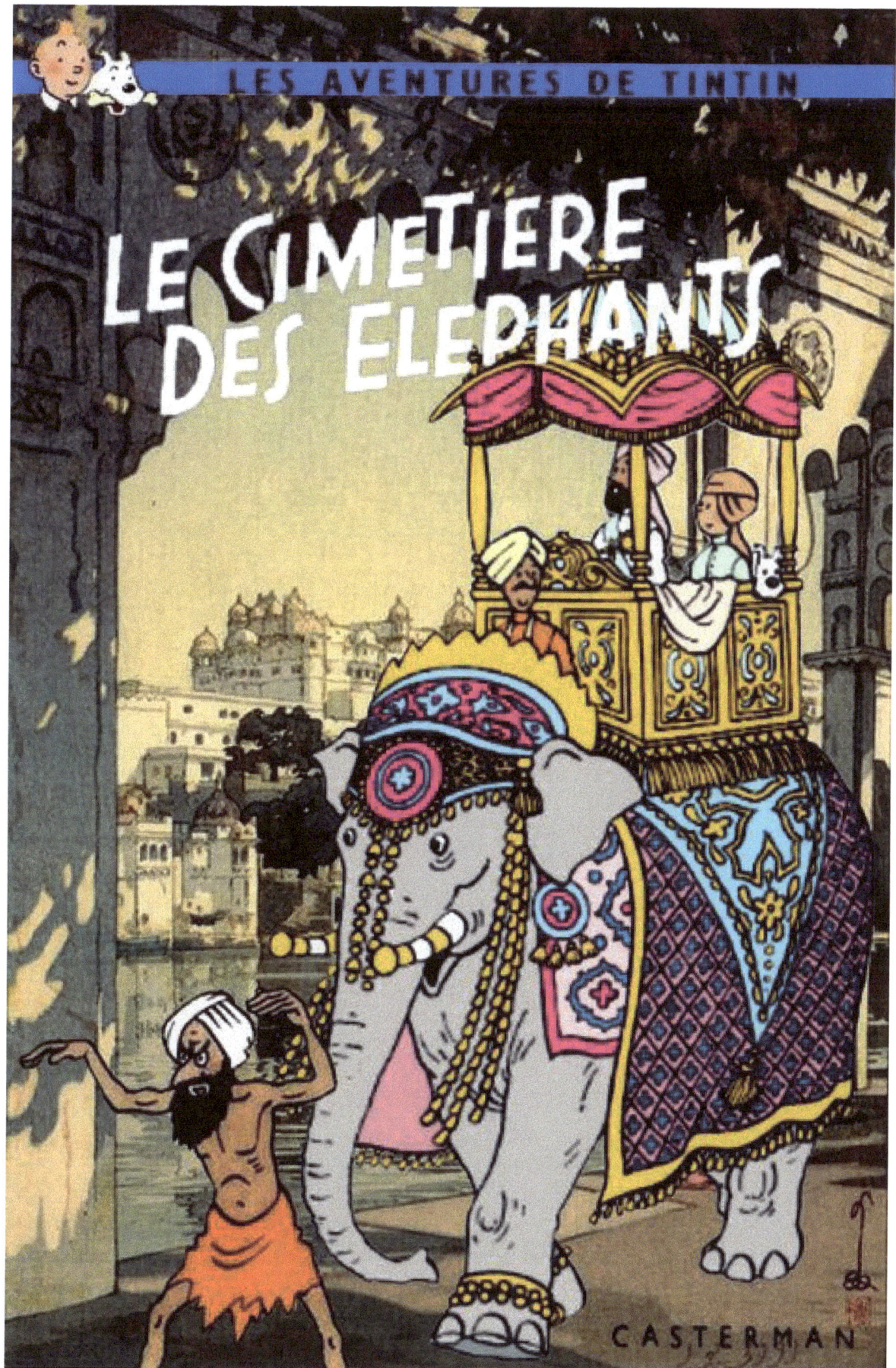

"Elephant Cemetery."

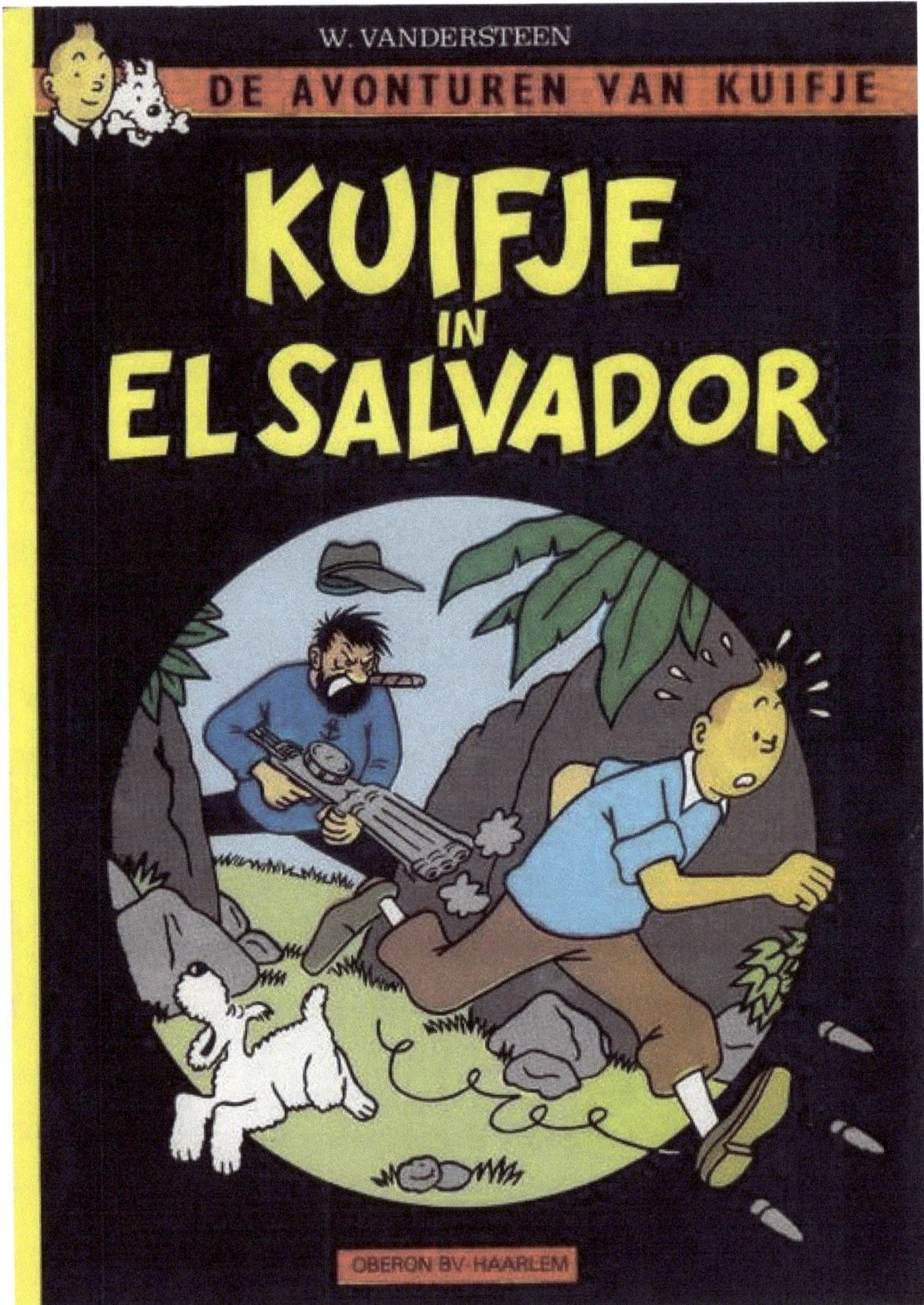

Dutch "Tintin" in El Salvador.

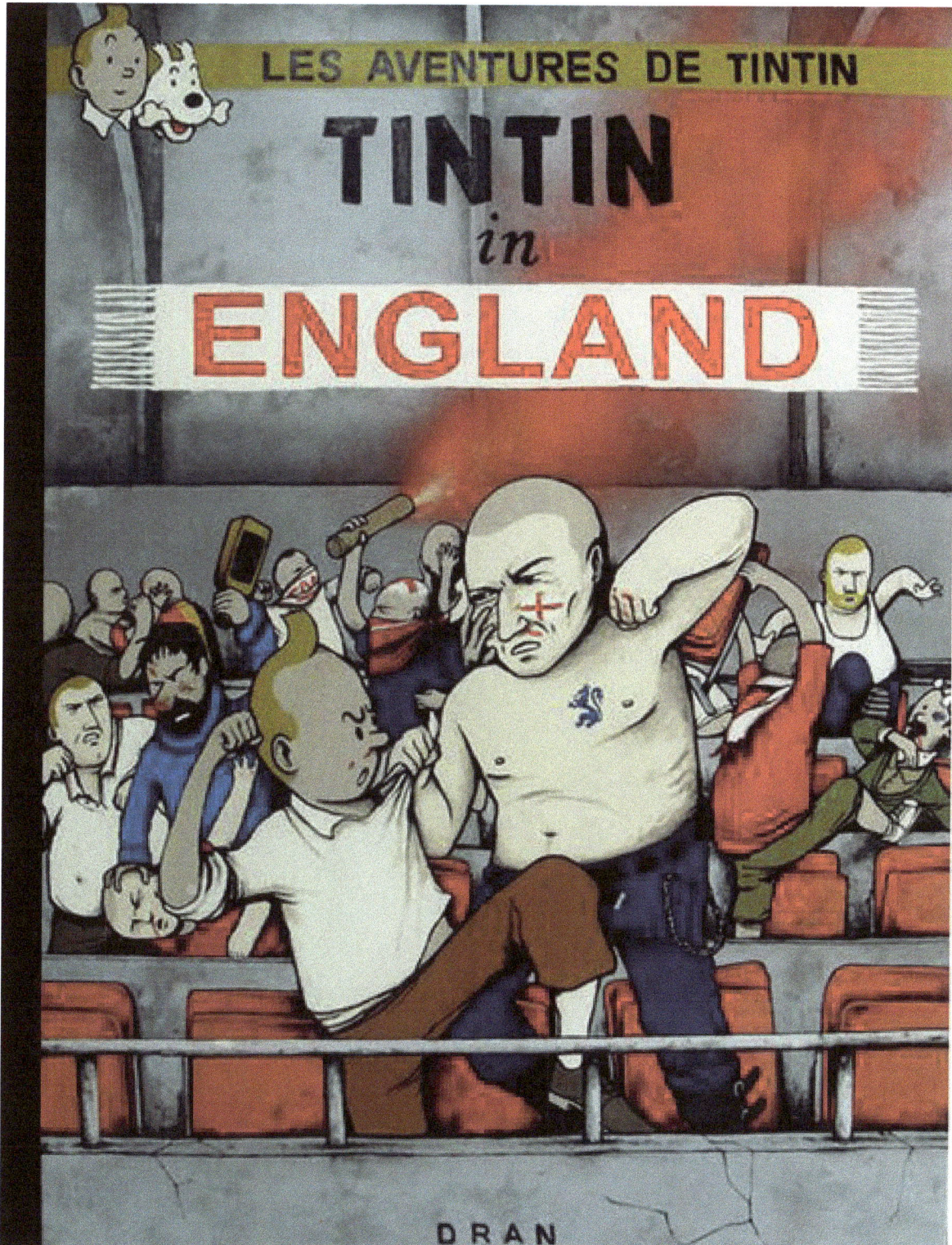

Tintin gets into a football brawl. The title is a soccer scarf. Haddock holds his own with some Loch Lomond but Calculus is worse for wear.

- HERGÉ -

LES AVENTURES DE TINTIN

VOYAGE À LONDRES

casterman

"Trip to London." Out on ol' London town with Nestor bringing up the rear. Our heroes are oblivious to IRA bomb blasts.

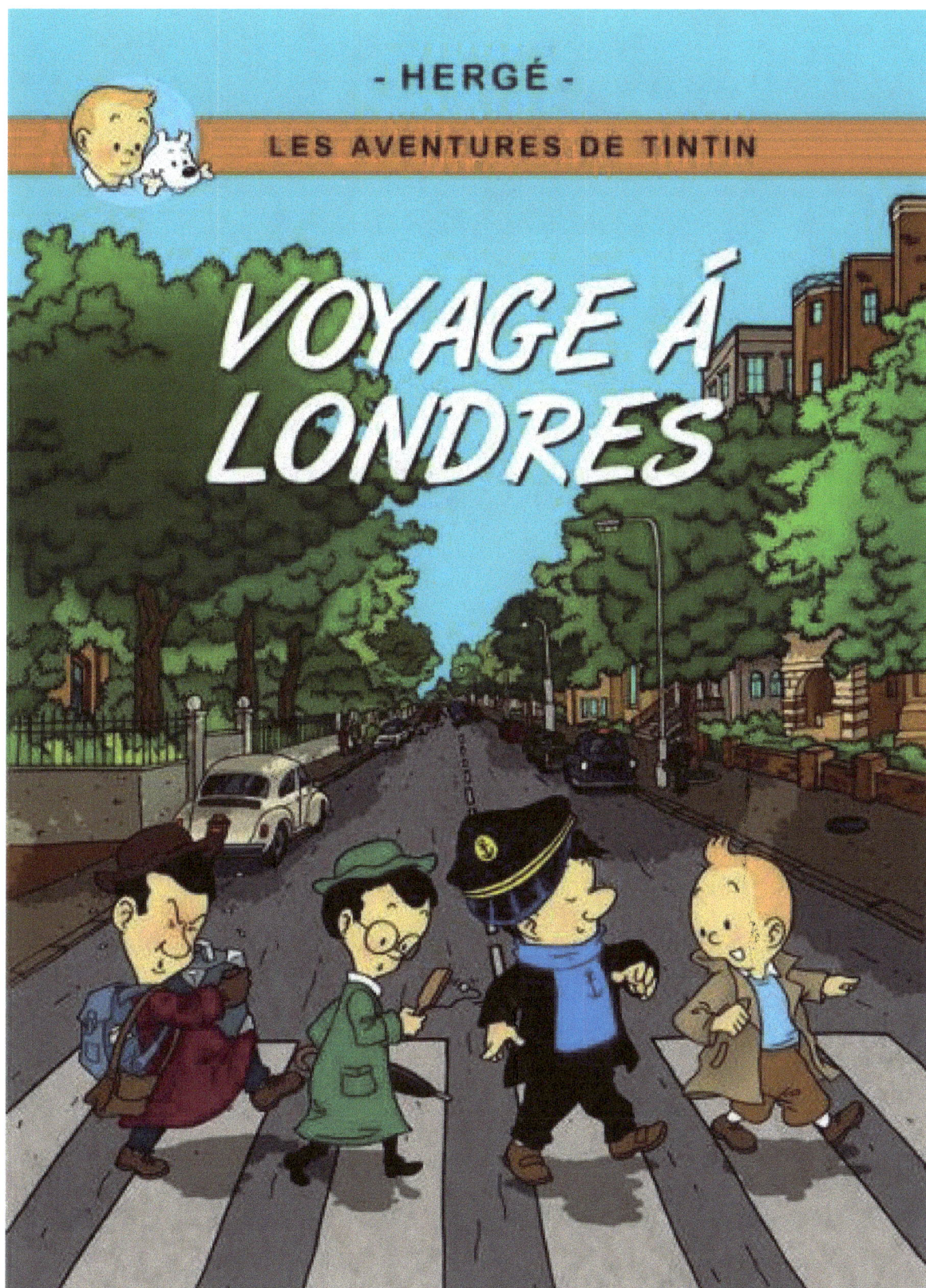

- HERGÉ -

LES AVENTURES DE TINTIN

VOYAGE Á LONDRES

Baby 'Tintins' walk Abbey Rd and the Beatles' album cover. See also **Plate 85.**

Plate 180

Another Hergé-Jacobs fusion.

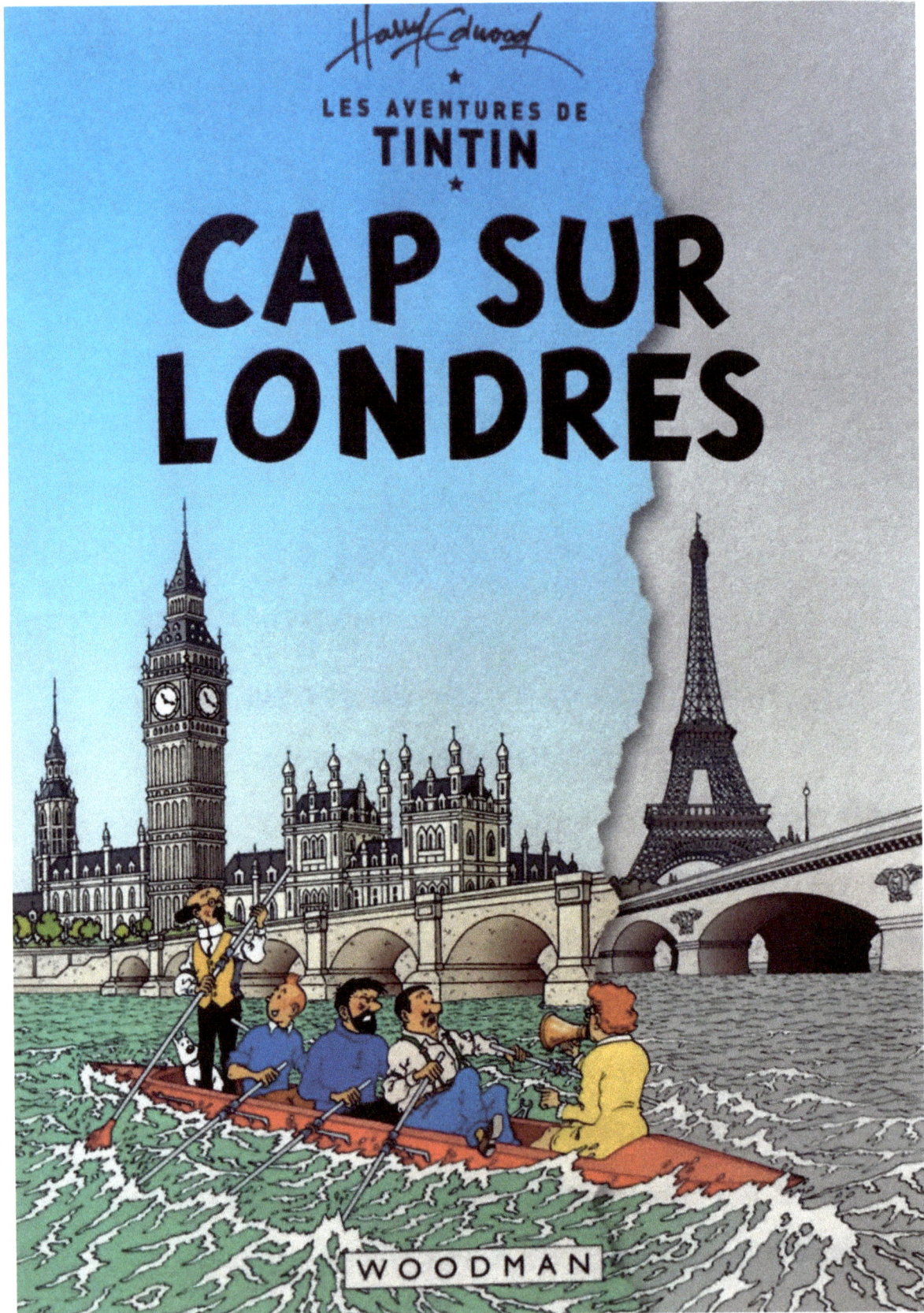

"Cape Town to London."

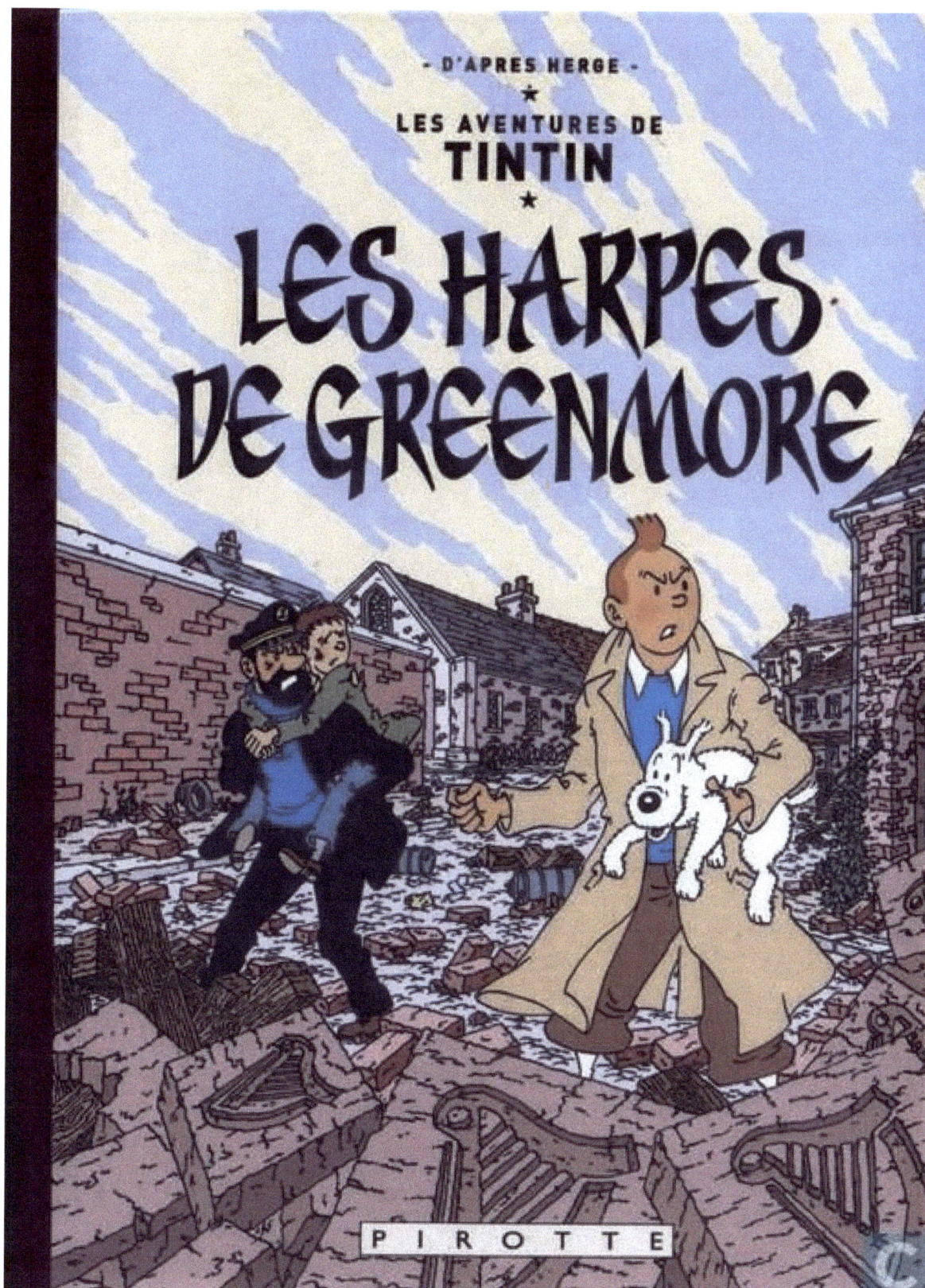

- D'APRÈS HERGÉ -

★

LES AVENTURES DE
TINTIN

★

LES HARPES DE GREENMORE

PIROTTE

"Greenmore's Harps."

"The Ruins of Stonehenge."

"A World Engulfed." Tintin meets Climate Change.

-GORDON ZOLA-
★
LES AVENTURES DE
SAINT-TIN ET SON AMI LOU
★
COQ EN TOC

Le Léopard Démasqué

"Rooster in Knock" or 'Knocked Up Rooster"? a pun on "Stock de Coque" ("Coke in Stock") the original French title for "The Red Sea Sharks."

Plate 188

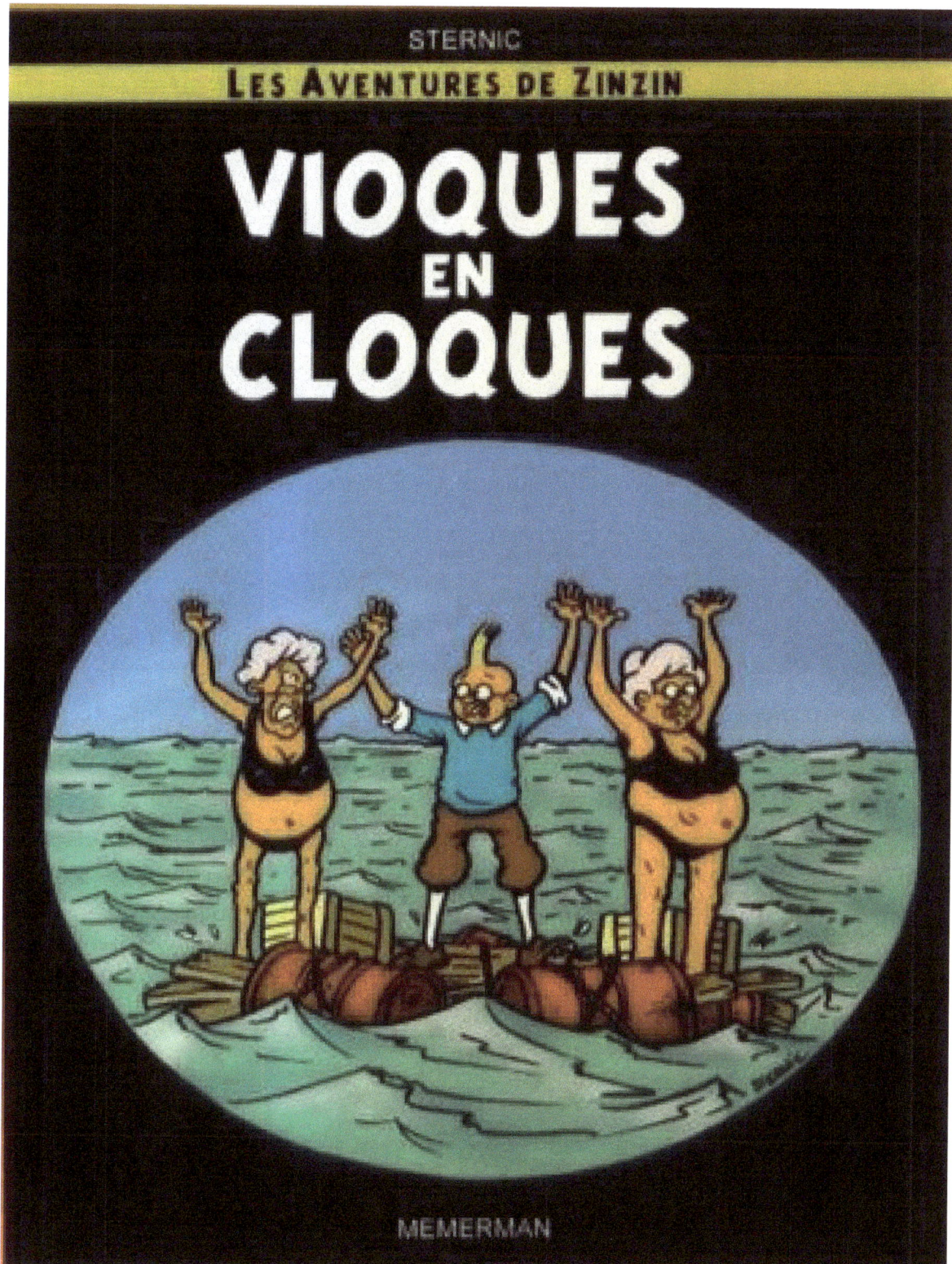

"The Pregnant Violets"? Probably a nonsense pun on the original title.

"The Fall." Tintin with *Flight 714* characters. The man top left is the driver in **Plate 314** (D'Archibald, the pastiche artist?). The gentleman with the umbrella is from *Calculus* p. 44, see **Plate 217**.

"The Fall of Icarus"

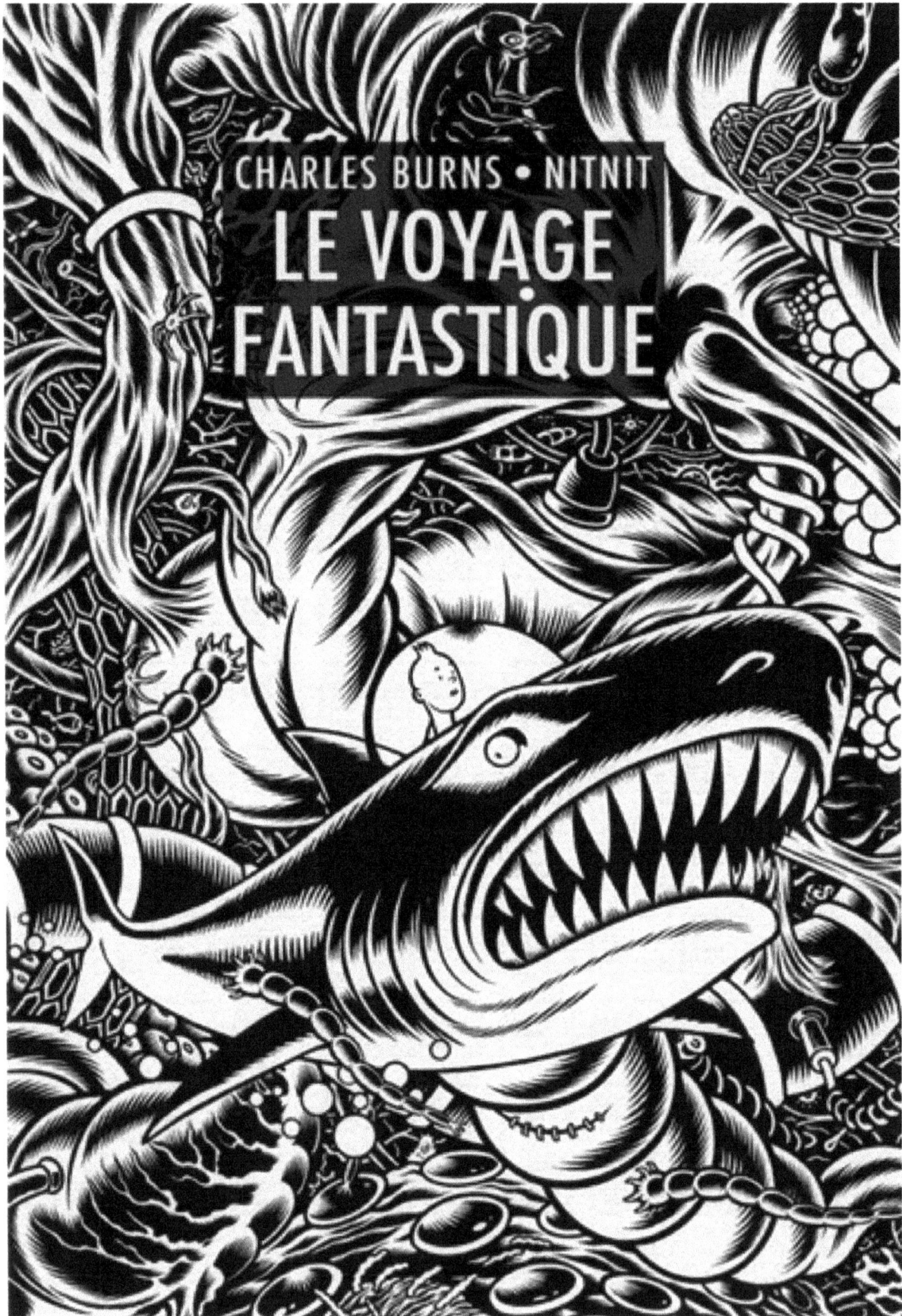

CHARLES BURNS • NITNIT
LE VOYAGE FANTASTIQUE

Burns parodies Tintin backwards as "Nitnit" more clever than my "TimTam" the Australasian chocolate biscuit, **Plate 223b.** Burns' Calculus submarine is alive.

LES AVENTURES DE TINTIN

TINTIN À LA FERME

casterman

"Tintin on the Farm."

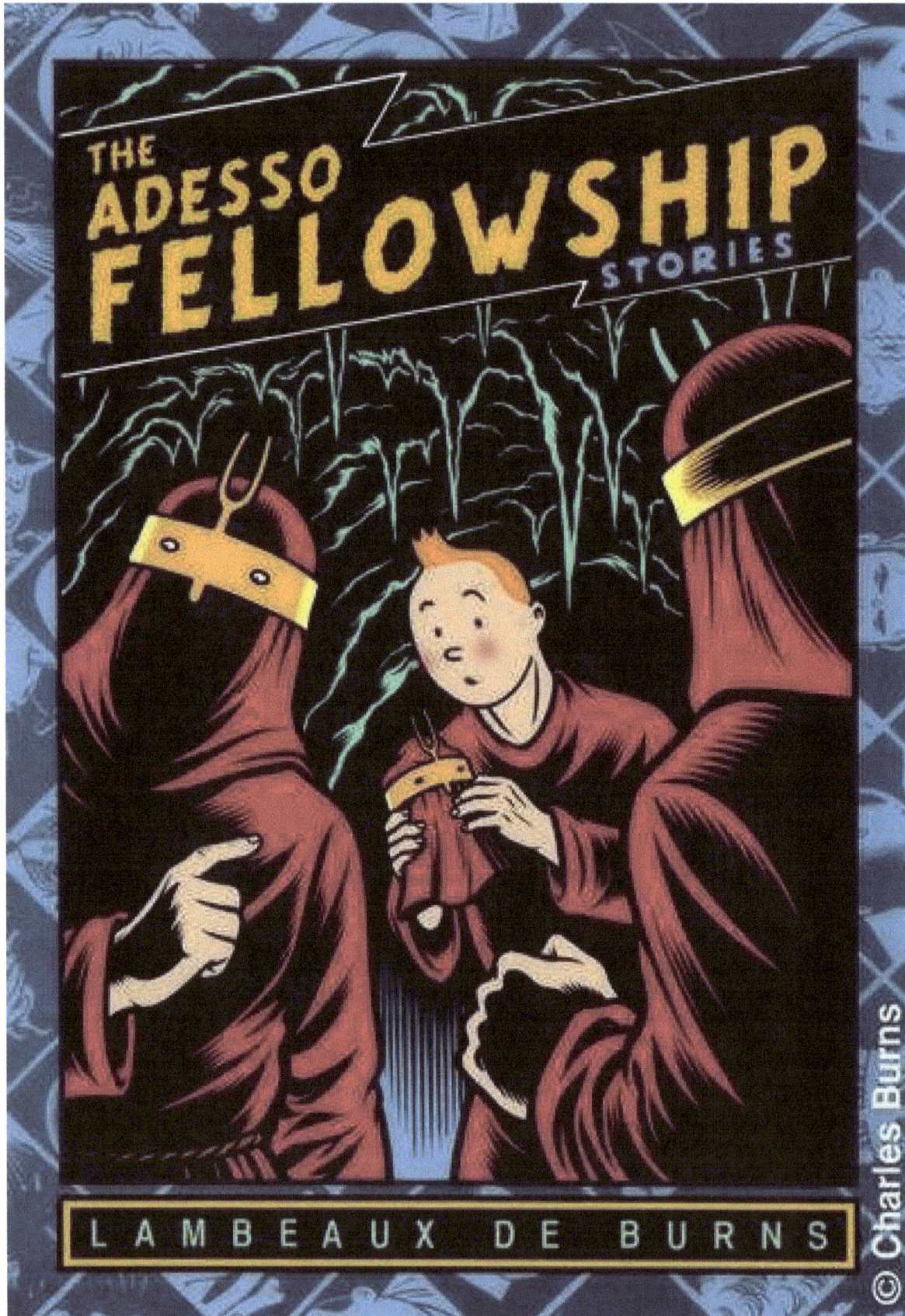

A Charles Burns reworking of the secret society from *Cigars of the Pharaoh*.

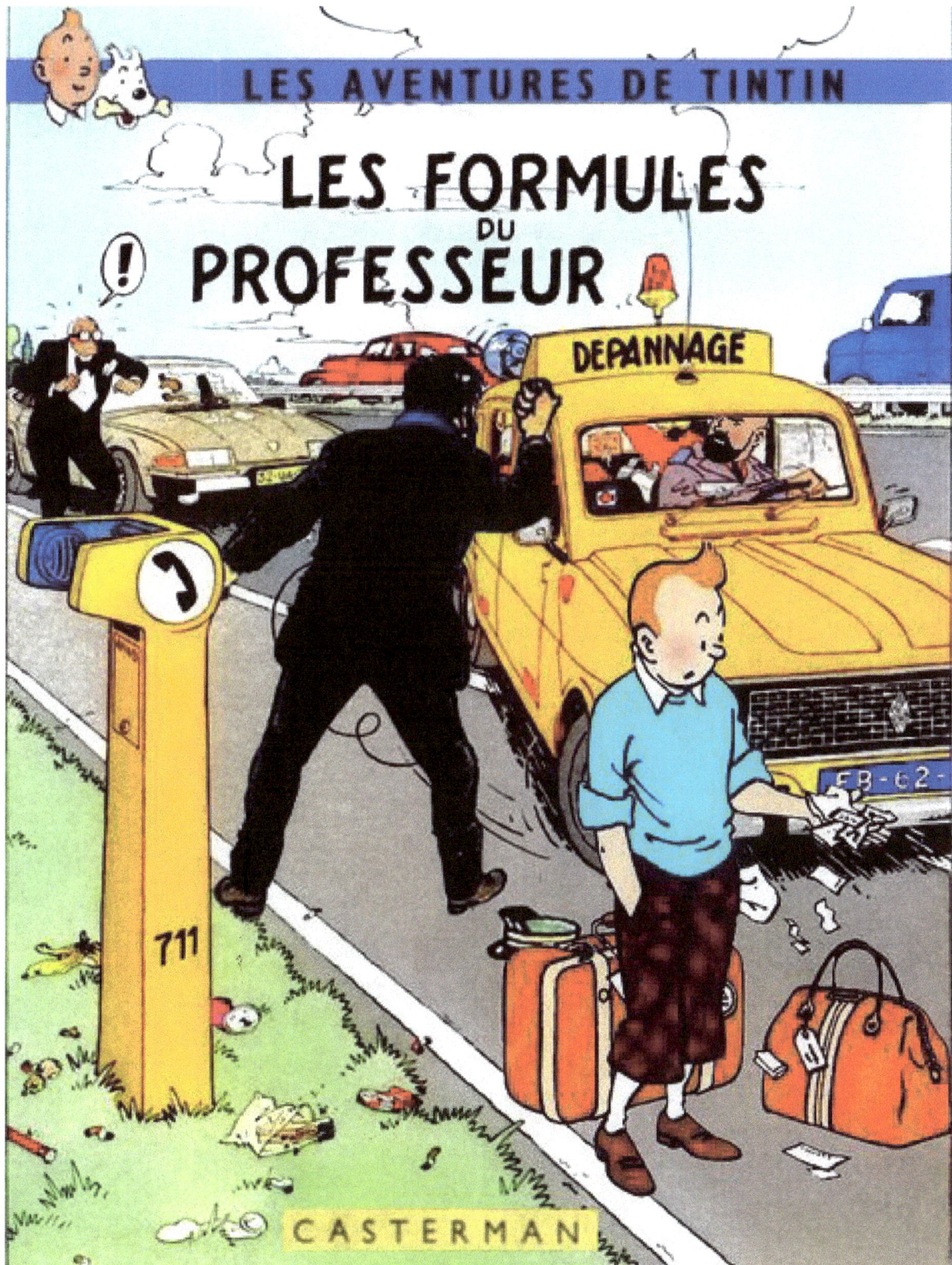

A Jacobs' title, see Section **8.B.** The Tintin artwork is partially repeated from **Plate 124** *Airport*. The Taxi is "Troubleshooting" and perhaps refers to Dr. Müller, the driver, who is always trouble and shoots at our heroes.

Tintin putt-putts down a French winter street in his Congo-mobile.

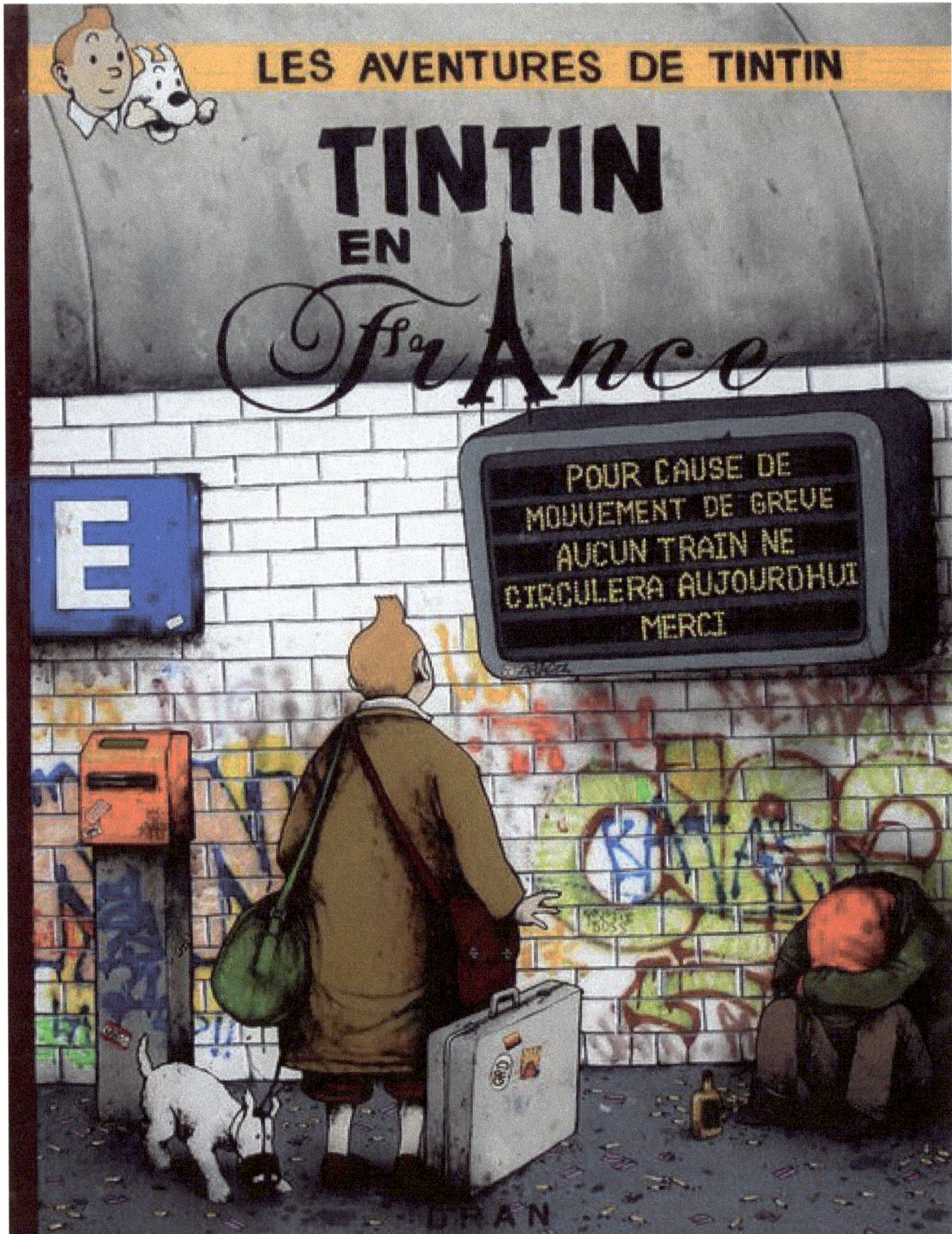

The digital sign reads, "Because of the strike no trains will run today Thank you."

Tintin in America artwork transposed onto a Fribourg landscape and coloured.
See also **Plate 21.**

"The Eiffel Tower Gold."

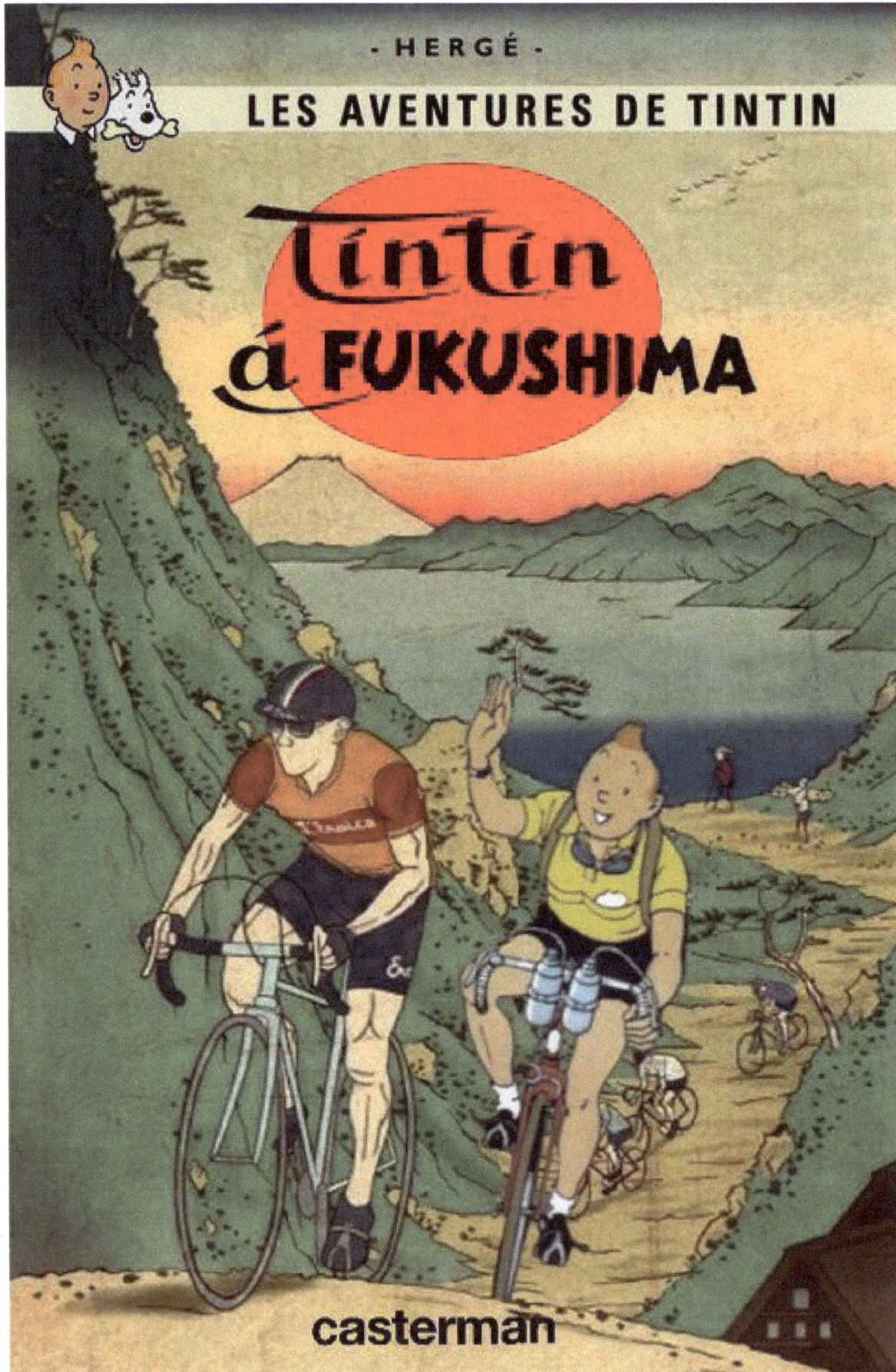

- HERGÉ -

LES AVENTURES DE TINTIN

Tintin á FUKUSHIMA

casterman

Fukushima or Japanese vignettes are popular. See **Plates 68, 69; 318.**

"The Useless Ghost." Both Calculus and Tintin have acted as sheet ghosts.

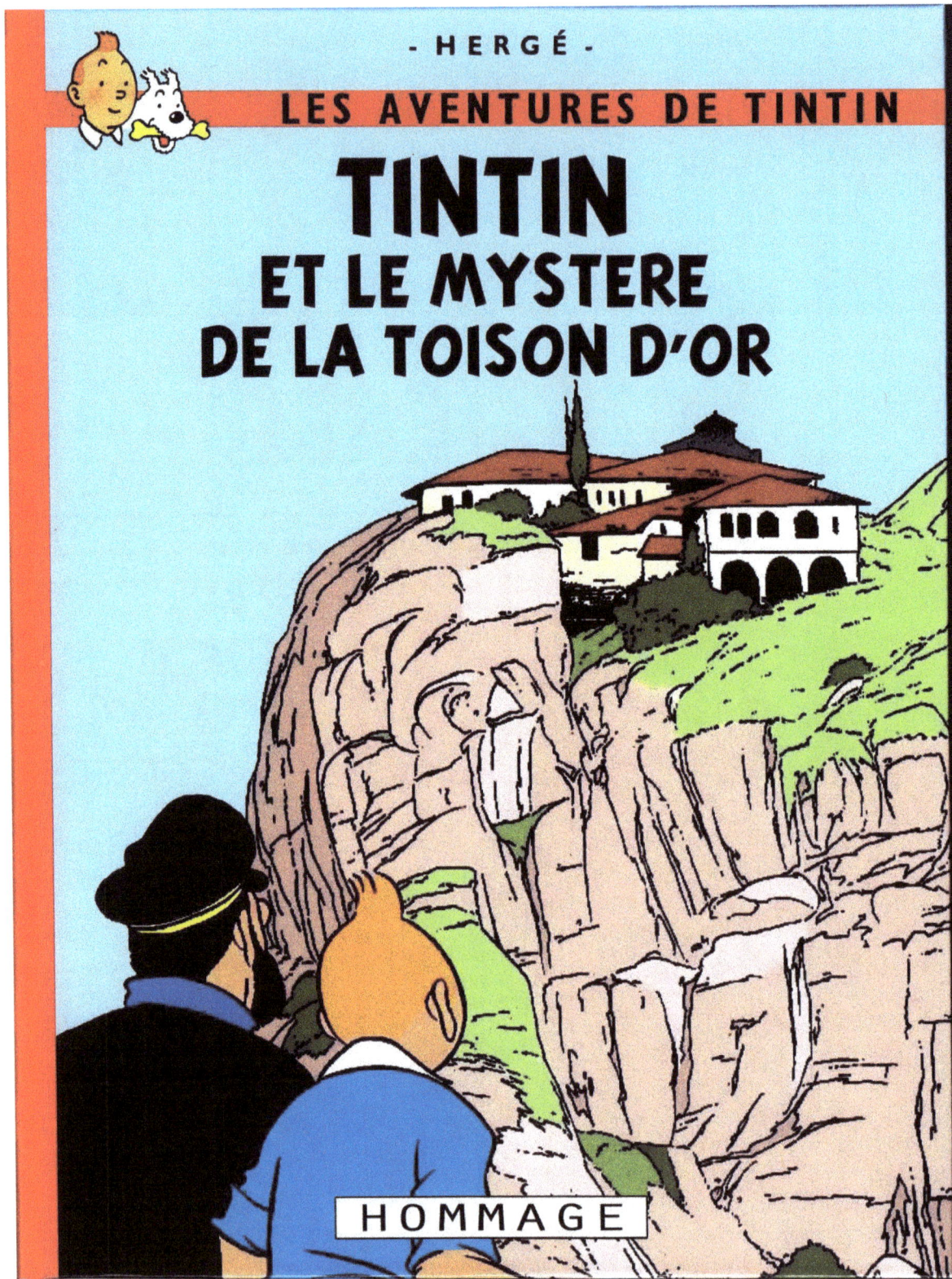

- HERGÉ -

LES AVENTURES DE TINTIN

TINTIN ET LE MYSTERE DE LA TOISON D'OR

HOMMAGE

"The Mystery of the Golden Fleece."

"The Green Perfume" (opium?). See also **Plate 277.**

"The Secret of the Green Egg."

LES AVENTURES DU PETIT PILOTE BELGE

CHASSE EN HAUTE MER

CASTERFLOT

"Hunting Hautemer." This is a re-conceived drawing from the helicopter chase scene in *The Calculus Affair*, p. 31.

"Hergé's Secret."

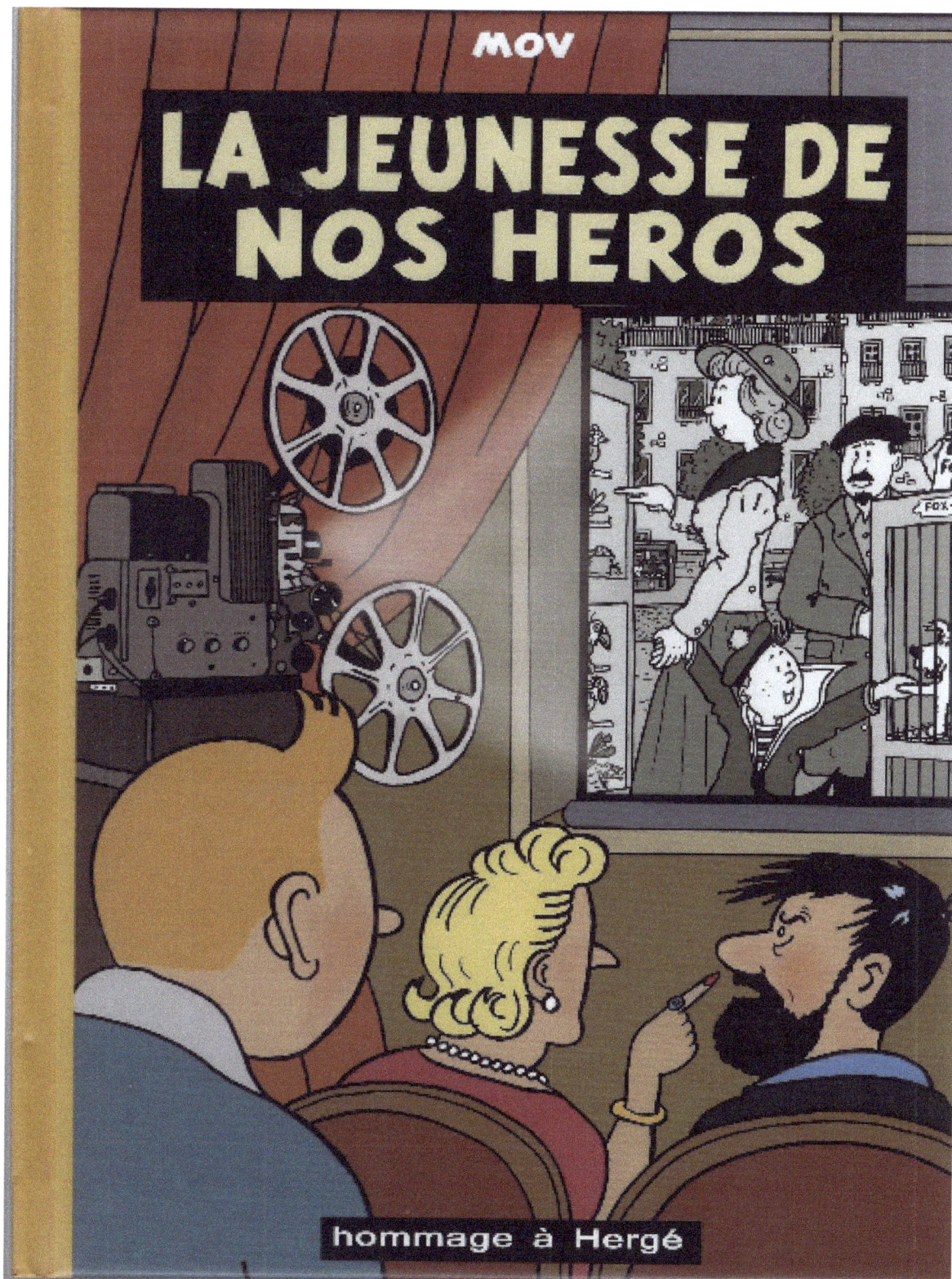

"Our Hero's Youth." The black and white home movie on the screen, is the art from pastiche **Plate 226** in which Tintin is a toddler and first meets Snowy as a puppy, suggesting a back life for Tintin. Notably it is Castafiore and Haddock watching this home movie (as parents?). See also **Plate 136**.

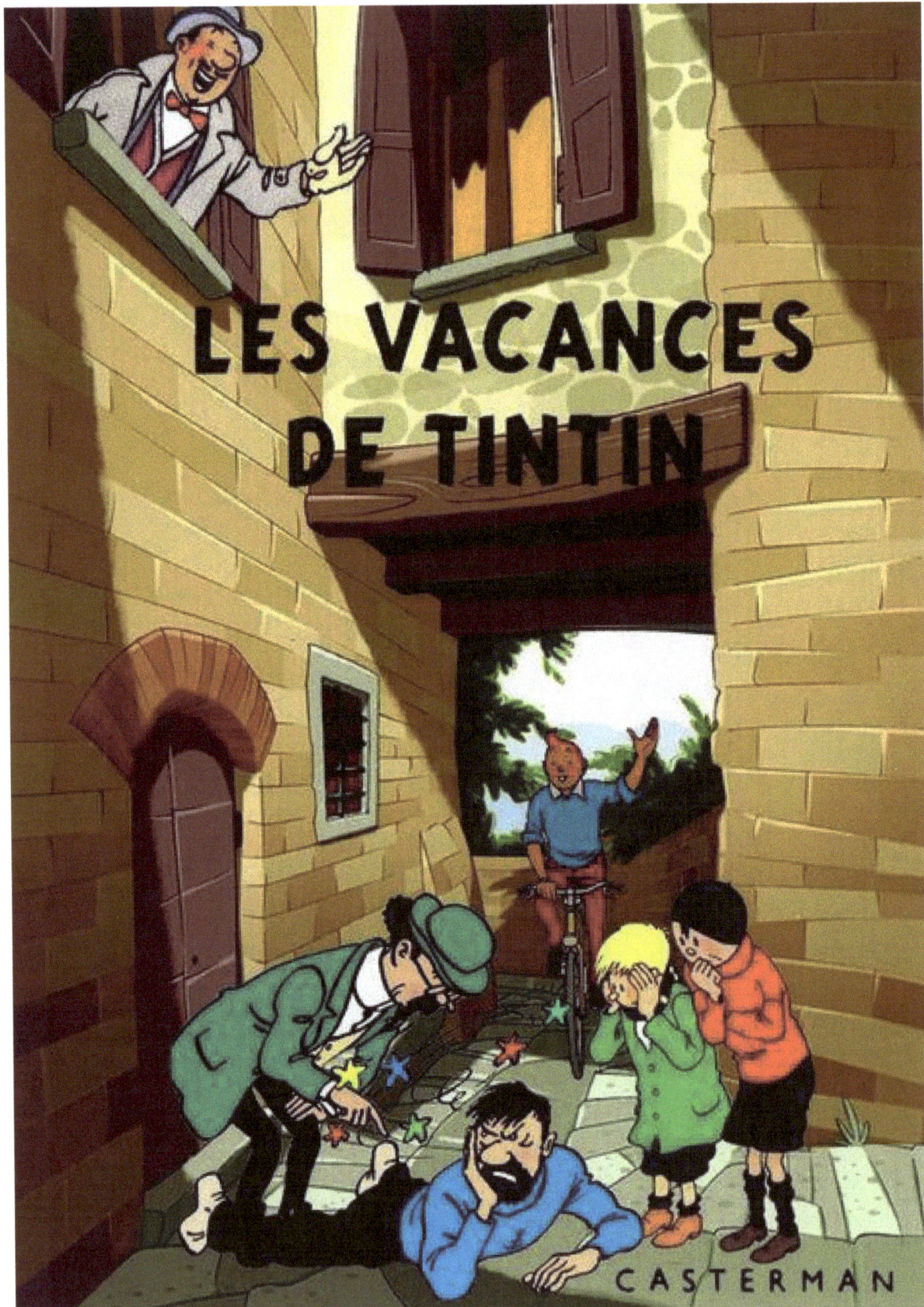

"Tintin's Vacations." Quick and Flupke are on this family holiday too. Haddock never seems to be able to escape Jolyon Wagg who is perhaps holding forth about accident injury insurance.

Is a buyer spotting a rare Tintin annual?

LES AVENTURES DE TINTIN ET MILOU

LE TRÉSOR DE L'INCA

casterman

"The Treasure of the Inca."

- HEMGI -

LES IMPROBABLES AVENTURES DE
TINTIN

le piege
javanais

"The Javanese trap"

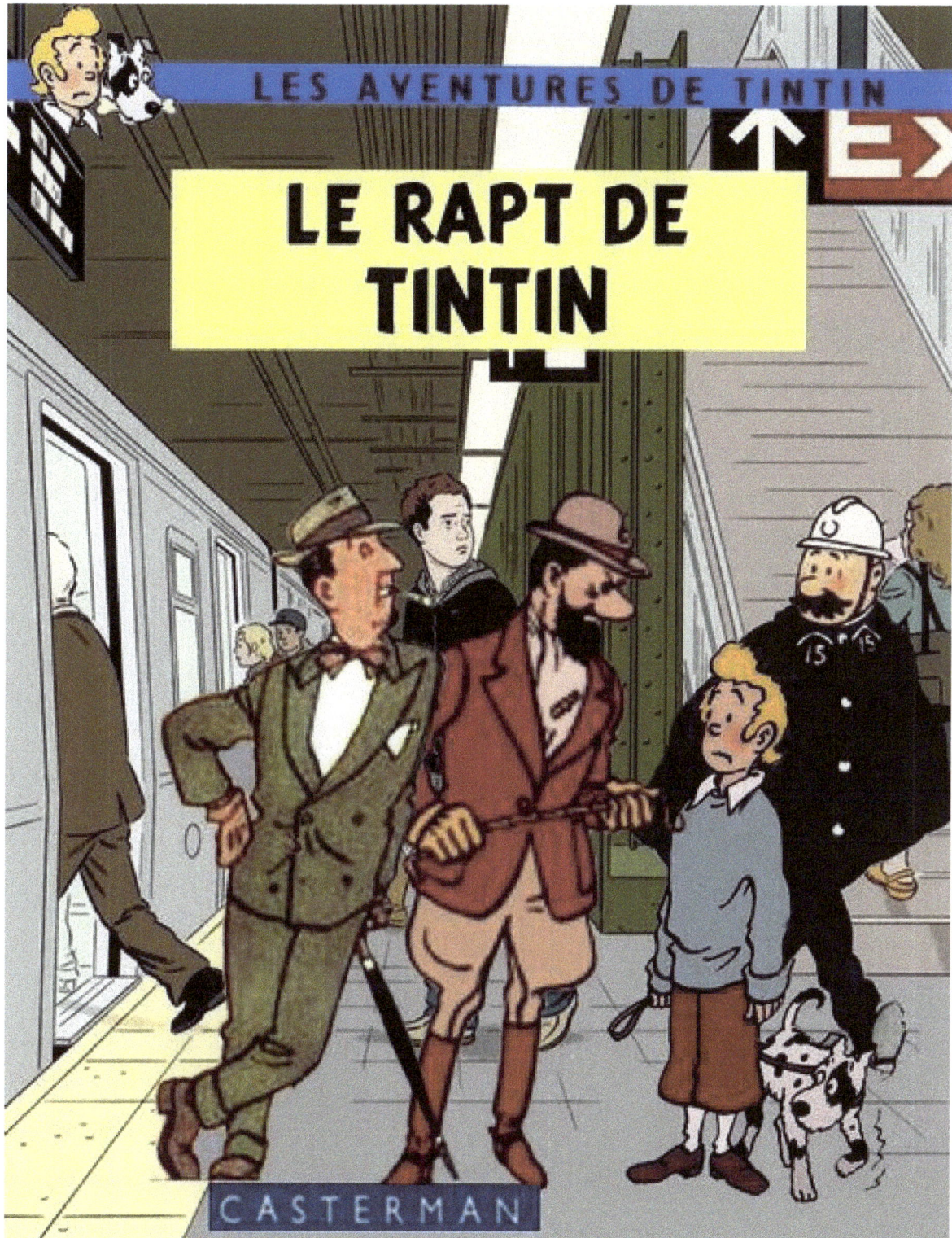

"The Abduction of Tintin." The man leaning on the umbrella is an incidental Casanova from p. 44 of *The Calculus Affair* with a bouquet of flowers, who has his umbrella pulled out from under him by Snowy. The young man center background is perhaps the pastiche artist?

"The Lair of Koltar."

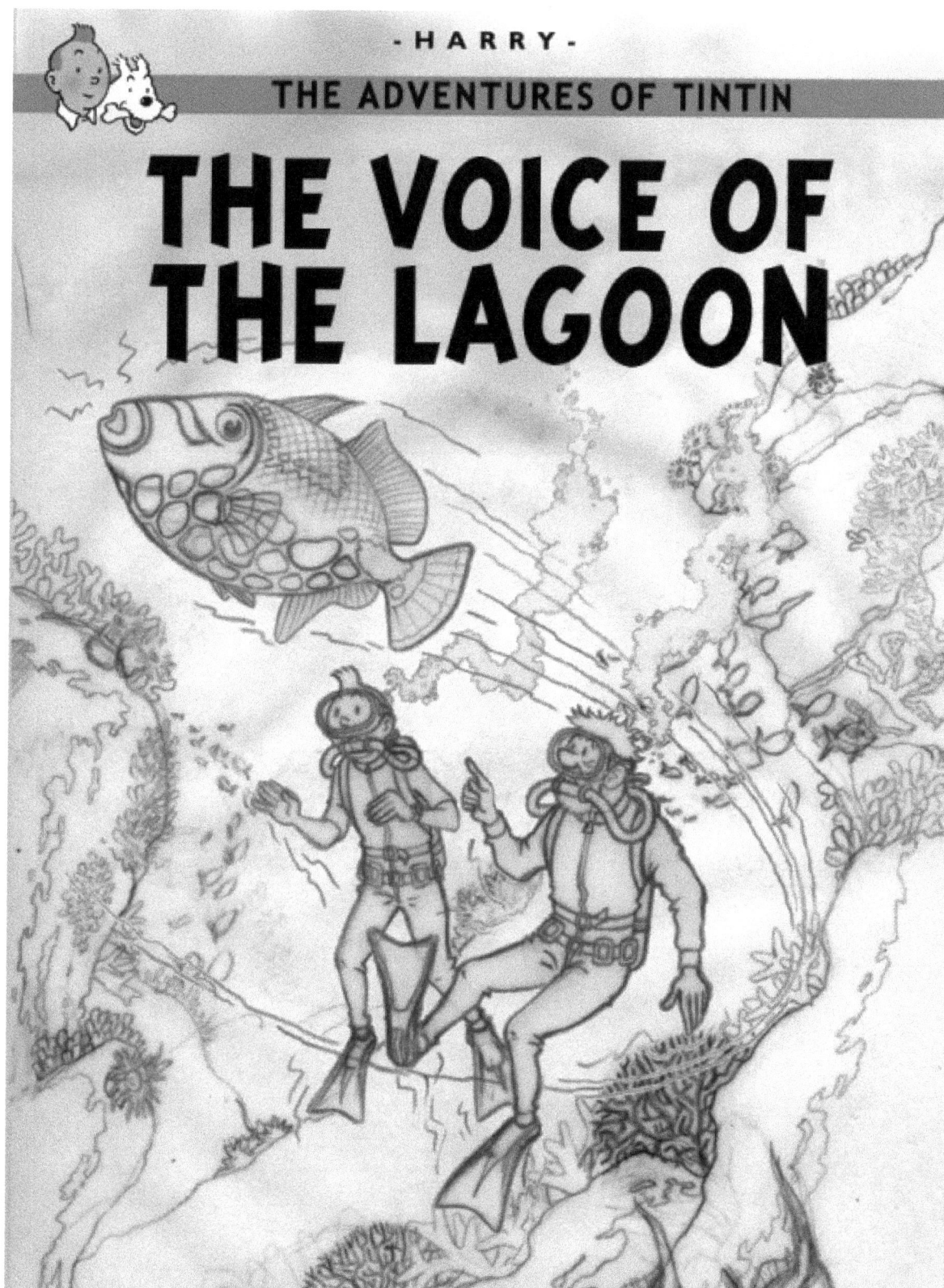

- HARRY -

THE ADVENTURES OF TINTIN

THE VOICE OF THE LAGOON

Harry Edwood pencils for the cover of *Lagoon*, realised in colour as **Plate 220.** See also **Plate 221.**

Harry Edwood

A NEW ADVENTURE OF TINTIN

THE VOICE OF THE LAGOON

Nosy Boraha, east cost of Madagascar. Tintin and the Captain are taking refuge in the tropics, away from the hustle and bustle of life at Marlinspike ...

Ah, the sea air! There's nothing like it – the waves, the spray ...

... the quiet ...

Exactly, lad! Here, there's no Jolyon Wagg! No Vagabond Car Club, no Jolly Follies ...

... the calm ...

?

A NEW ADVENTURE OF TINTIN

THE VOICE OF THE LAGOON

DRAWINGS AND ORIGINAL TEXT BY HARRY EDWOOD, TRANSLATED BY RICHARD
BASED ON THE CHARACTERS CREATED BY HERGÉ

Ten thousand thundering typhoons! Is this shack falling apart or are we under attack?

What's that thingummy?

A stone ... but made of lead ...

Lead? Another piece of junk from those blistering Sputniks?

Possibly ... it could well be an aerolite...

What's that you're calling me? Aerolite yourself! I'm not ...

No, Captain - a meteorite ...

Ah, a shooting star ... and it had to fall on me! That's a good start!

Strange, all the same.

A bit of the local tobacco... a siesta... that'll do me nicely.

YEAARGH!

331

A NEW ADVENTURE OF TINTIN
THE VOICE OF THE LAGOON
DRAWINGS AND ORIGINAL TEXT BY HARRY EDWOOD, TRANSLATED BY RICHARD
BASED ON THE CHARACTERS CREATED BY HERGÉ

Hukkh ! Turn it off ... quickly !

There, you're fine now - you've deflated nicely.

Nothing serious, Captain ! It was only the air valve ...

You think so ? Ha ! To be turned into an underwater blimp is nothing serious ?!

You come up with some good ones. I'm at the end of my tether with all these happenings !

RKMPXKFRTZRVT ! Come free, you blistering ...

... thundering rubber-necked cytoplasm ! ... Aha, that's it !

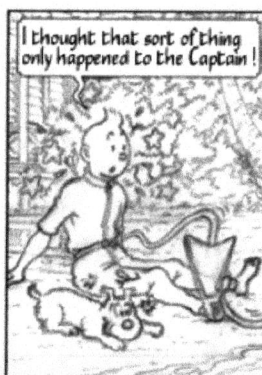

I thought that sort of thing only happened to the Captain !

Ah ! ... Peace ! ... ... finally !

What's that blistering pisciform ?

Thundering typhoons ! It's a ... ... and it's coming right for me !

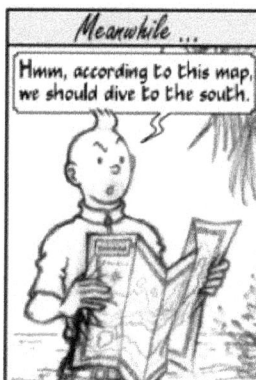

Meanwhile ...

Hmm, according to this map, we should dive to the south.

Snowy, you wait here. I'm just going to join the Captain and ...

HELP ME!

"The Voice of the Lagoon." In my view a less successful realised colour cover than the earlier drawing or the plate opposite.

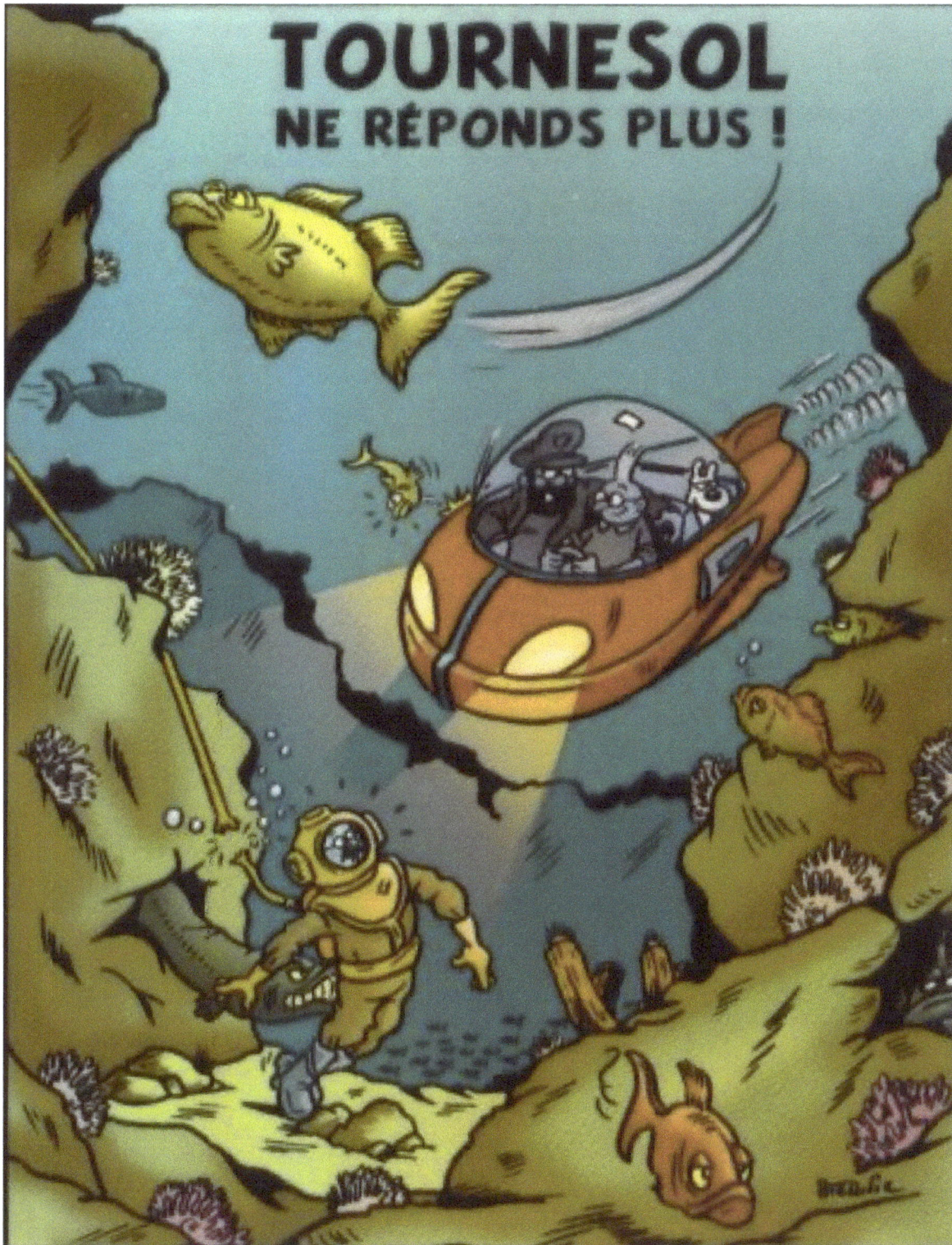

"Calculus (Tournesol) Does Not Respond" (his air pipe is severed). Haddock and Tintin traverse in a more modern Calculus submersible, and the fish top left is a variation on Edwood's pencil sketch composition for *Lagoon* **(Plate 331).**

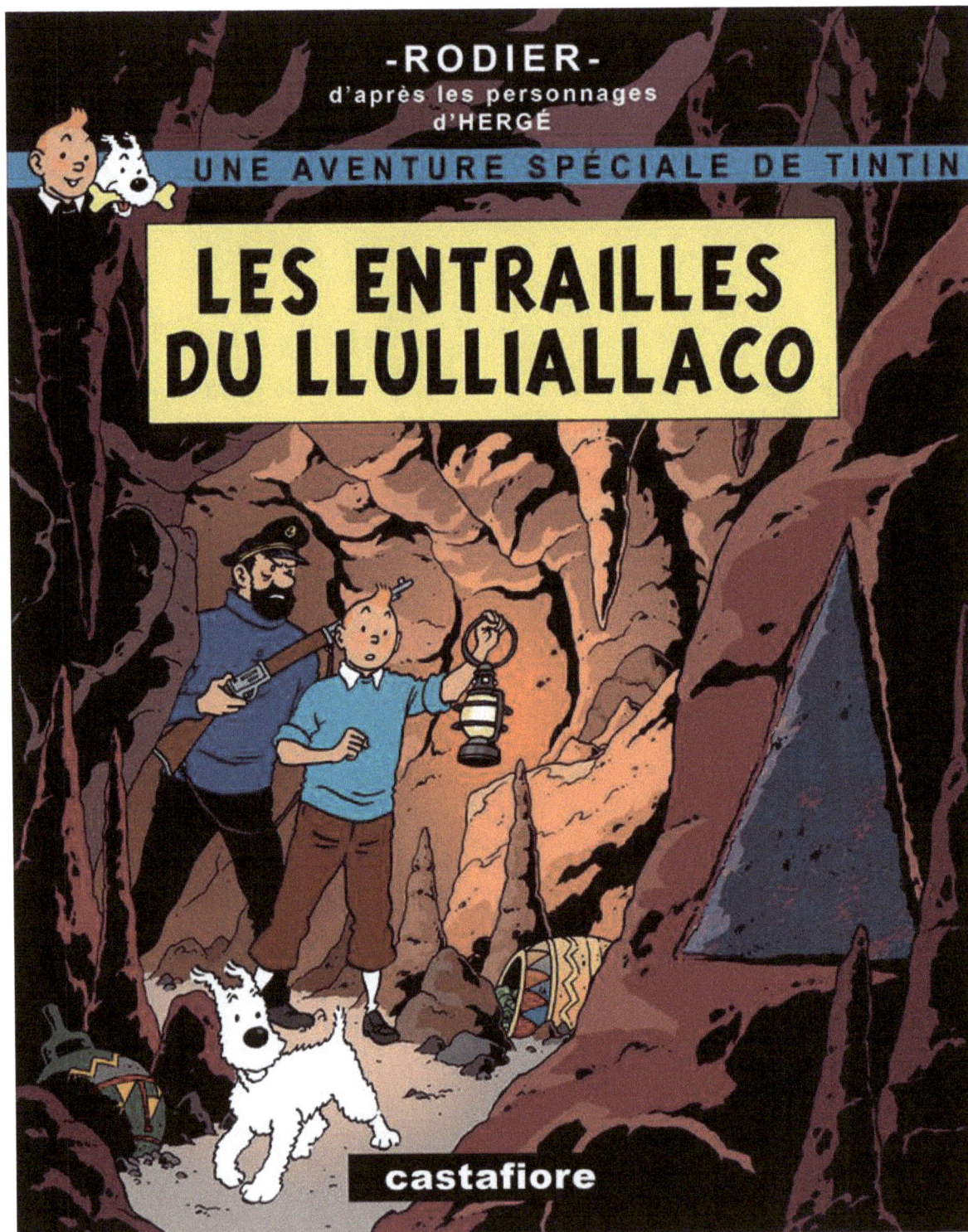

-RODIER-
d'après les personnages
d'HERGÉ

UNE AVENTURE SPÉCIALE DE TINTIN

LES ENTRAILLES DU LLULLIALLACO

castafiore

"The Bowels of Llulliallaco" a dormant volcano on the border of Argentina and Chile in the Puna de Atacama. It is therefore a good candidate as the exploding volcano in *Flight 714* or an actual geographic location for *Prisoners of the Sun*.

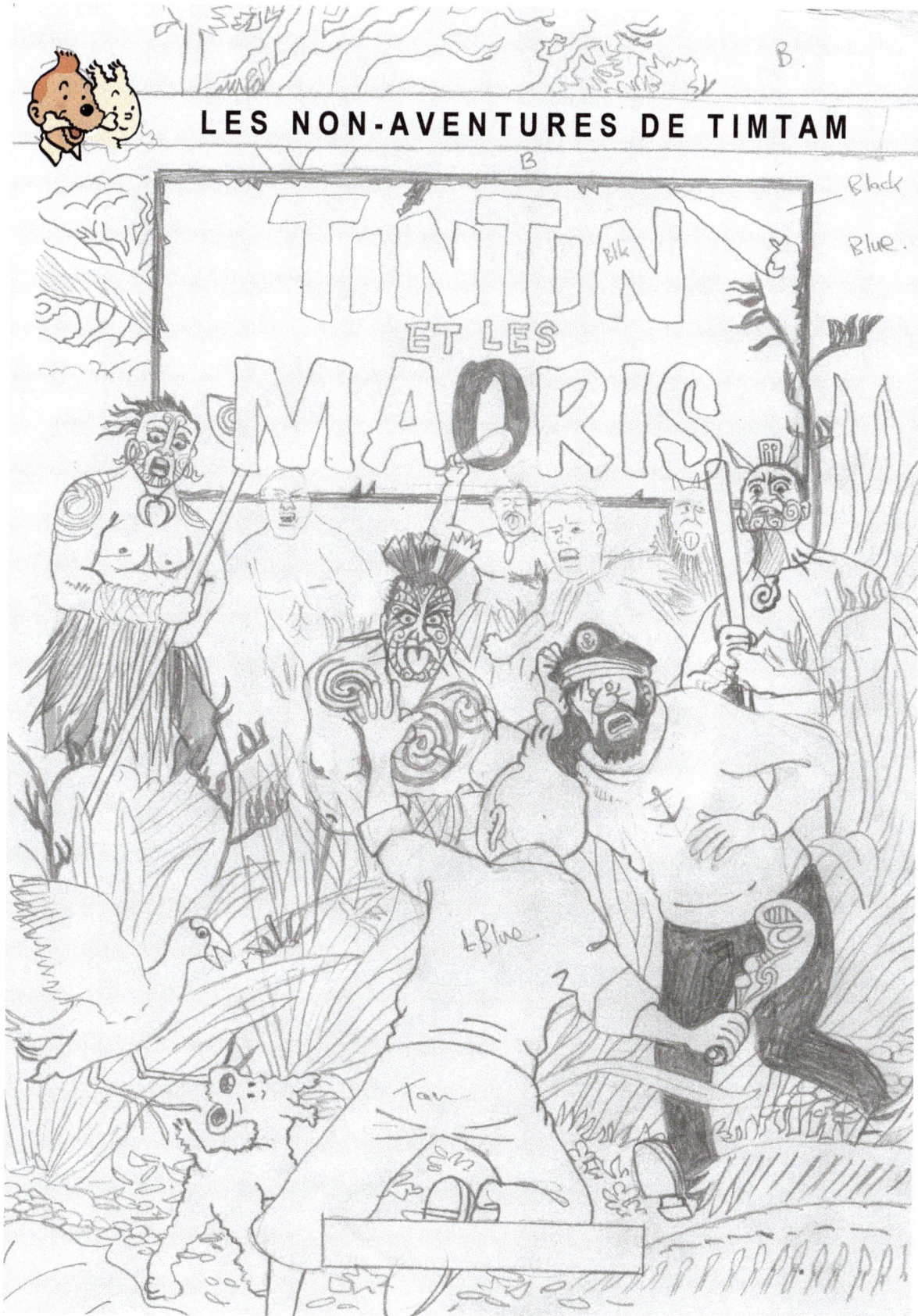

Tintin meets New Zealand Maoris. He wields a prized kotiate and Snowy is confronted by a pukeko (swamp hen). Pastiche sketch by the author.

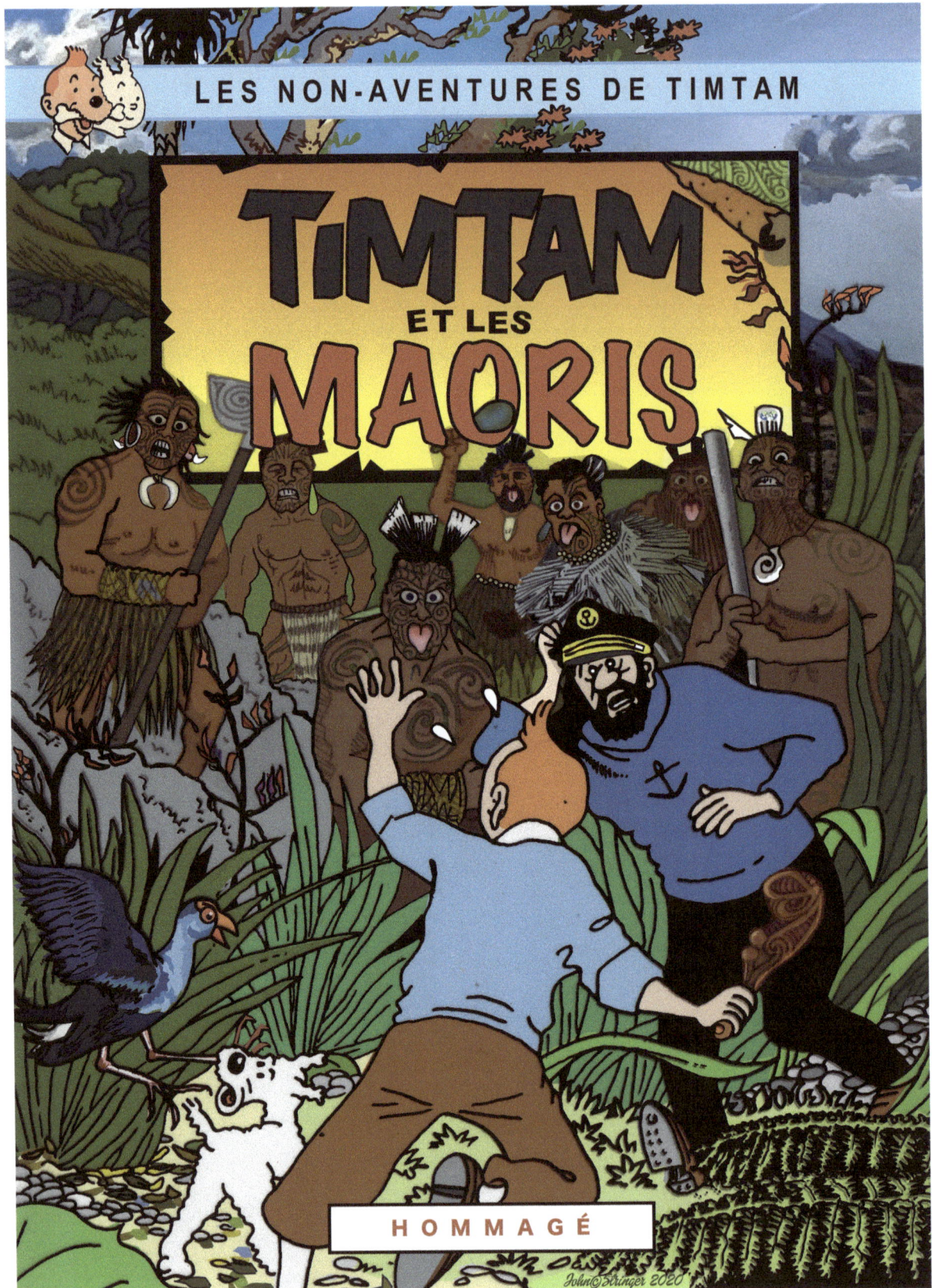

LES NON-AVENTURES DE TIMTAM

TIMTAM
ET LES
MAORIS

HOMMAGÉ

John©Stringer 2020

In the colour rendering I changed Tintin's name to "TimTam," a celebrated Australasian biscuit by Arnotts invented in 1983 –their most popular biscuit of all time (669 million eaten in Australia every year). Biting off both ends and used as a straw to slurp up your coffee it is known as the 'TimTam Slam.' Tintin eventually made Sydney after being hijacked (*Flight 714*). Here I shift him across the Tasman to visit New Zealand.

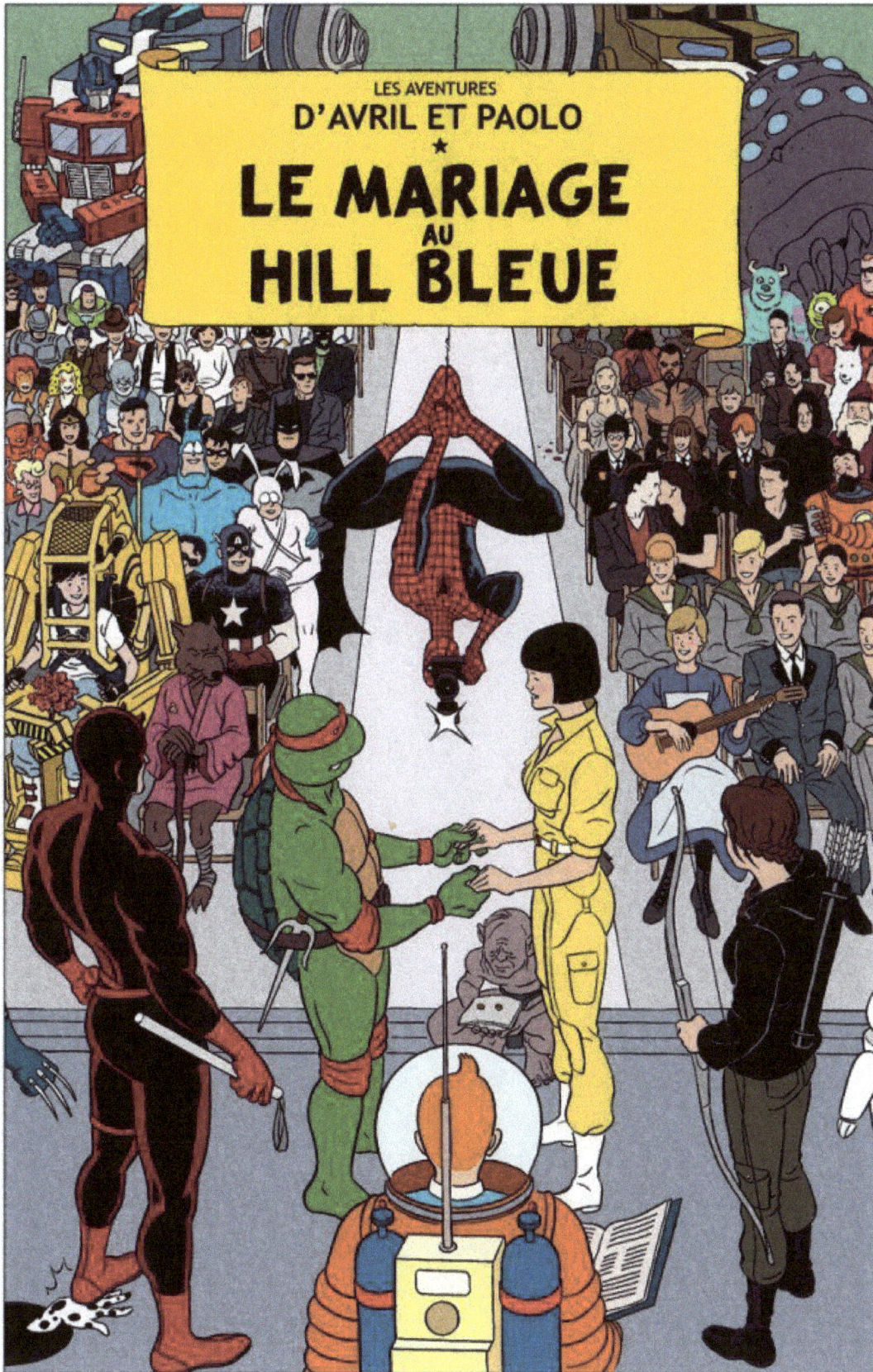

LES AVENTURES
D'AVRIL ET PAOLO
★
LE MARIAGE
AU
HILL BLEUE

"Blue Hill Weddings" (a NY restaurant). Tintin officiates a pop culture wedding as moon astronaut with Haddock top right. Sigourney Weaver in *Alien* fork lift is at left next to Captain America, along with *DC*, *Disney* and *Marvel* characters and the Von Traps from *The Sound of Music*. Peter Parker provides wedding snaps as erstwhile stringer for *The Daily Bugle*. *Daredevil* and Hunger Games' *Catniss* are best persons.

"The Forgotten Messerschmitt." Continuing the Nazi late-war technology theme seen in **Plates 247.** The Hergé moon rocket is a close replica of the WWII V2.

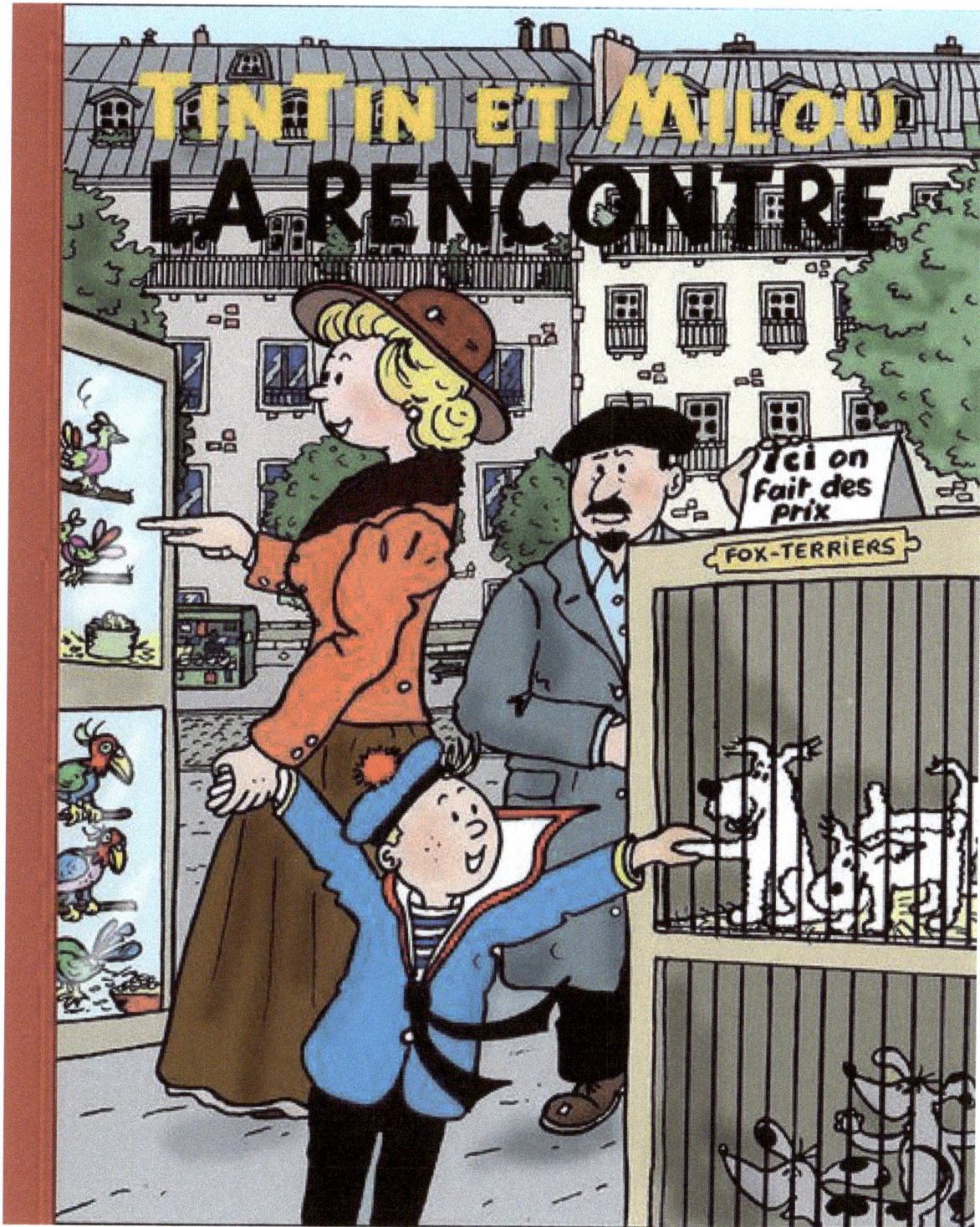

"The Meeting of Tintin and Snowy." Tintin with his unknown parents meets Snowy for the first time. See **Plate 209.**

"Tintin in the Middle-East." A variant on the Middle-East adventure. The saw is from the storyboards in which Tintin cuts his way out of the back seat of the car to escape before this crash and explosion.

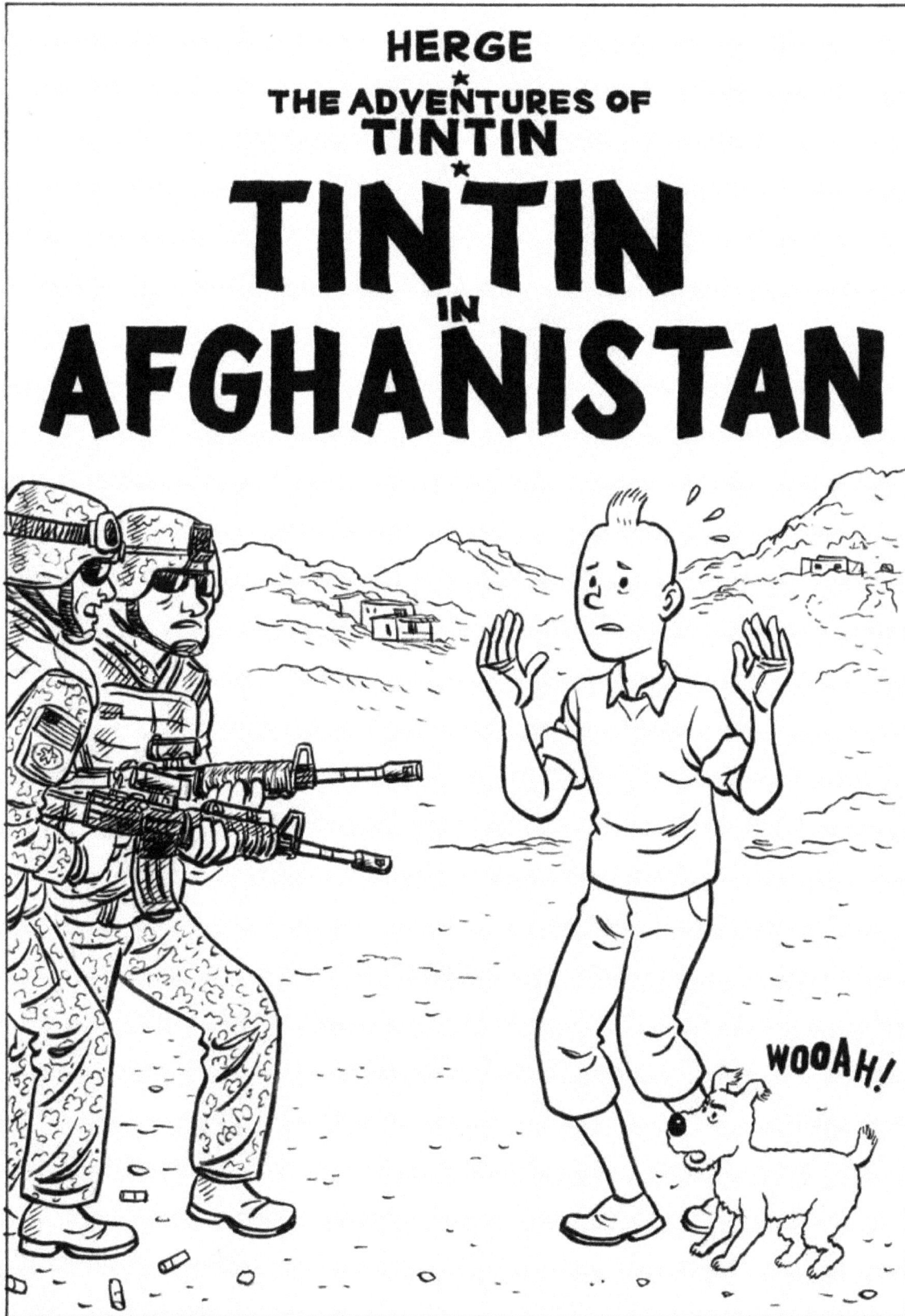

The pastiche artist is Dylan Horrocks a fellow New Zealand cartoonist.

Tintin in Damascus.

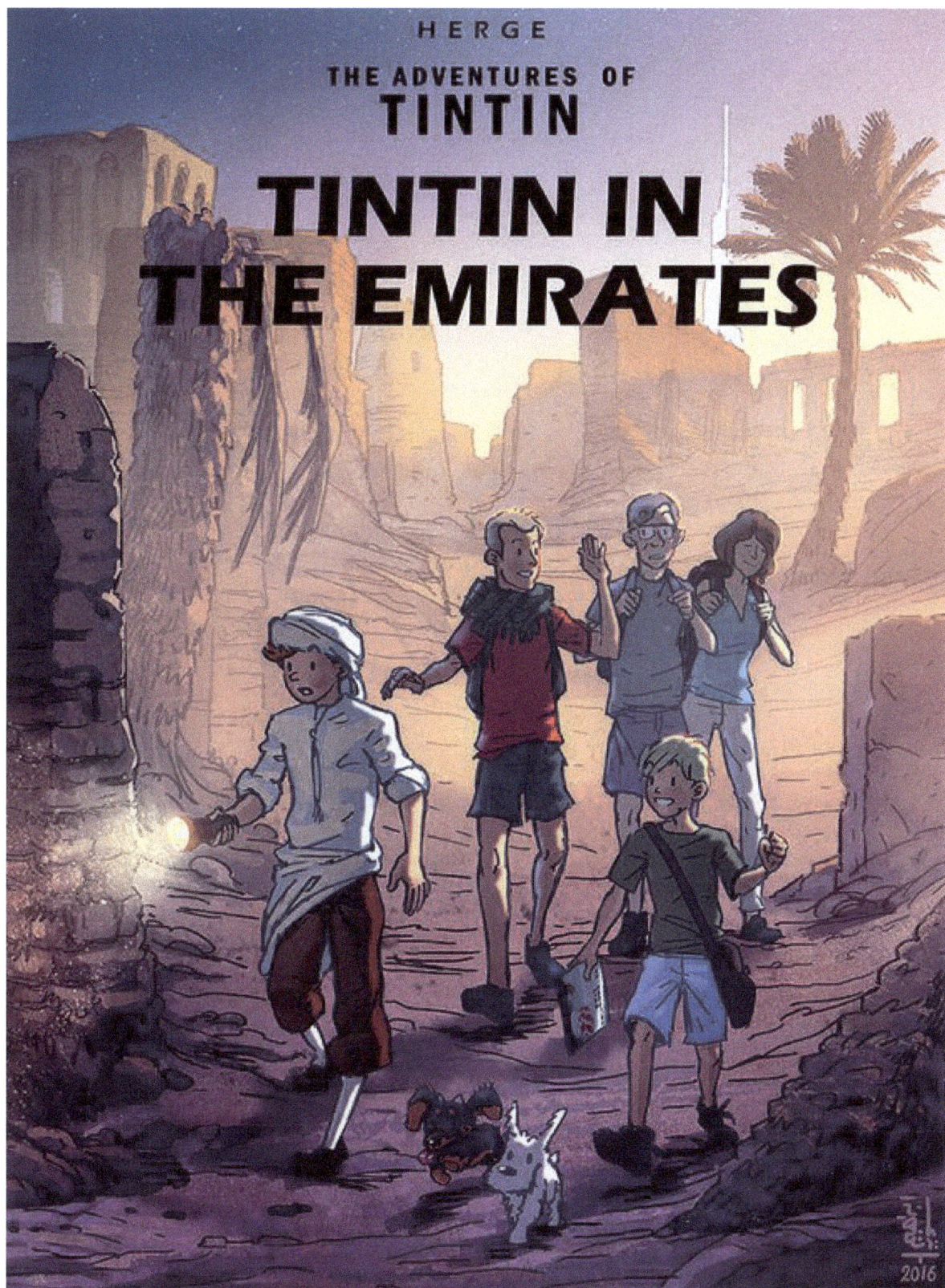

Plate 233

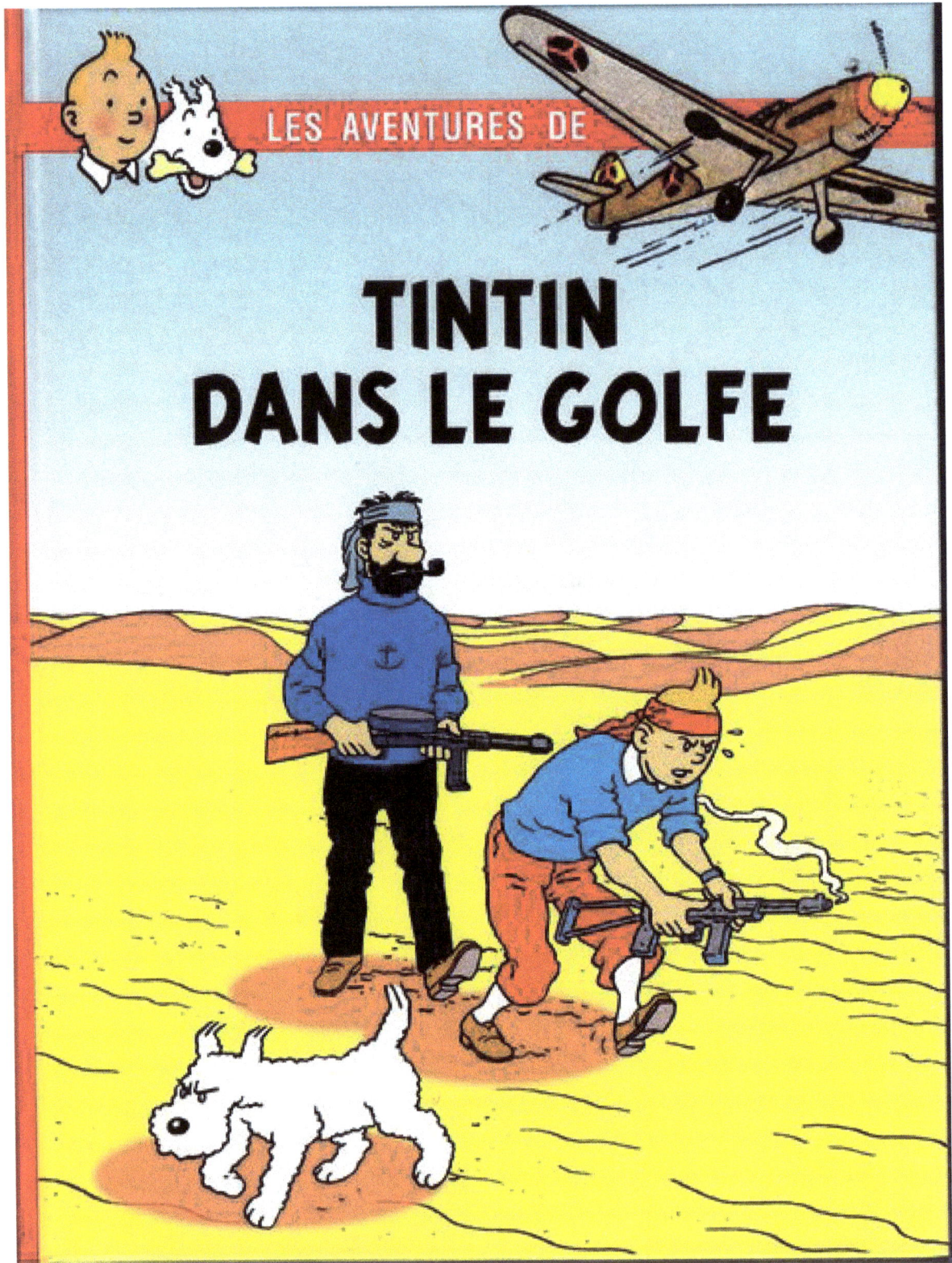

"Tintin in the Gulf (States)."

Tintin à Jérusalem
Hergé et la Politique

Tintin as a French correspondent reporting from Jerusalem (a copy of *Le Monde* cast aside). Castafiore is a camel-riding tourist, while the Thom(p)sons are Hasidic elders. Note the explosive 'cigarettes of the Pharaoh' (used by Abdullah) bottom left and the moon rocket as minaret top right.

The Tom(p)sons blend in as Saddams.

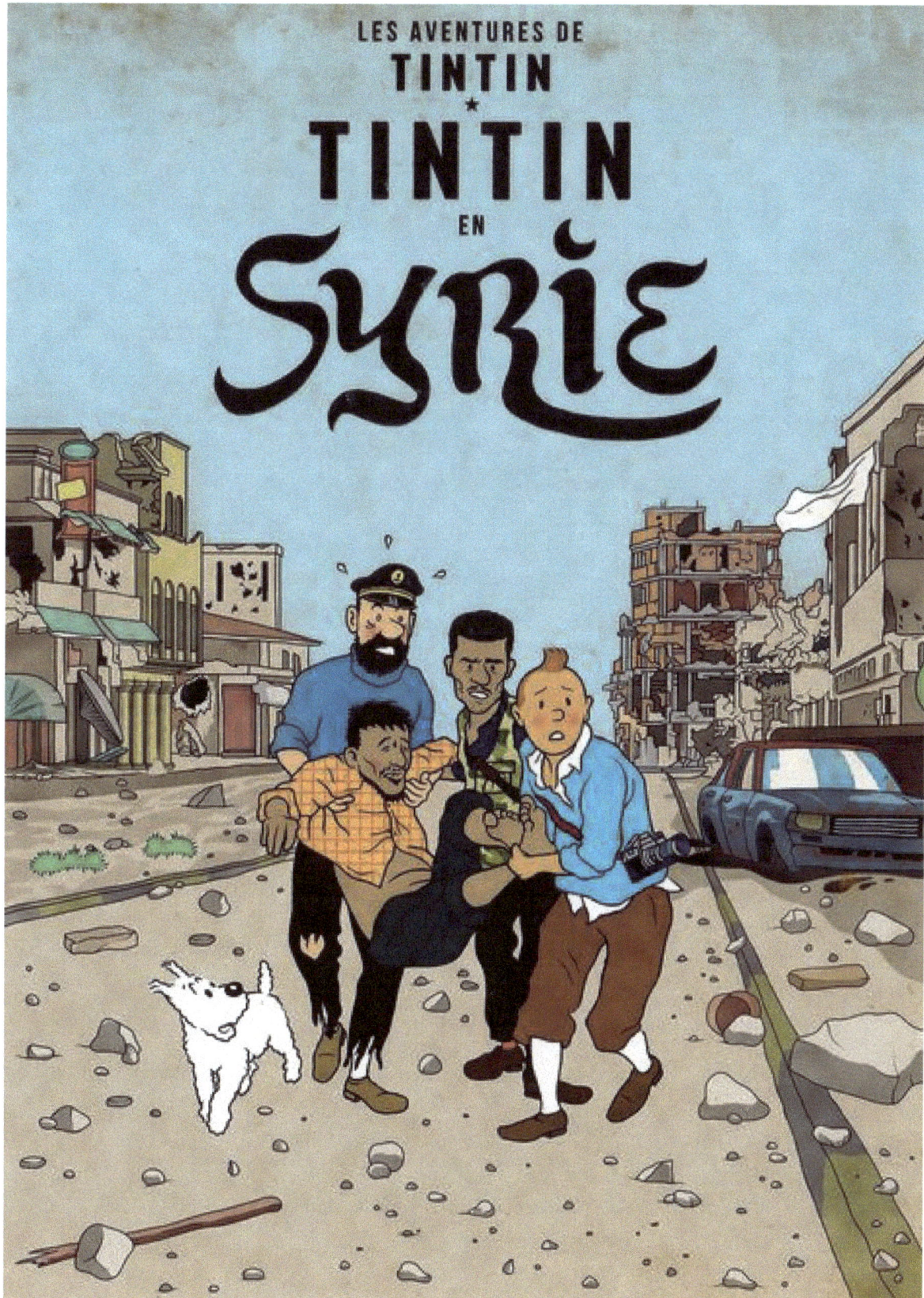

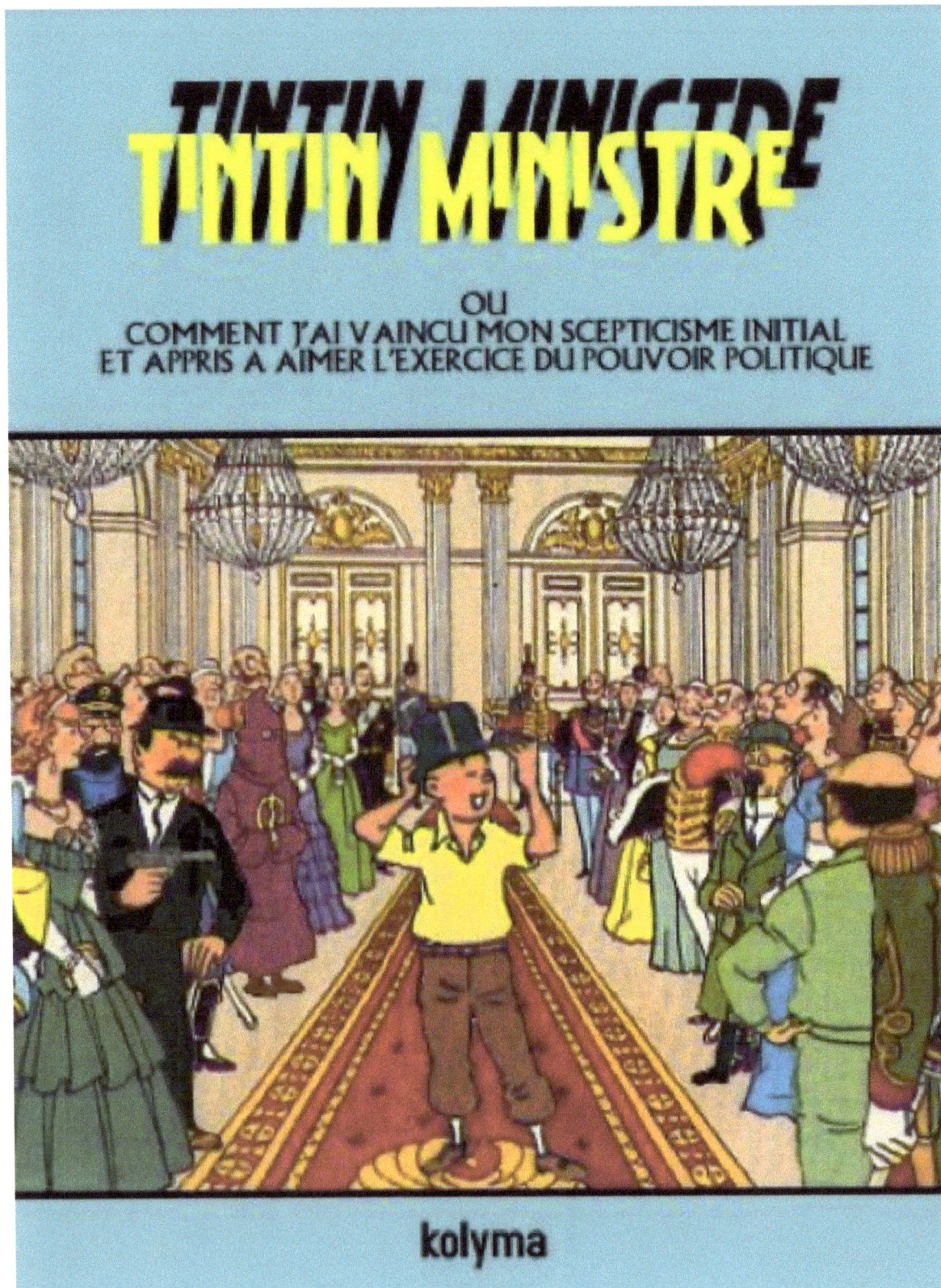

"Minister Tintin" or "How I overcame my initial skepticism and learned to love the exercise of political power." Probably a French political critique via Tintin.

A variant on **Plate 237.**

Peggy Alcazar and a companion have "Marched in to sh*t." This can only be Snowy's (?) who has already visited the moon.

"We Walked Under the Moon." A romantic variation on the Moon title.

This is a visual reference to the 1902 silent movie *Le Voyage Dans la Lun* ("A Trip to the Moon") by Georges Méliès.

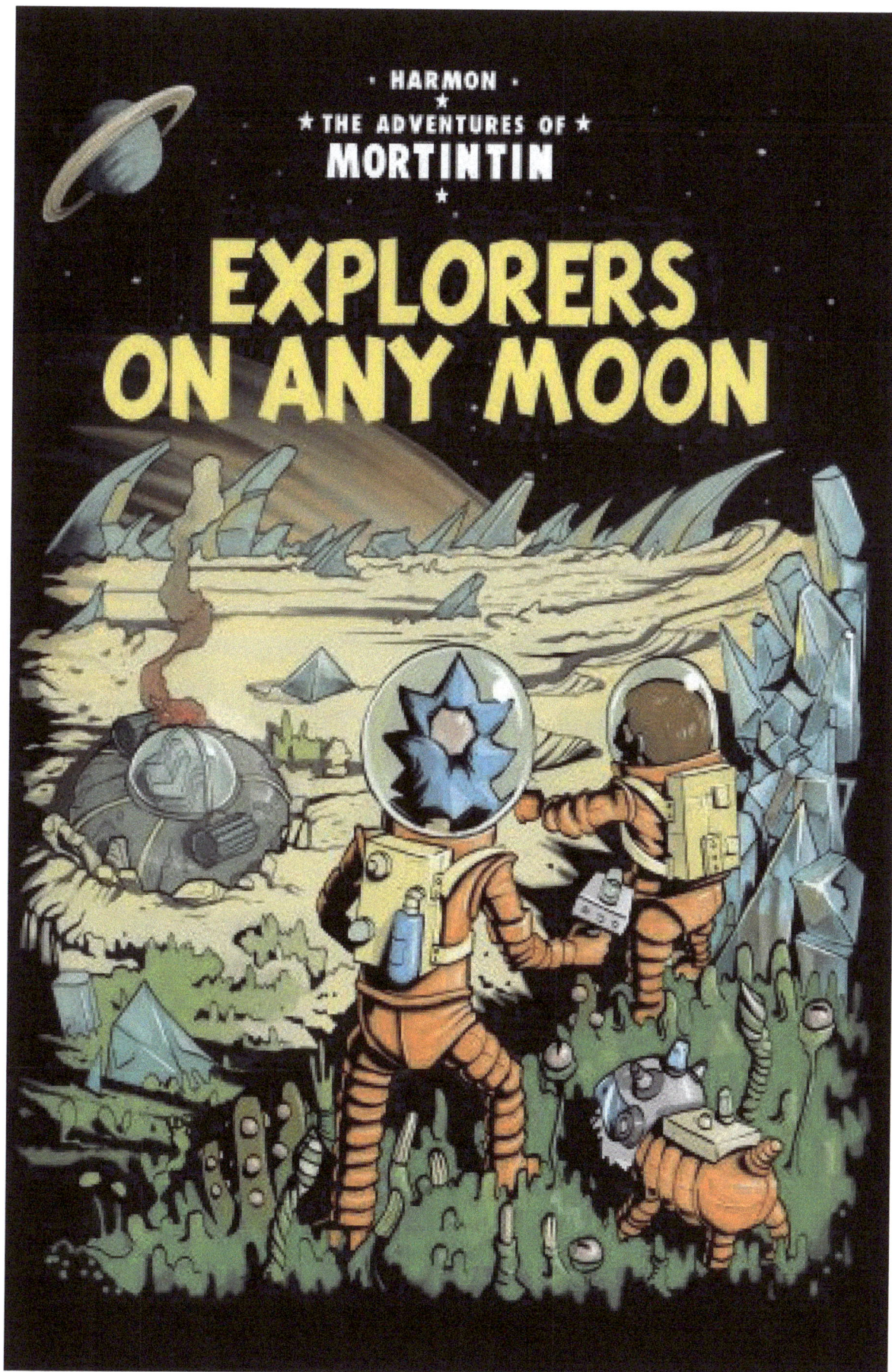

· HARMON ·
★
★ THE ADVENTURES OF ★
MORTINTIN
★

EXPLORERS ON ANY MOON

Jacobs would have loved this version of *Explorers*.

"We Have a Crowd on Mars." The gravity of Mars affects our heroes like magic mushrooms might, which are shown as per the outer space asteroid from *The Shooting Star*, now a Tintin icon.

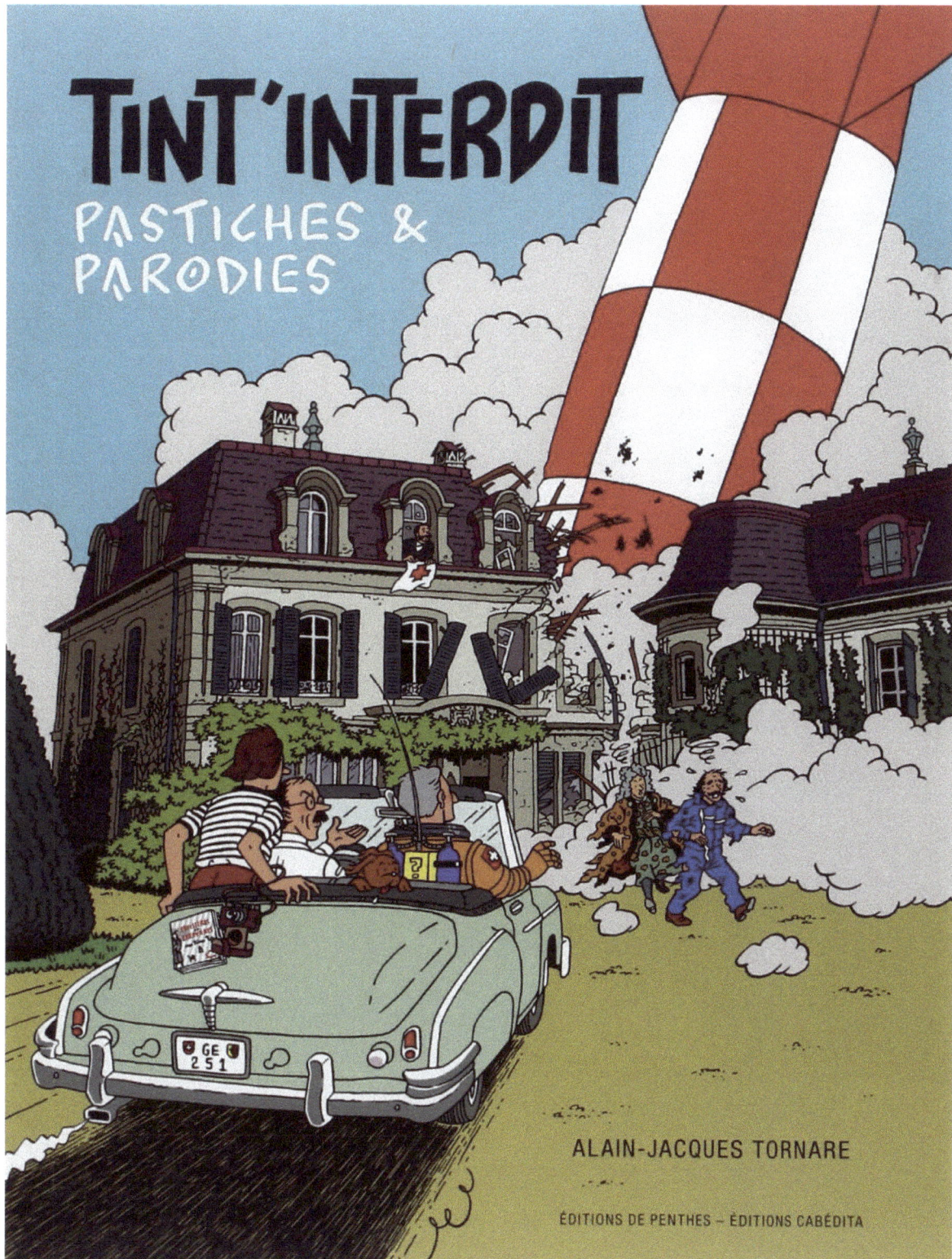

TINT'INTERDIT
PASTICHES & PARODIES

ALAIN-JACQUES TORNARE

ÉDITIONS DE PENTHES – ÉDITIONS CABÉDITA

"Forbidden Tintin." An actual publication similar to this tome, addressing the Moulinsart copyright controversies, similar to **Plate 102** in which the rocket takes out Tintin and Haddock. Here the moon rocket wrecks the Moulinsart chateau (the ancestral country manor in Brussels near Sart-Moulin, *Le château de Moulinsart*, which is the logo for Moulinsart and an inspiration for Marlinspike). The passengers are perhaps Fanny and other trustees? The little brown Pekinese dog is "Chang" verbally mistaken for Chang, in *Tibet* (p. 6). Chang the dog appears in several pastiches, such as **Plate 53, 306.**

A panade is a baked pie, thus "Moulinsart Pie."

HERGÉ
THE ADVENTURES OF
TINTIN
AT THE
MOUNTAINS
OF MADNESS

MUZSKI

Tintin in Tibet meets a *2001 a Space Odyssey*-esque monolith in an assemblage Jacob's could easily have sketched for *Blake & Mortimer*.

"Mystery Island." See **Plates 126, 148, 225.**

L'ILE MYSTÉRIEUSE

THE JOURNEY

casterman

"Mystery Island." Tintin, Chang and Haddock in a *Jurassic Park* like scene. See **8.I.**

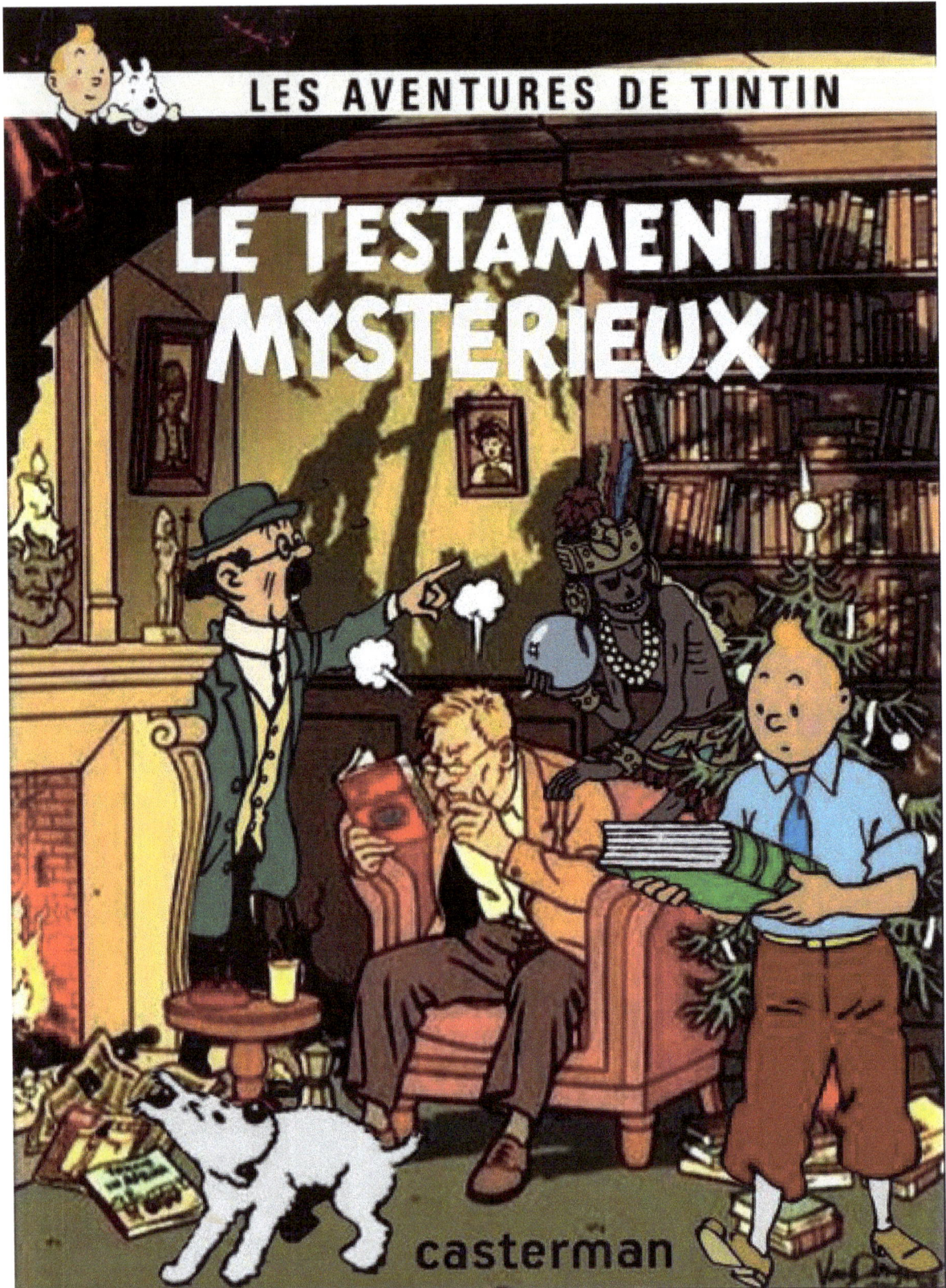

LES AVENTURES DE TINTIN

LE TESTAMENT MYSTÉRIEUX

casterman

"The Mystery Will." Hergé and Tintin investigate clues while the hallucination from *Seven Crystal Balls* sits astride Hergé's chair with his hand on the shoulder. This may be a reflection on the Dutch courts decision on reproduction rights in Hergé's will. Calculus and Snowy react to some unwelcome intrusion frame right.

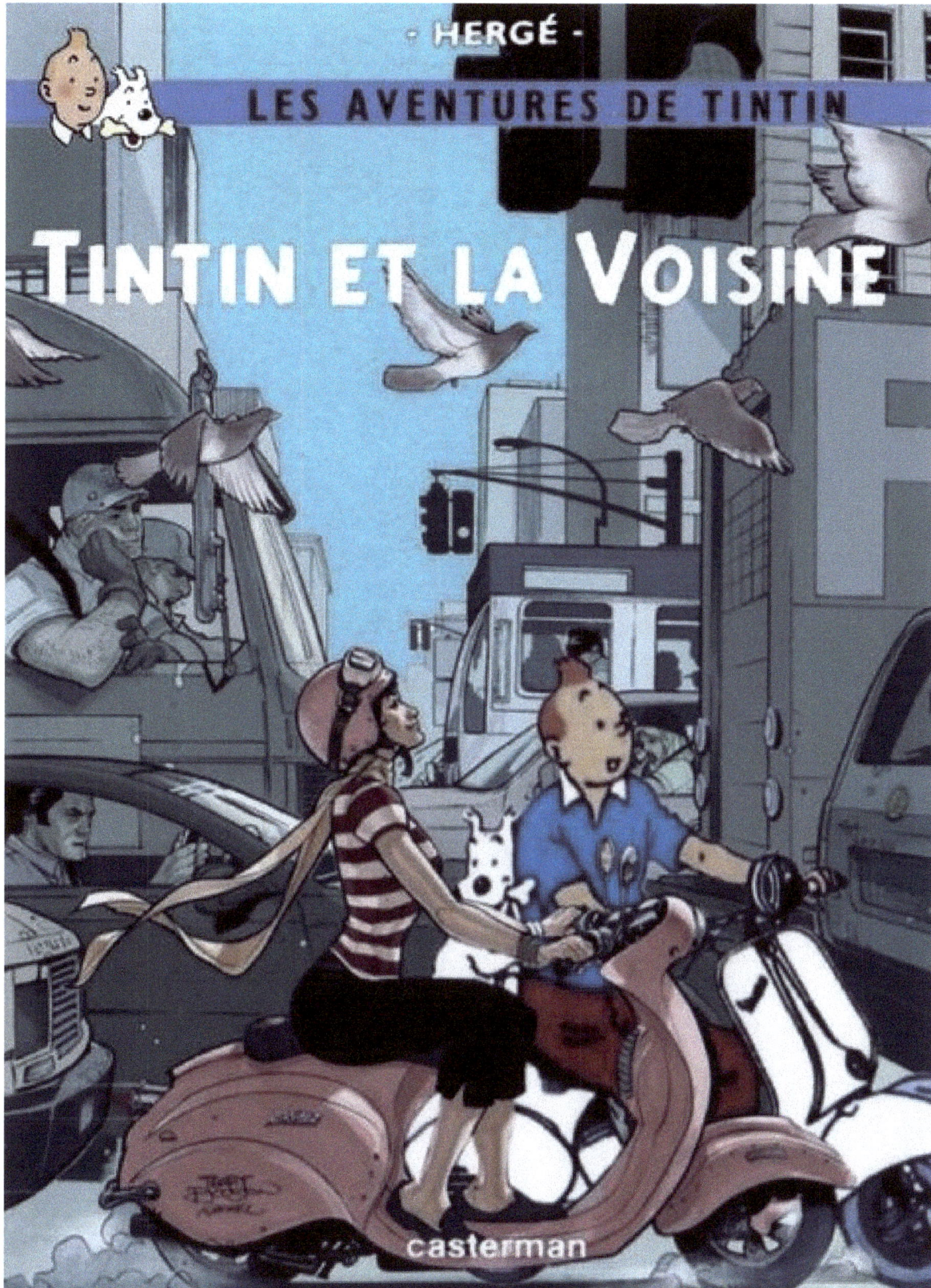

"Tintin and the Neighbour." Perhaps some romance for Tintin with a Fanny Vlamynck type prospect? Snowy is certainly enamoured.

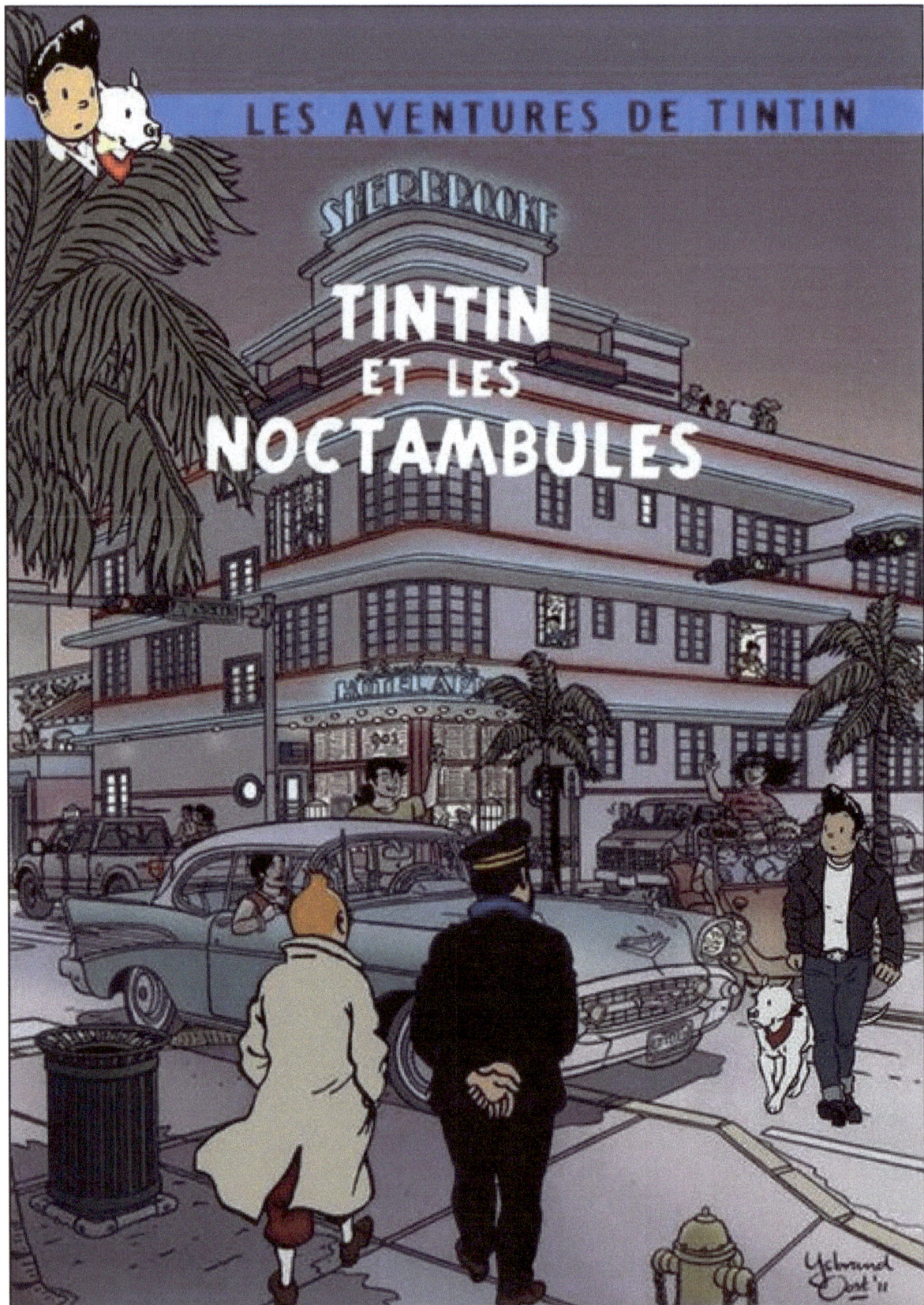

LES AVENTURES DE TINTIN

SHERBROOKE

TINTIN ET LES NOCTAMBULES

"Tintin and the Night Owl." A *Happy Days* Fonz-Tintin with an American white pit-bull approaches a more traditional duo.

Franklin hommage à nos héros

UNE AVENTURE DE TINTIN

TINTIN EN NORMANDIE

SOUVENIR

Nous Tintin is a 1987 tribute art book to Tintin by American pop-artist Keith Haring, thus "Haringland," a good segue to *Omega-Art* opposite.

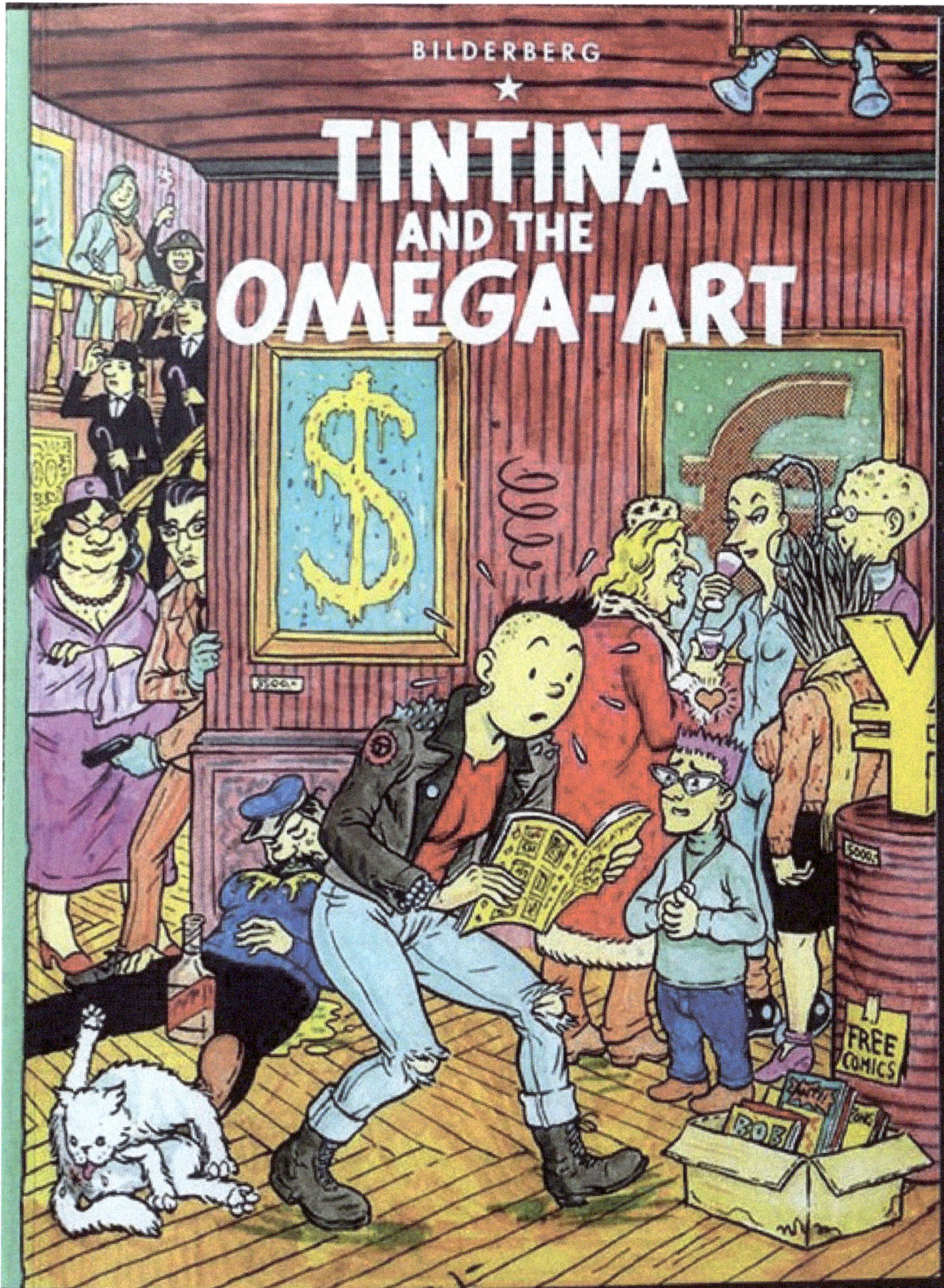

The other end of *Alph-Art*, Omega, with a female Tintina as a British boot-girl. Castafiore is in red and trans Thom(p)sons are coming down the stairs. and a trans Haddock is drunk on the floor.

"Peru."

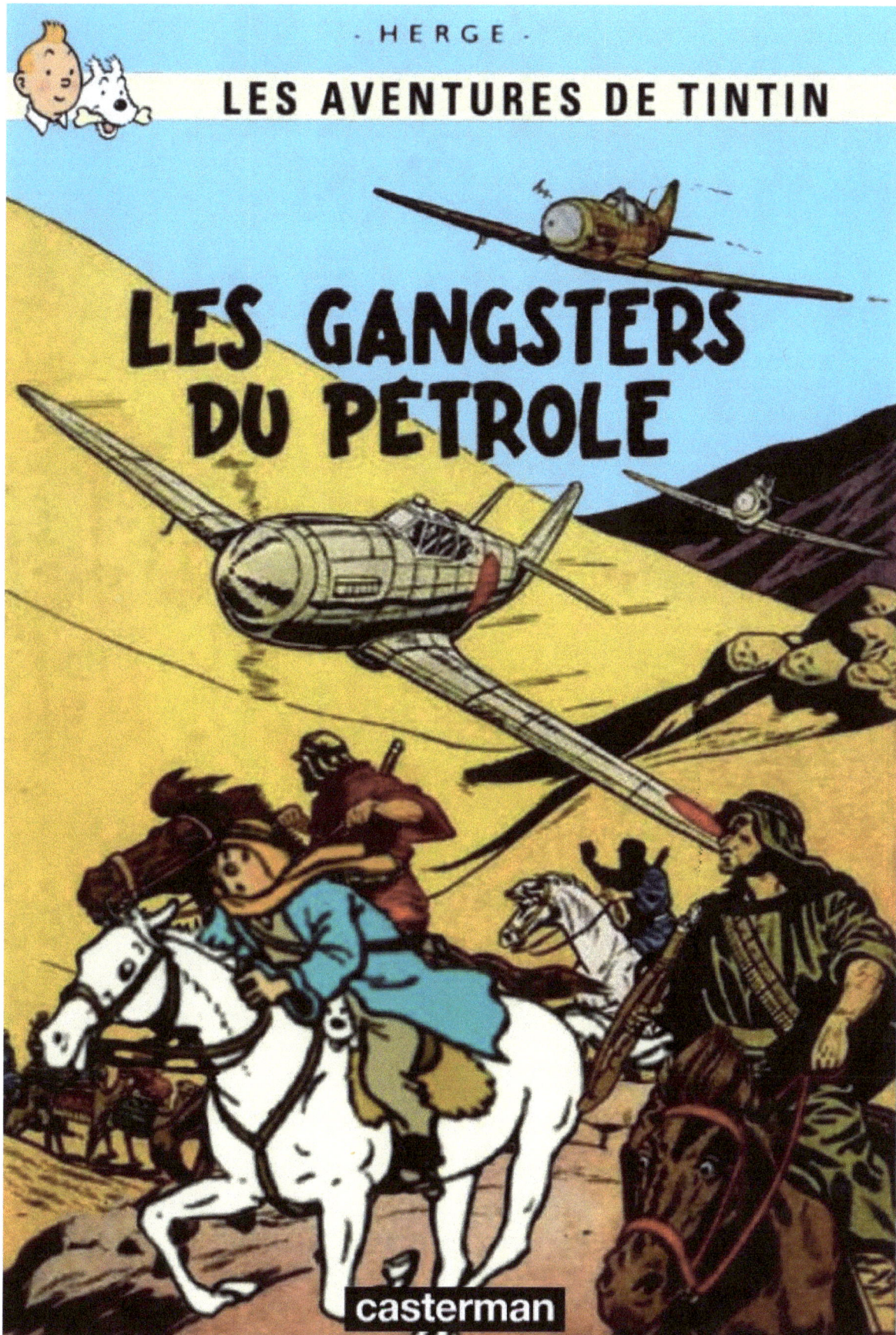

- HERGE -

LES AVENTURES DE TINTIN

LES GANGSTERS DU PÉTROLE

casterman

"The Oil Barons" or "Petroleum Gangsters."

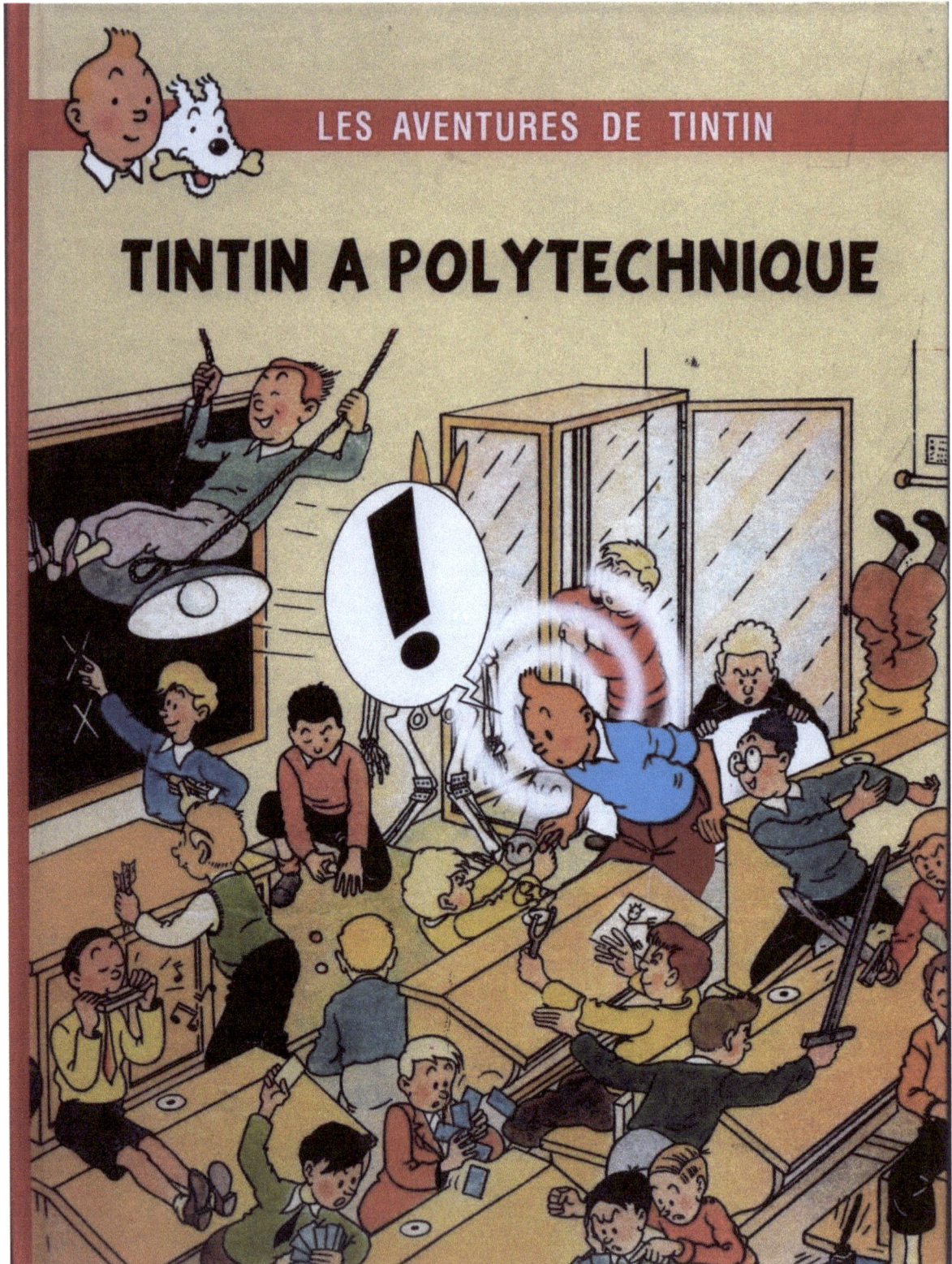

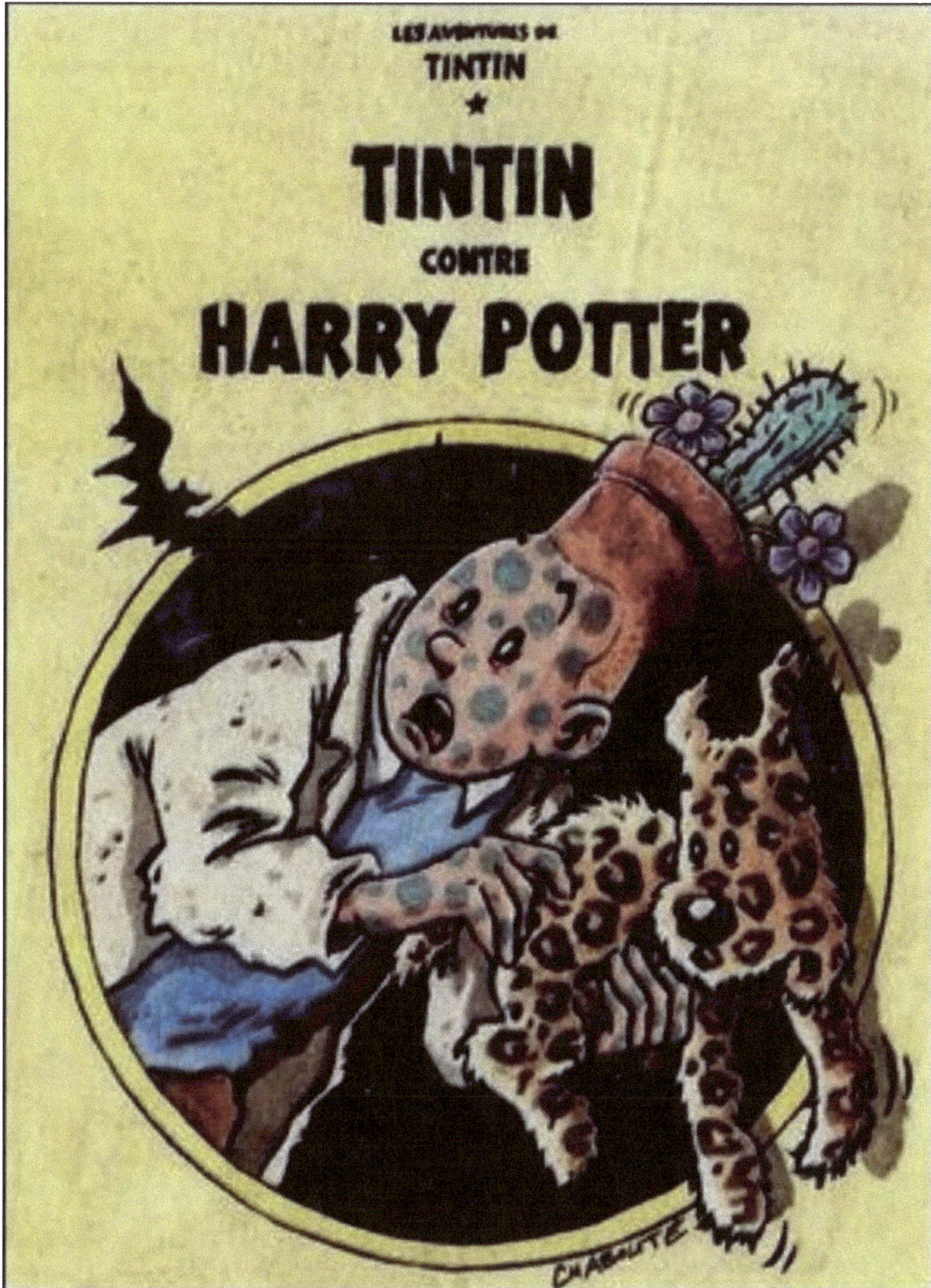

Snowy takes on a Tigger/*Calvin & Hobbes* look as Tintin morphs magically.

"The Secret of the Forgotten Pyramid." Reminiscent of the *Cigars of the Pharaoh* hallucinations, Haddock morphs into a hieroglyph. Tintin has taken to wearing a tie and is all in white like Snowy. See section **8.N** p. 450.

LES AVENTURES DE TINTIN

RODIER

TINTIN A QUEBEC

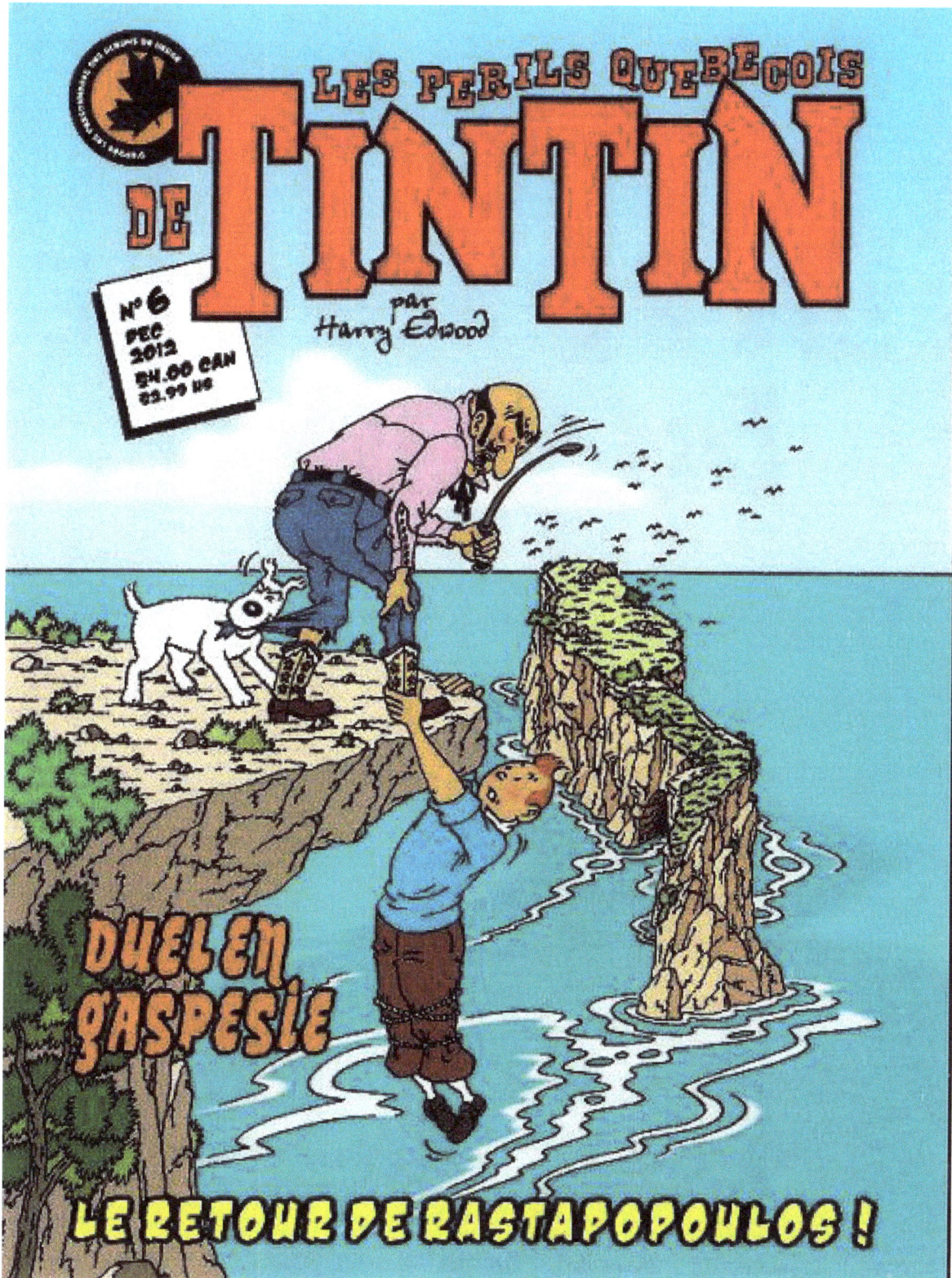

"Tintin's Perils in Quebec…the Duel in Gaspie" (a peninsula in Quebec, thus the background). "The Return of Rastapopoulos."

LES AVENTURES DE
TINTIN
★
LA RÉSIDENCE DU SOLEIL

"The Residence of the Sun." A pun on *Prisoners of the Sun*. Snowy, Haddock and Tintin at the retirement home past their prime.

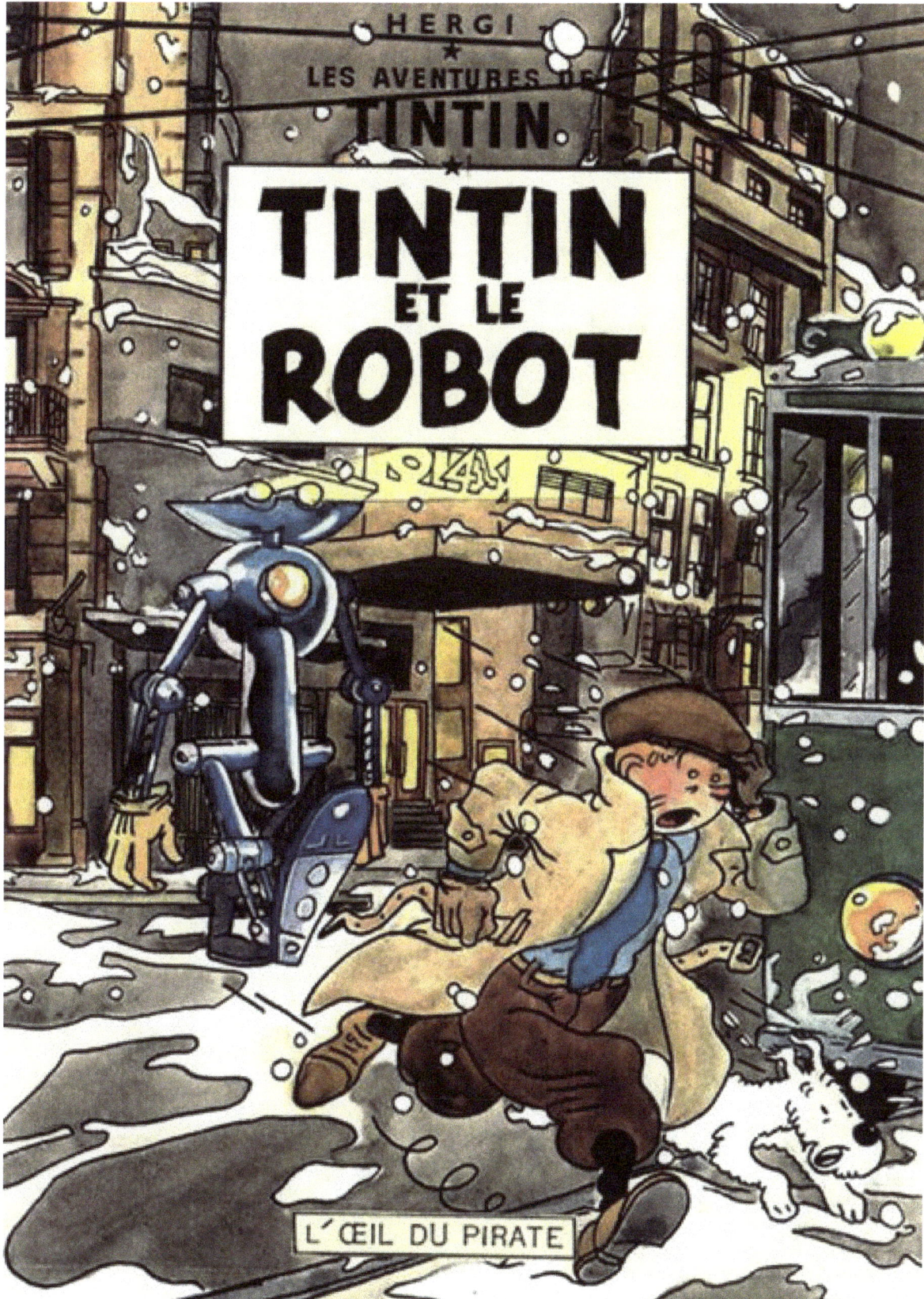

In this plate and the one opposite, Tintin merges with various Jacobs or *Star Wars* robots.

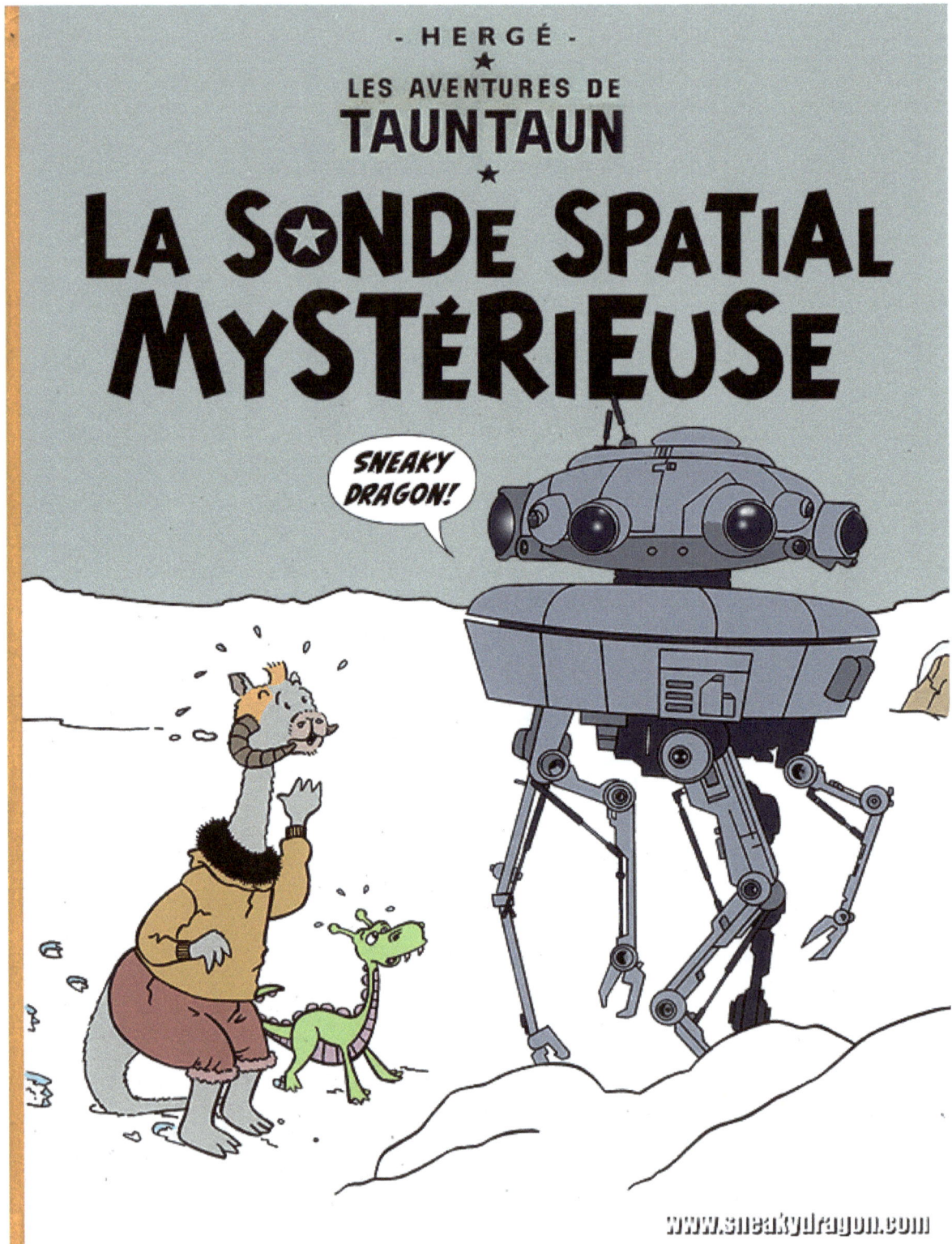

"The Mysterious Space Probe." *Sneaky Dragon* is a pop-culture and cartoon podcast series by Ian Boothby and David Dedrick. In 2015 the two men made a comprehensive podcast series *Totally Tintin* covering every Tintin adventure. The green dragon is the *Sneaky Dragon* logo.

"Master of the Rock" ie ice or meth, as per the pipe in the title. Note Haddock.

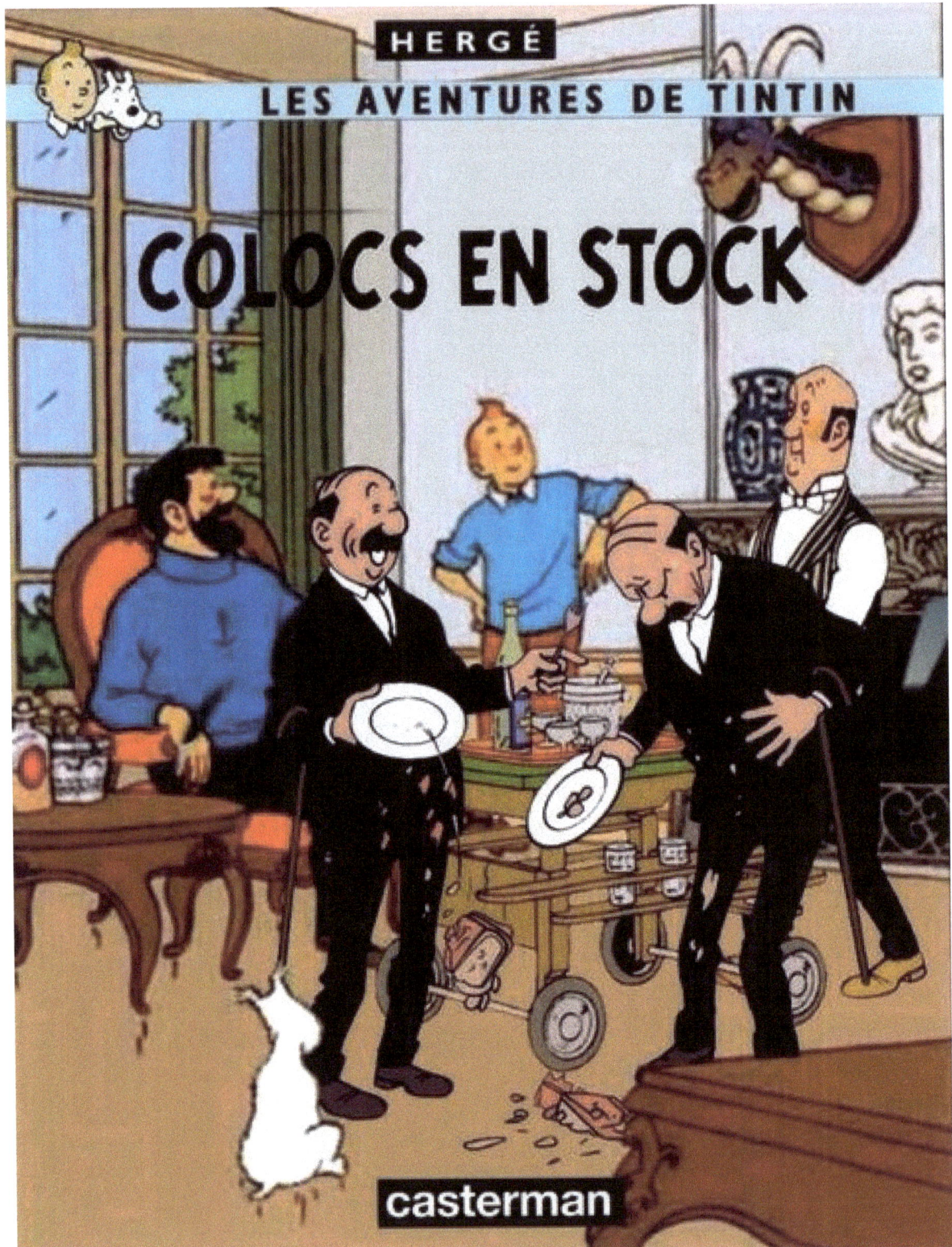

"Taking Stock of Room mates." The dragon on the wall belongs to the Rodier pastiche *La Bete de la Sorciere*, **Plate 328.**

LES AVENTURES DE TINTIN

TINTIN FAIT LES SOLDES

CASTERMAN

"Tintin Makes the Sales " (or Dutch) "Makes the Soldiers." In his *Soviets* attire Tintin battles Arumbaya Indians from *The Broken Ear*.

MICHEL DE BOM · ERWIN DREZE

LES AVENTURES DE LOUIS VALMONT

LE PIÈGE DES SABLES

casterman

"The Sand Trap." This Haddock also appears in *Tintin in Penrith*, **Plate 31.**

SCOTLAND

BY THE SEA

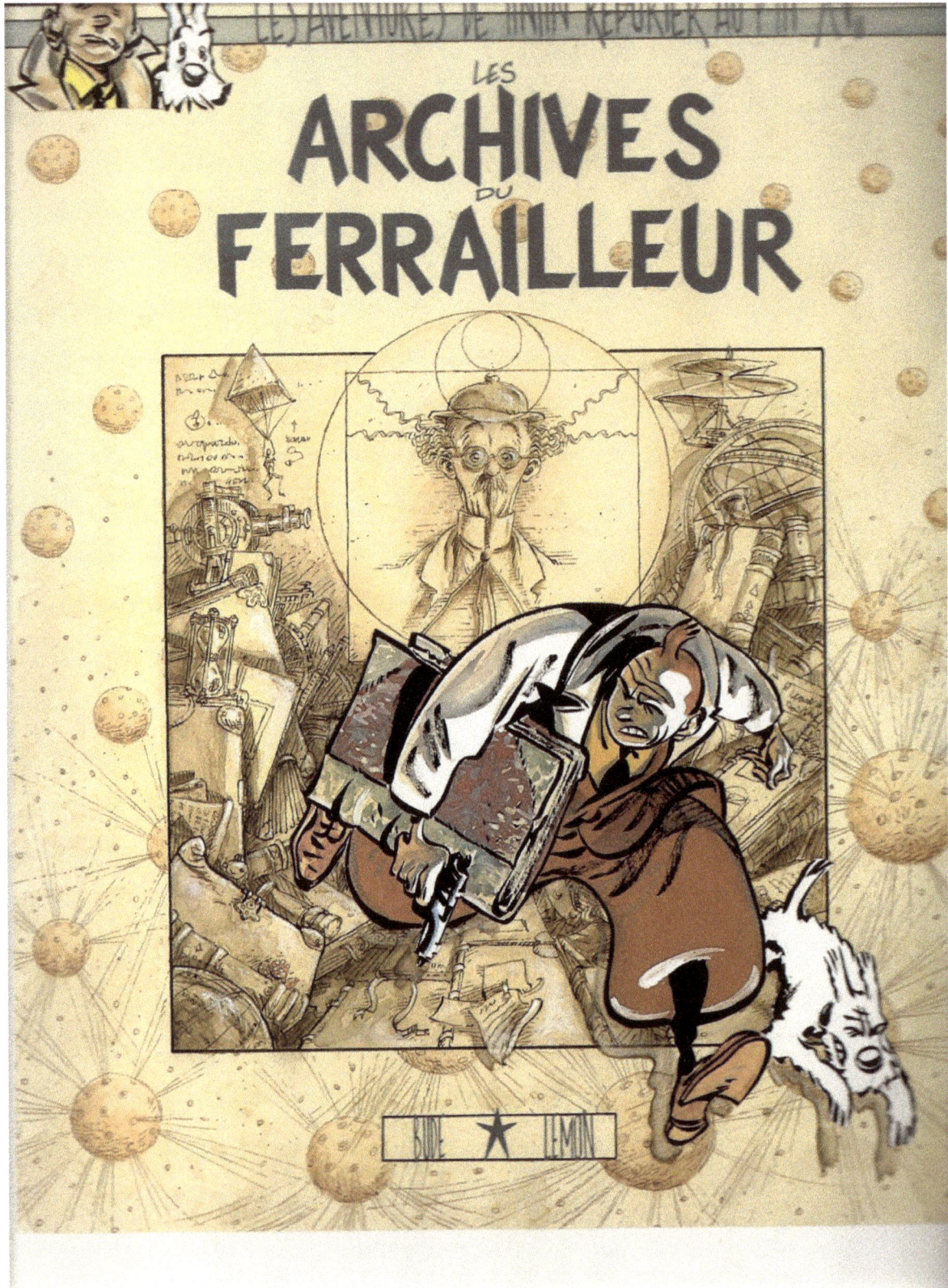

"The Archives of the Scrap Merchant," perhaps a reference to 'cut n paste' polyploid pastiche artists. Tintin flees with a Hergé art folder, as seen on the cover of *The Adventures of Hergé* (2011) (Vol. 1, p. 12) and in **Plate 306** bottom right.

"The Serenade." Another family Flinflin holiday pastiche. See p. 213-218.

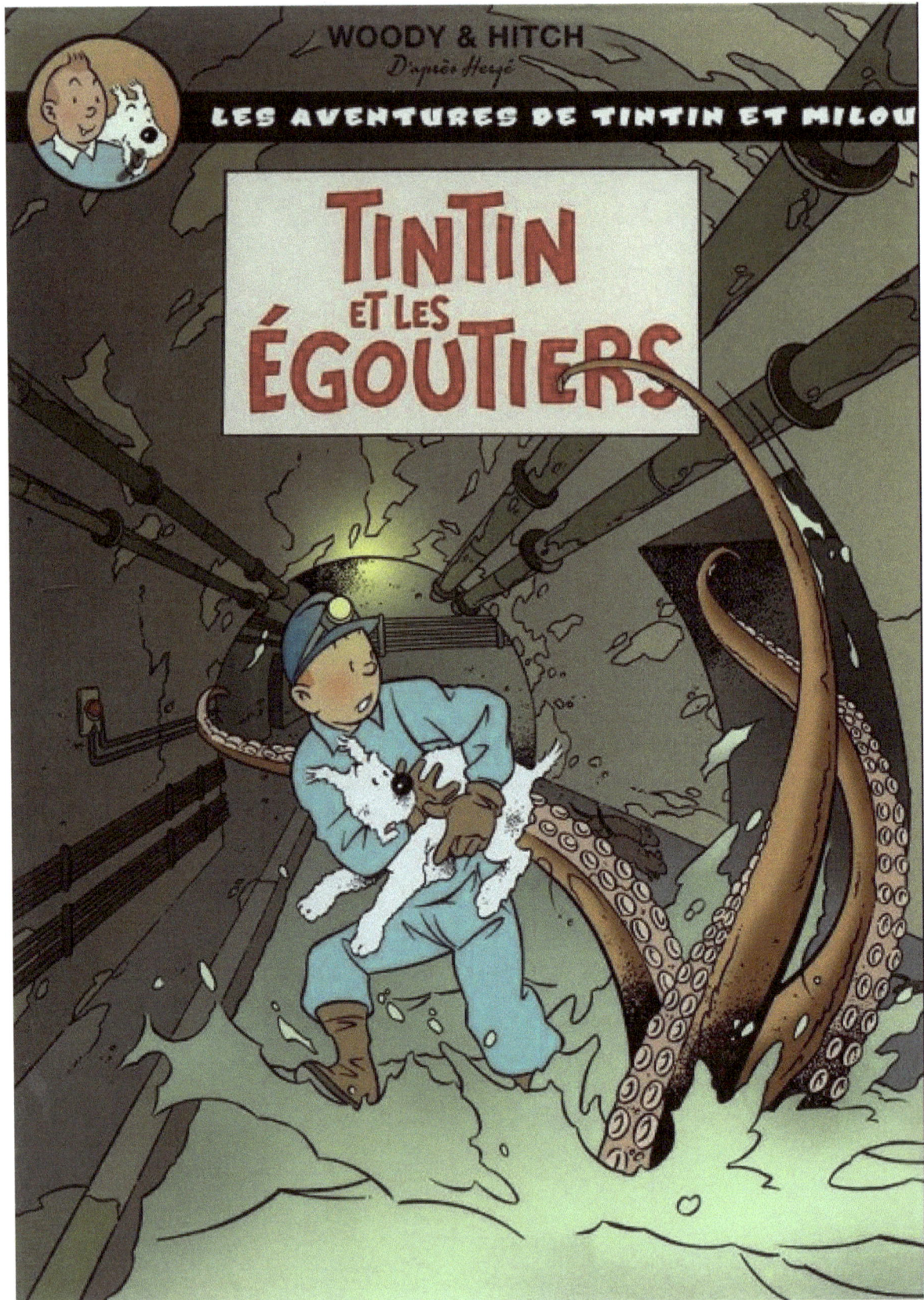

WOODY & HITCH

D'après Hergé

LES AVENTURES DE TINTIN ET MILOU

TINTIN ET LES ÉGOUTIERS

"Tintin and the Sewers."

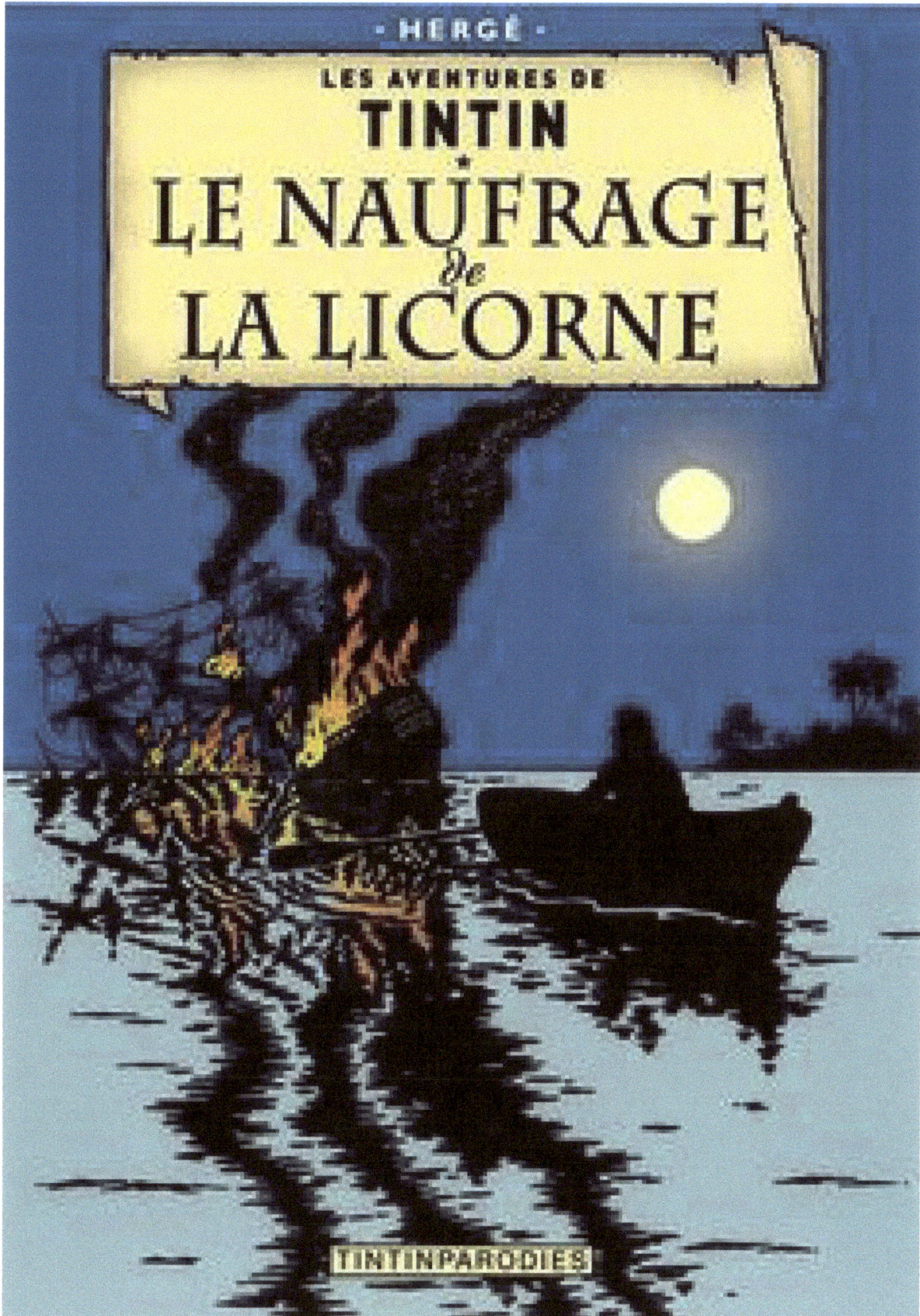

Several ships plates follow: "The Shipwreck of the Unicorn."

"The Green Perfume."

"Return of the Unicorn."

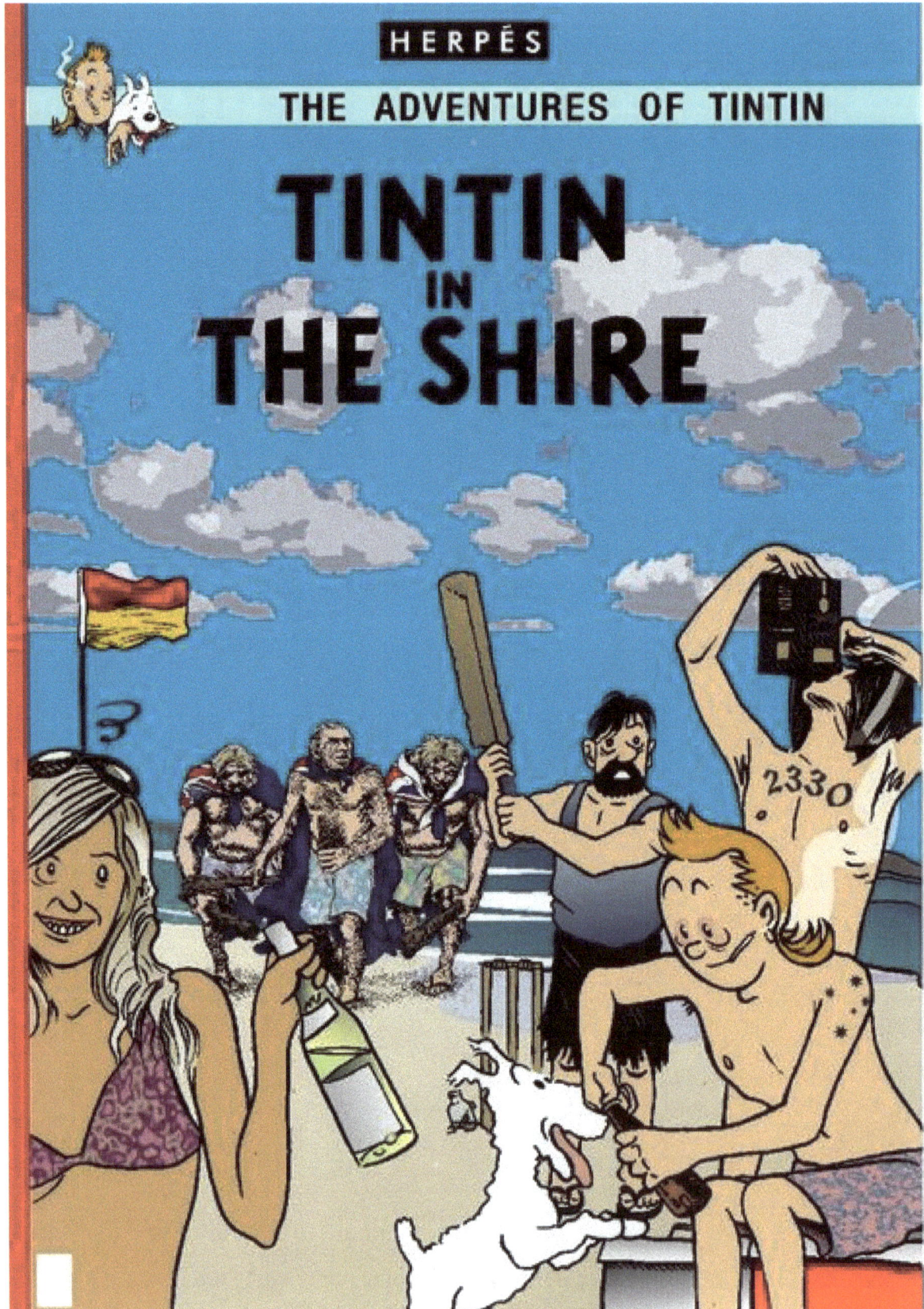

HERPÉS

THE ADVENTURES OF TINTIN

TINTIN IN THE SHIRE

Literary allusions abound. The Union-Jack Neanderthals are perhaps those from the first episode of *Dr Who*, 1963. *The Shire* is Tolkien, and "2330" may be a reference to the Angel Number, helping others (or in this case, helping oneself to a cask of wine) while Tintin cracks a tinny with a mullet. Haddock wants to play beach cricket.

A more alien variant of *The Shooting Star* mushroom.

"Tintin Remembers." Looking across to the Black Island. He is driving a NIVA Russian LADA.

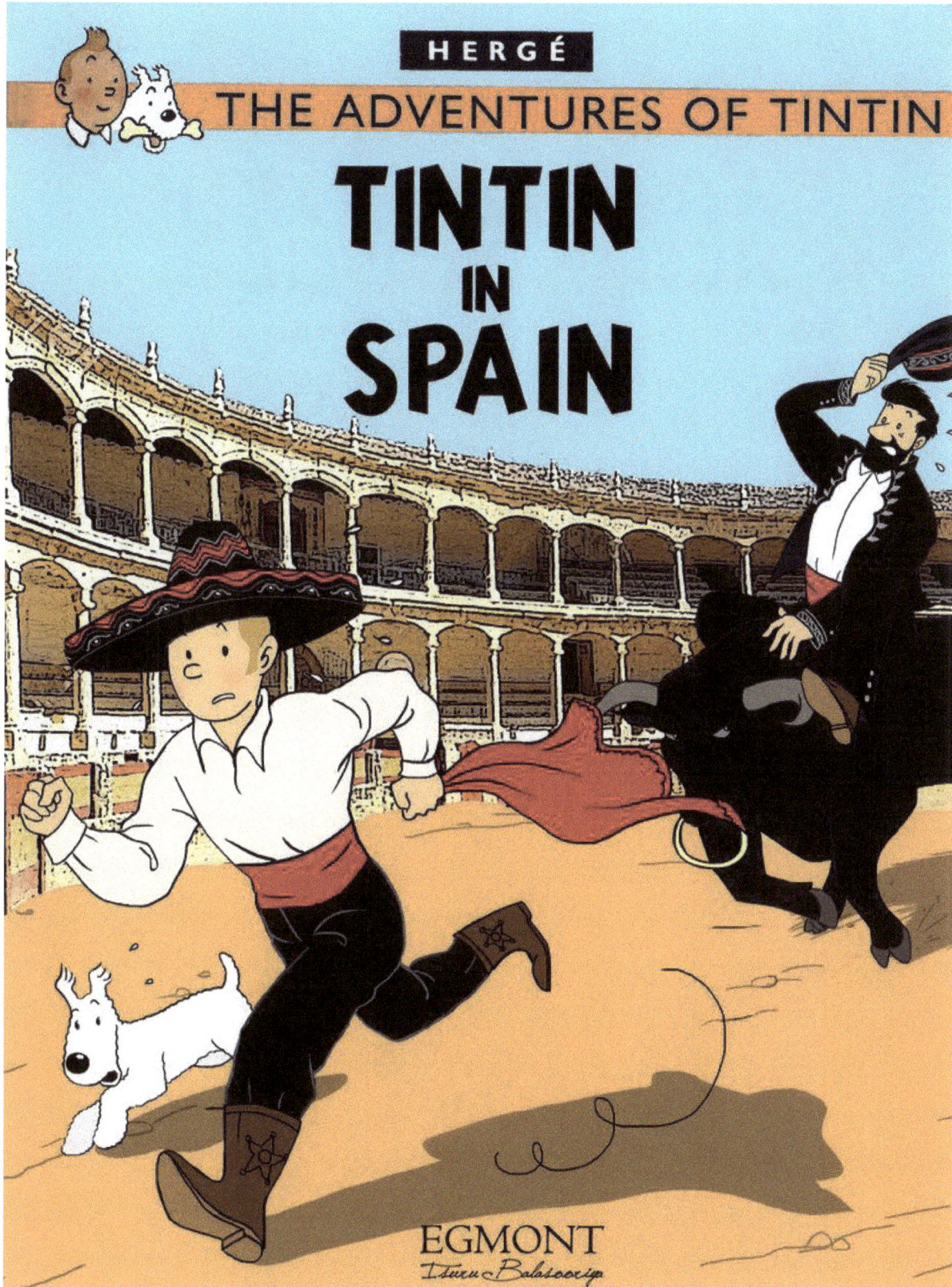

HERGÉ

THE ADVENTURES OF TINTIN

TINTIN IN SPAIN

EGMONT

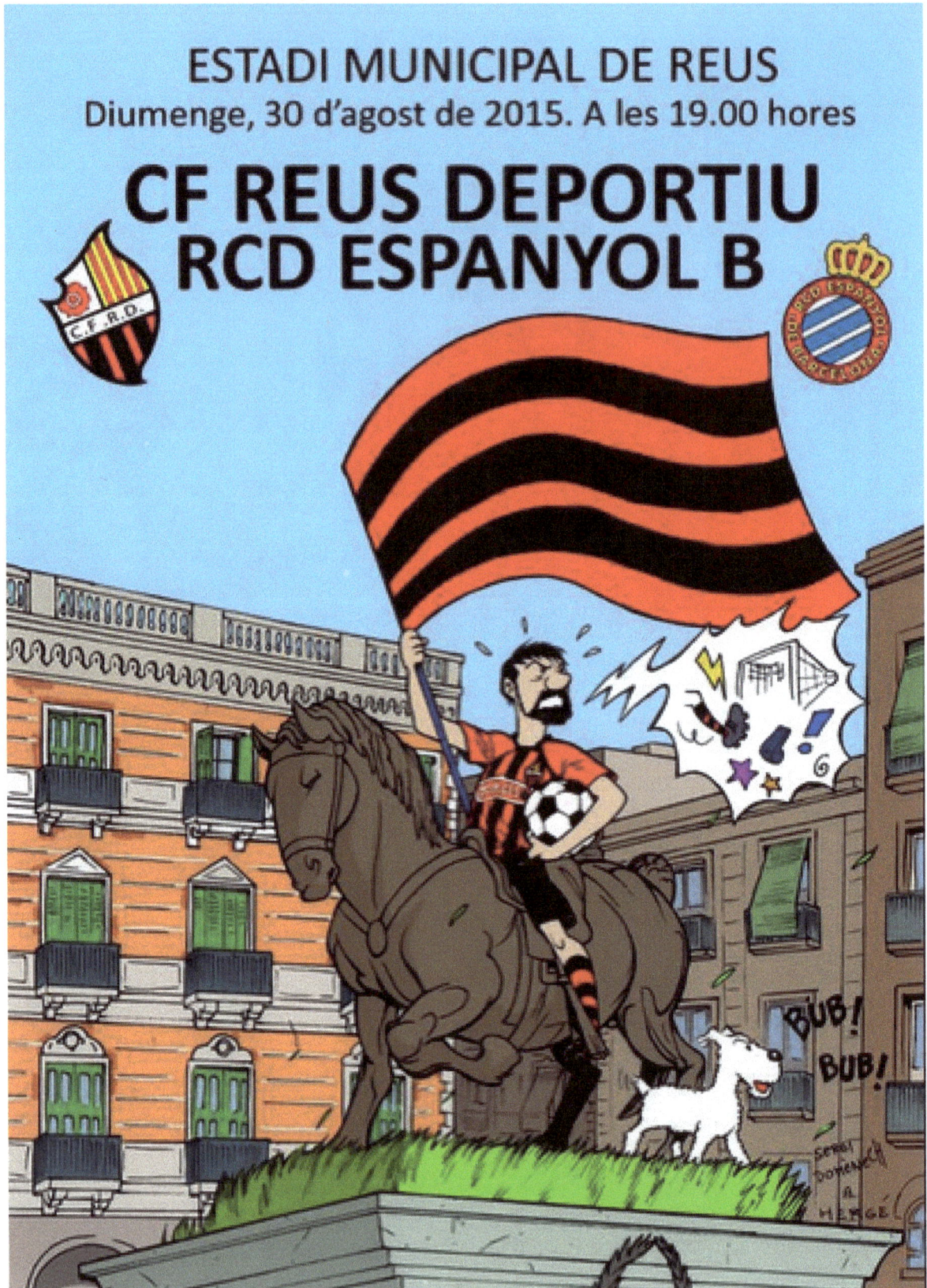

Reial Club Deportiu Espanyol de Barcelona "B" is the reserve team of the RCD Espanyol club, Barcelona, in Catalonia.

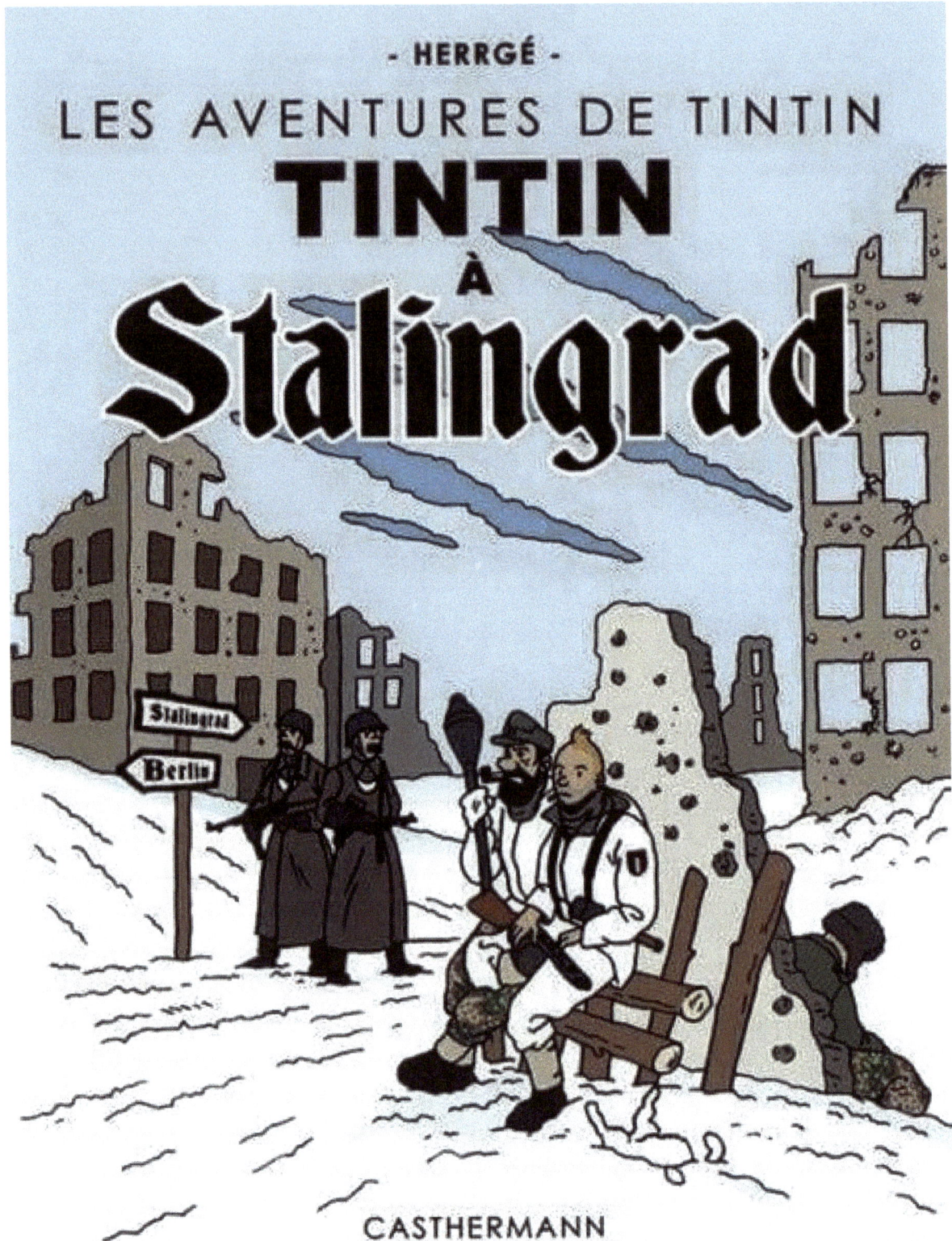

An obvious variant on the *Land of Soviets* adventure. Snowy did not survive the battle and the Thom(p)sons are on guard..

This and following plates feature Tintin with or as a Taun Taun from *Star Wars*. Note the *Star Wars* android from **Plate 267** in the background.

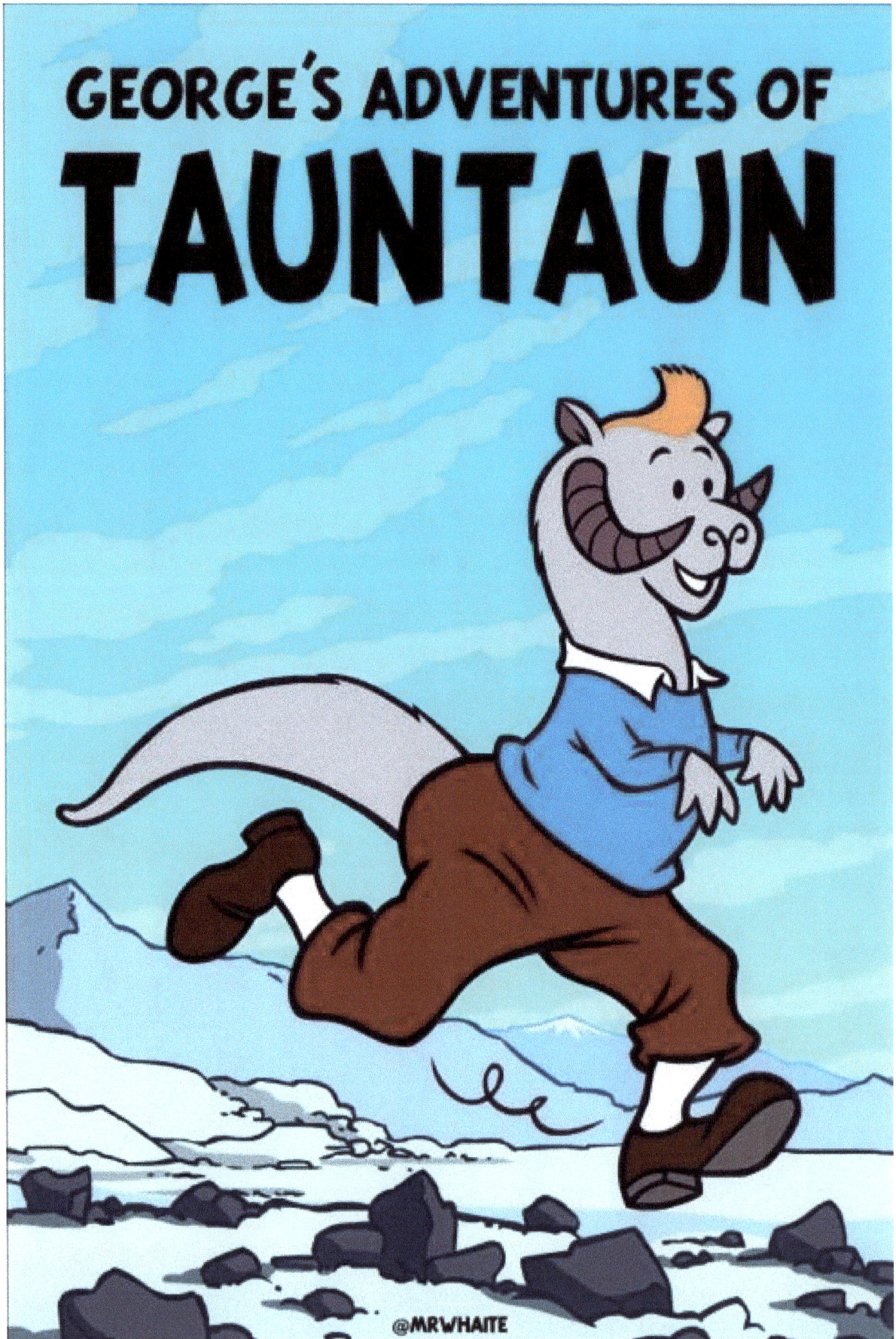

GEORGE'S ADVENTURES OF
TAUNTAUN

@MRWHAITE

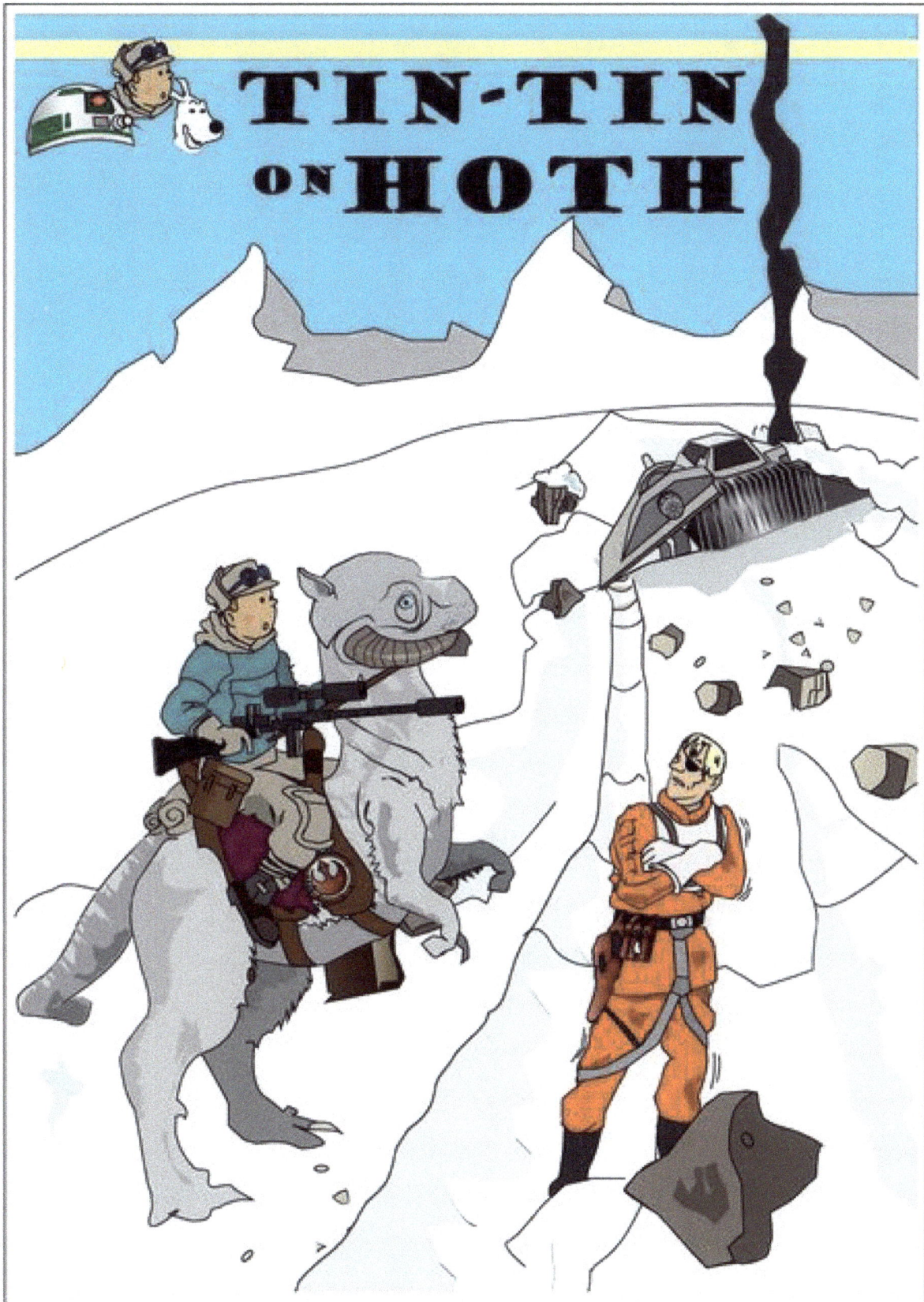

Skut the pilot from *Flight 714* and earlier, *The Red Sea Sharks,* joins Tintin on Hoth as the downed pilot of a *Star Wars* rebel fighter.

LA GUERRE DES ÉTOILES - ÉPISODE 4

LUKE
AU PAYS DU
Lord Noir

WWW.AVVD.NET

"Luke in the Land of the Black Lord." Tintin is top right beneath the floral design opposite the Death Star floral. The Ottoman frame is from *Land of Black Gold*.

Dutch "Tintin." Curiously, everyone sports red shoes and Castafiore has become burlesque cabaret. Even Snowy is drunk.

Is the woman in the car Fanny Vlamynck? See **Plate 323.**

Taravana is a diving decompression disease suffered by early native Polynesians diving for pearls or sponges. This is perhaps set in Tahiti (note Tintin's Polynesian shirt). The mushroom may suggest an alternative cause of taravana? Tintin's Hawaiian shirt matches the *Shooting Star* mushroom.

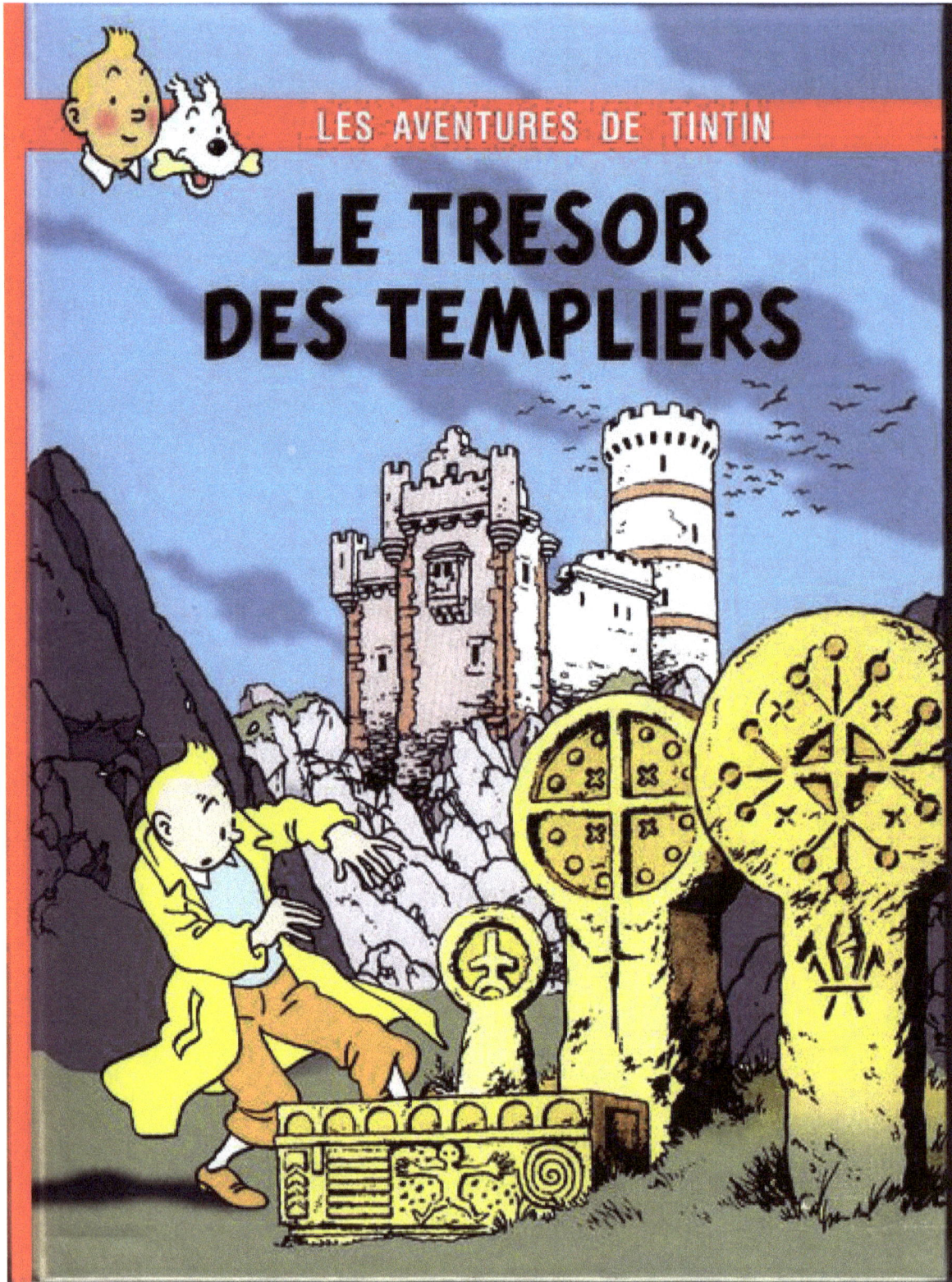

The Templars previous and above, long associated with mysterious adventures, druids and mystical Freemasonry.

LES AVENTURES DE TINTIN

TRAFIC SOUS HAUTE TENSION

WOODMAN

"High Voltage Traffic." Jolyon Wagg (Seraphin Lampion) is electrocuted while erecting Christmas lights.

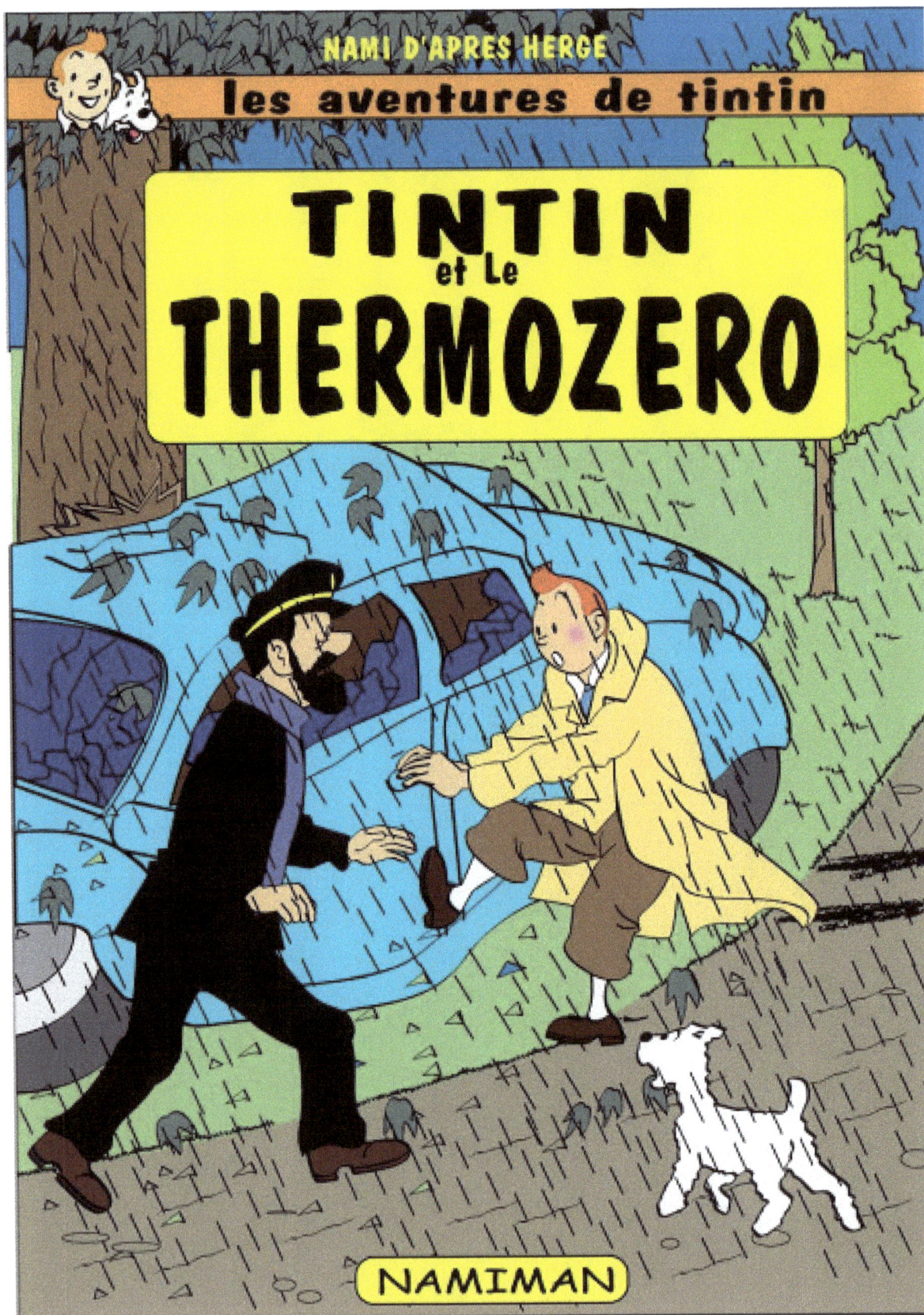

NAMI D'APRÈS HERGÉ

les aventures de tintin

TINTIN
et le
THERMOZERO

NAMIMAN

A naive rendering of *Thermozero* by Nami.

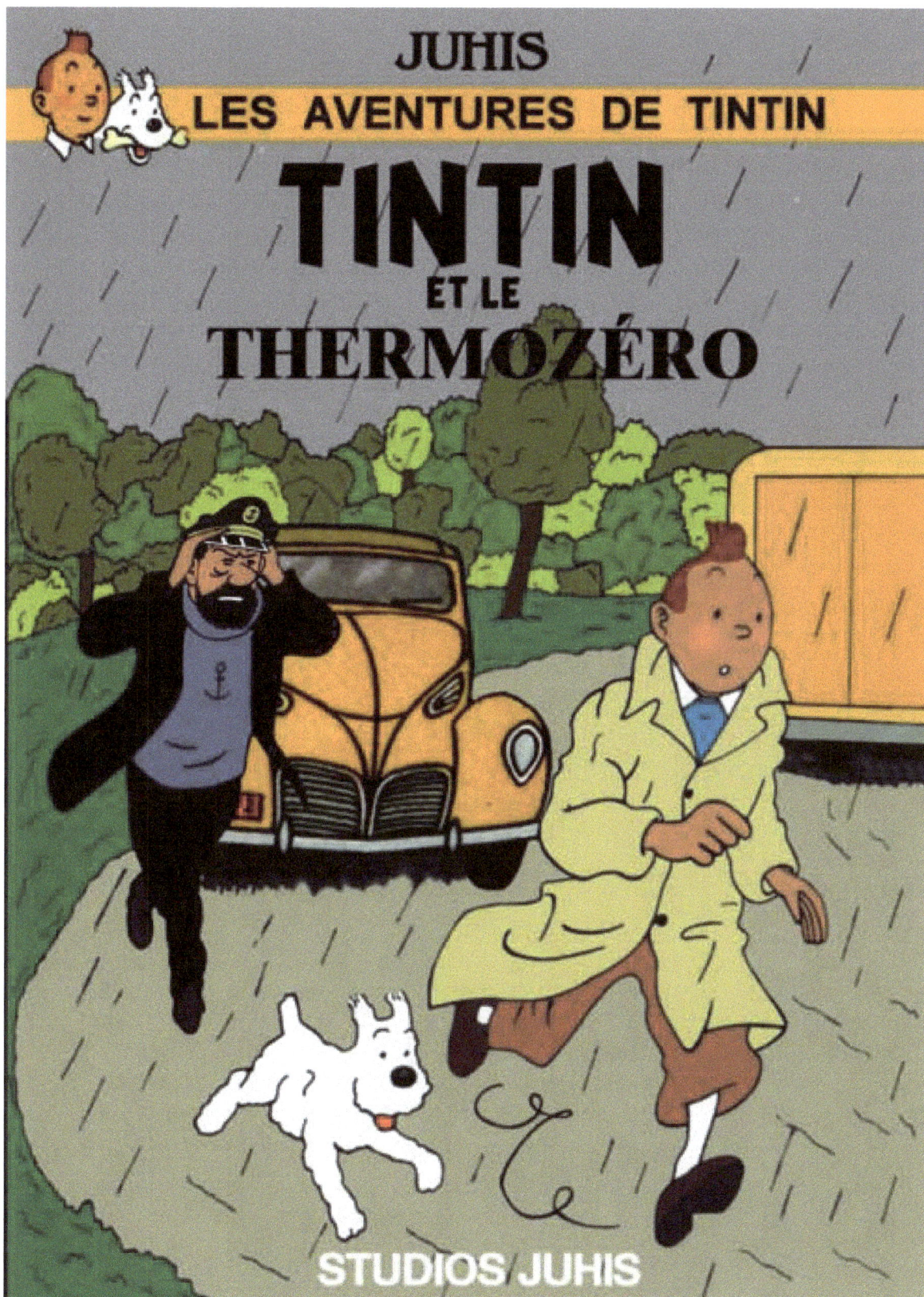

A better version by Juhis.

(A suivre)

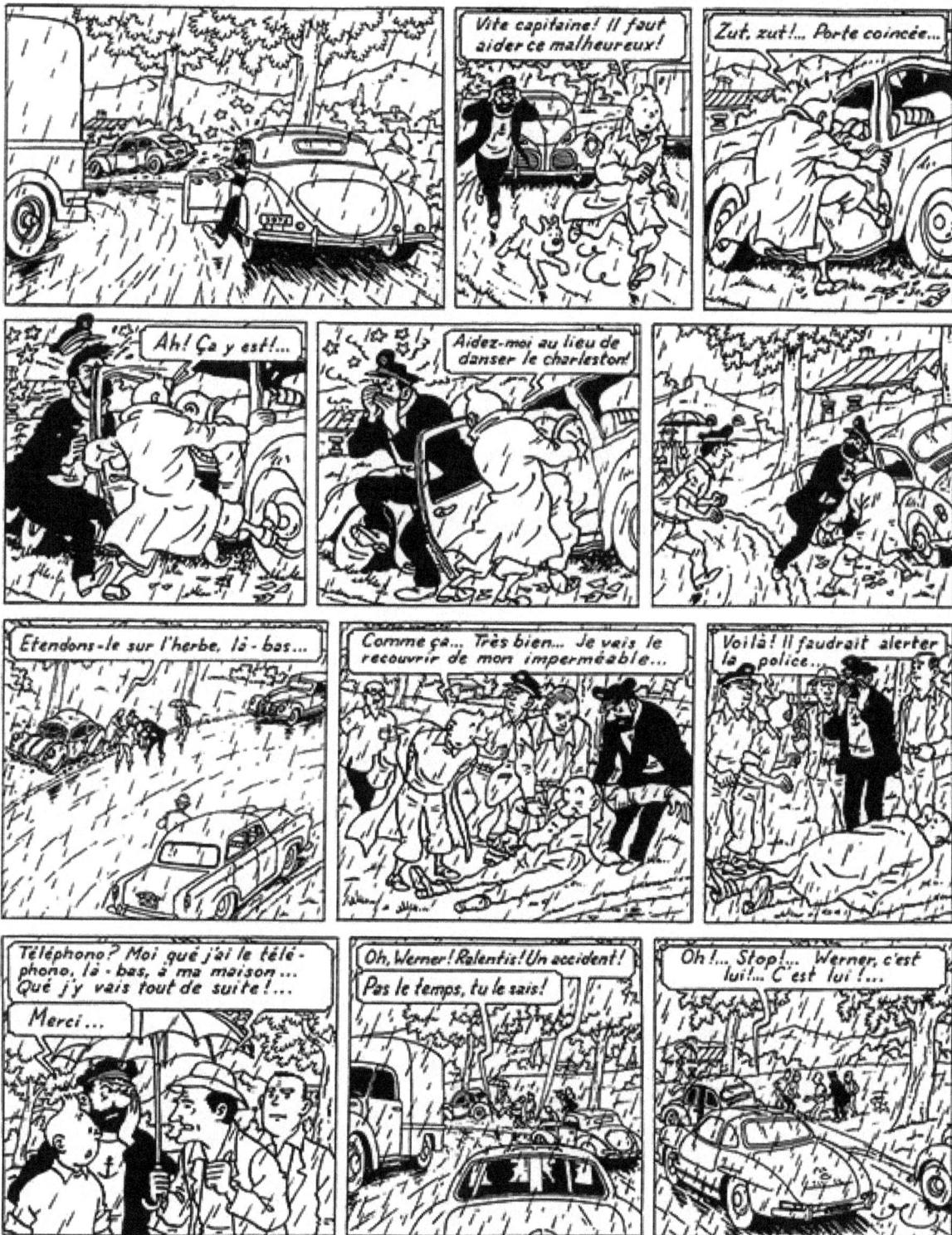

A Hergé *Thermozero* sketch panel edited and inked much later by Rodier ("29/150"). The latter made several judicious changes on his copies of the original pencils much like a comic book editor and Hergé himself would.

TINTIN ET LE THERMOZÉRO

Rodier's inked "29/150" Hergé sketch panel coloured by Henri Blum.

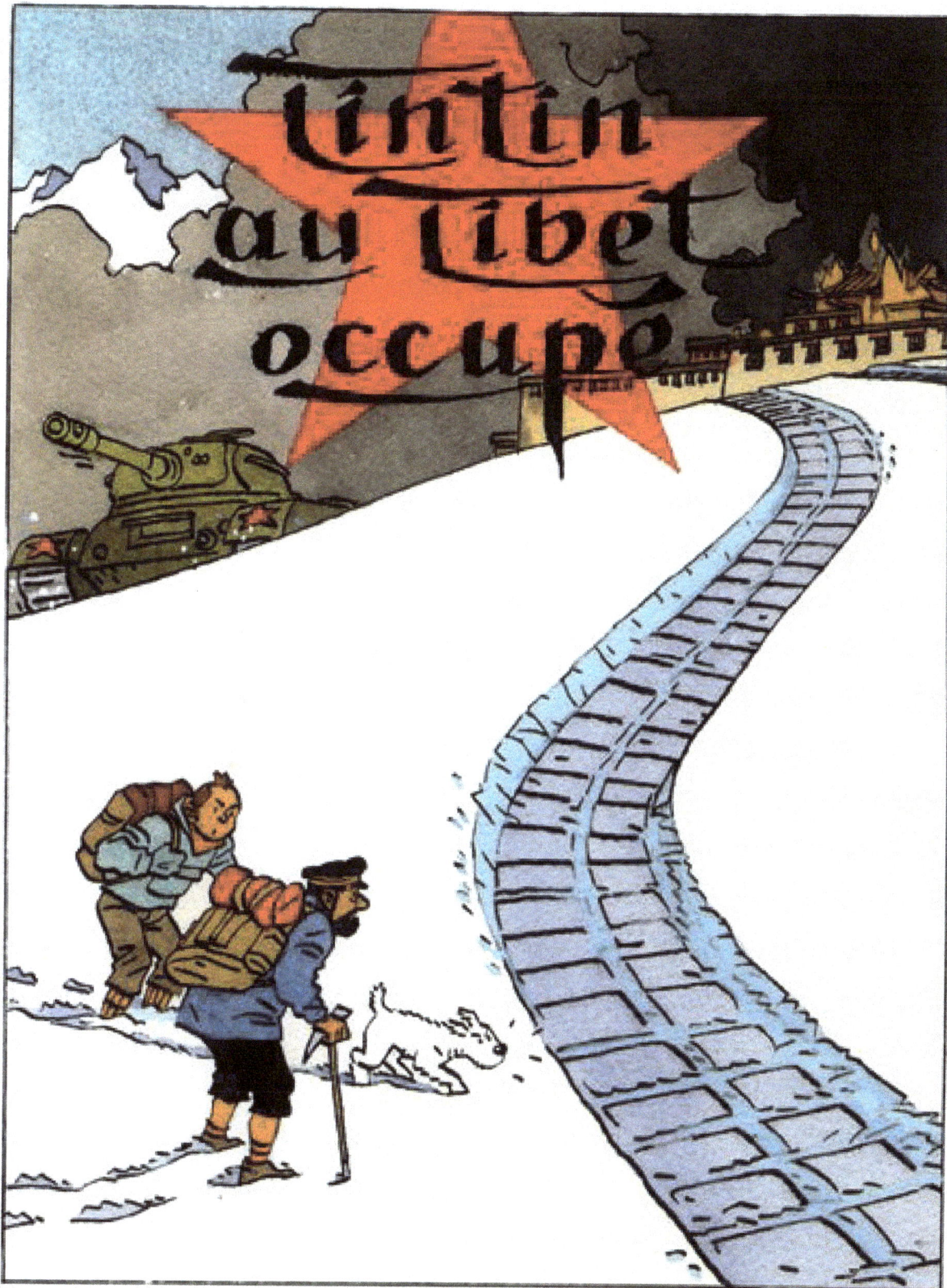

The Chinese abominably invade Tibet replacing the yeti tracks. It's enough to make you sneeze "CHANG!"

Composed as the *Tibet* cover are exemplars and later *ligne claire* cousins from American comics Hergé copied to learn to draw and from which he developed first *Totor* and then *Tintin*. The characters are examining a ligne claire in the snow rather than yeti tracks as they climb the cartoon mountain. For a run down on who is who, see p.197, especially the theory *Jiggs* (top) is Tintin's creative 'father' and *Becassine* next to him (with white hat) is his creative 'mother.'

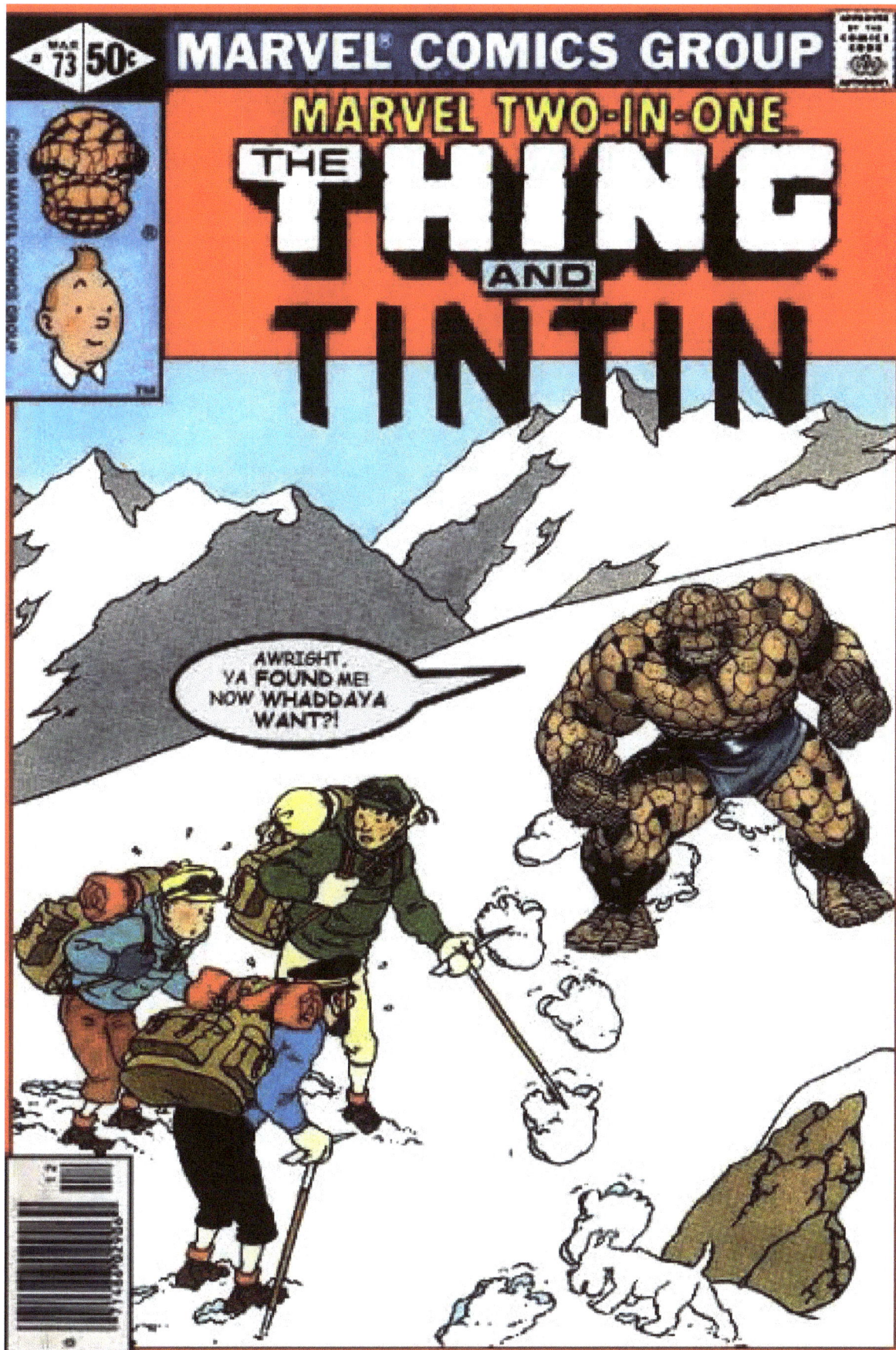

Ben Grimm's footprints may easily be those of the yeti. One of the Marvel *Two-in-One* comics in which The Thing featured alongside other comic characters.

Plate 308

"In the Footsteps of Tintin."

"Tintin (made) with Tipp-Ex." A visual pun on the use of Tipp-ex (Twink) that has eradicated the yeti footprints. Tintin says, "Yes, you'd think we'd know how to do (draw) snow in comics."

"Return to Tibet."

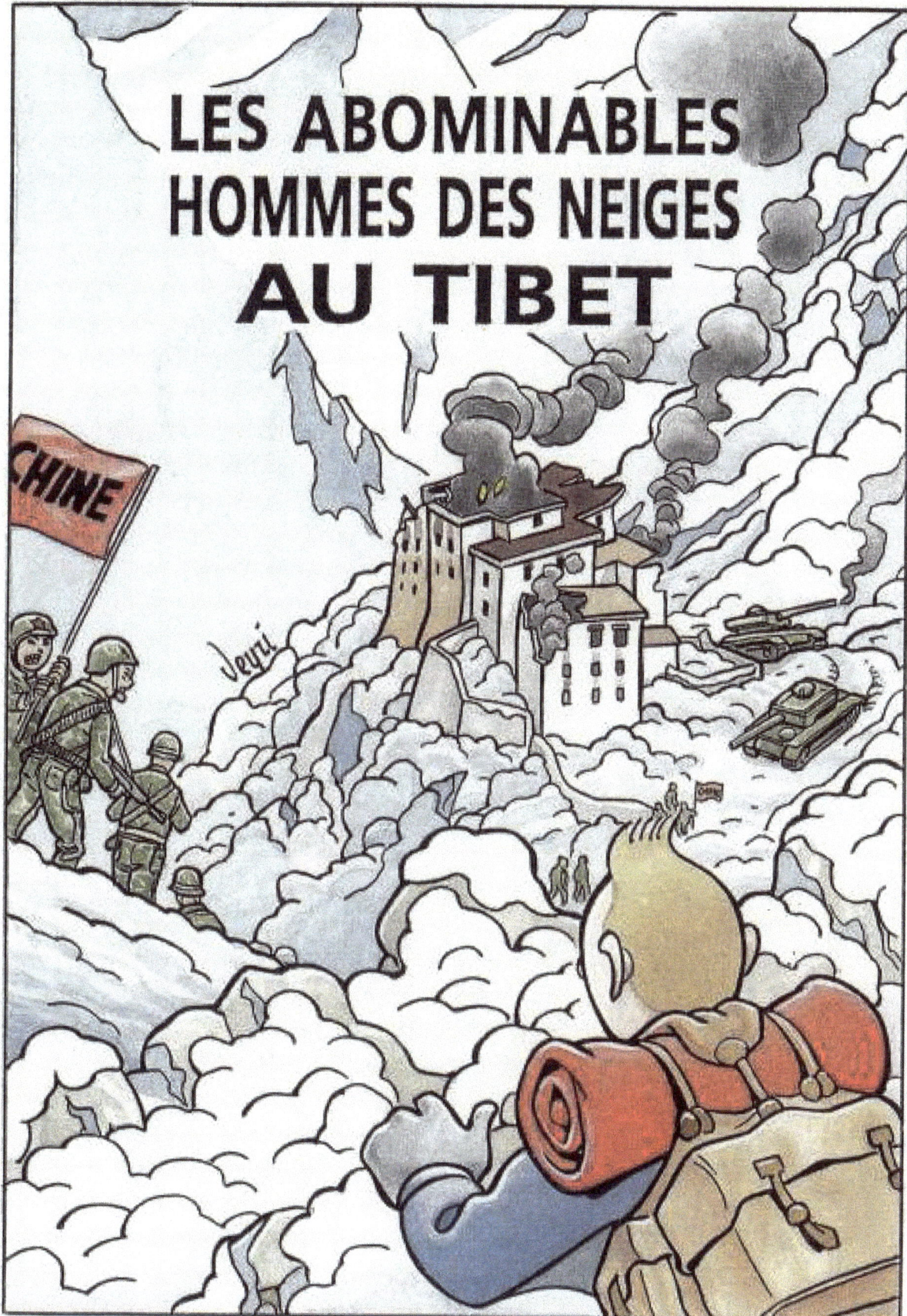

"The Abominable Snowmen in Tibet." Another variation on the Chinese invasion of Tibet. See **Plate 305.**

Tintin is Marty McFly in *Back to the Future* consulting his watch.

LES AVENTURES DE TINTIN

LE MYSTÈRE DU TEMPS

Les gardiens du temps

casterman

"The Mysteries of Time." Tintin as an enrolled Hitler Youth (scout) with Abbot Wallez (?) behind him and Tintin as Himmler investigating one of his paranormal obsessions.

"It's Raining Sunshine" or "The Time it was Sunny" a variation on "Le Temple du Soleil" (*Prisoners of the Sun*). The woman in this pastiche is also depicted in **Plate 56** (also the cover of Vol.1) and is probably Herge's widow Fanny Vlamynck. She may also be the woman in **Plate 296.** The old man on the bridge holds a red flower. Is this Hergé courting Fanny later in life with his wife behind him on the footpath?

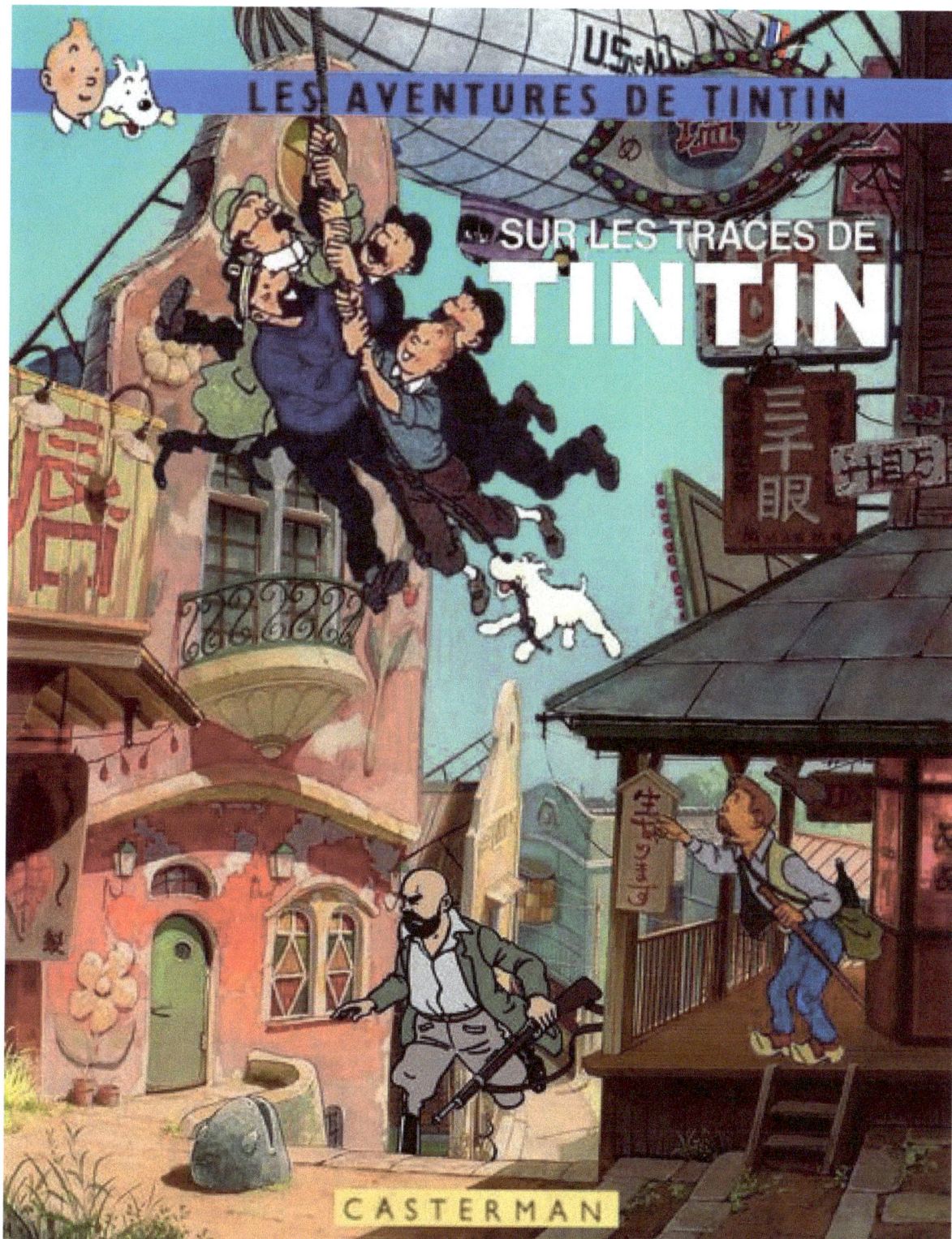

"On the Tracks of Tintin." A US blimp surveys a Chinatown movie lot. An older Tintin in Dutch clogs sports a moustache and fuller set of hair while Dr. Müller hunts down his prey.

TINTIN

Volume 283: Still Looking For That Goddamn Unicorn

http://phoscomicart.tumblr.com

Tintin goes 21st century Manga style with a Pokemon Snowy, a steam pump Haddock (and Fanny Vlamynck?).

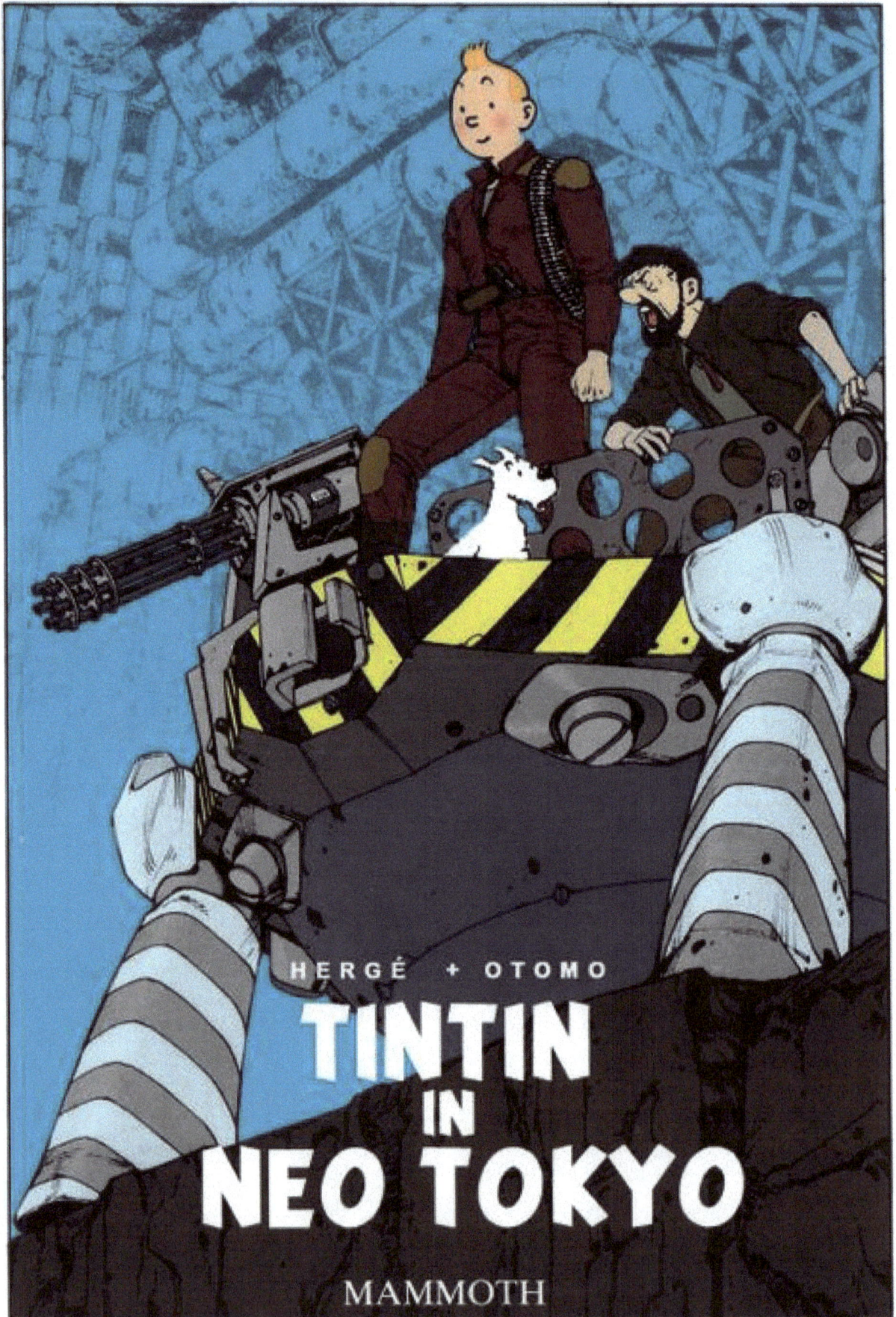

HERGÉ + OTOMO

TINTIN IN NEO TOKYO

MAMMOTH

"Transgender Calculus." Calculus' name in French is Tournesol (Sunflower). Dr Krollspell, one of the *Flight 714* hijackers, later switches sides, which is a pun here on switching genders. He 'courts' (?) two Calculus clones while Haddock and Tintin look on suspiciously.

Tintin is confused in Asia, as are Calculus and Haddock (who cannot comprehend the name of his whiskey). The publisher is Adesso.

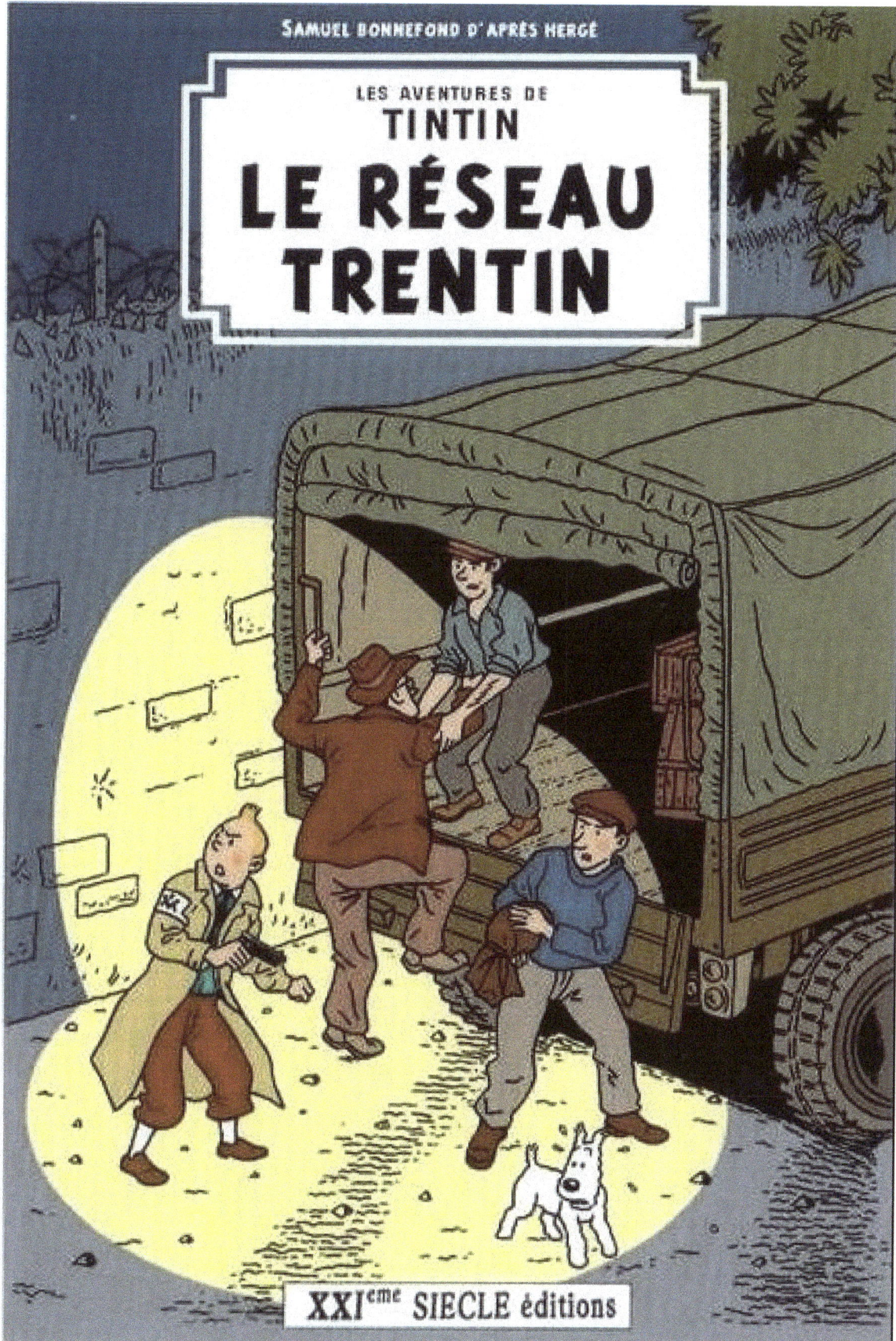

SAMUEL BONNEFOND D'APRÈS HERGÉ

LES AVENTURES DE
TINTIN
LE RÉSEAU
TRENTIN

XXIème SIECLE éditions

"The Trentino Network." Tintin as a French WWII Resistance fighter. Hergé was accused of collaboration but was rescued by well-known Resistance hero Leblanc who published him.

Plate 322

BOB DE MOOR

OVNI 666 POUR VANUATU

BOOGALOO

"UFO 666 for Vanuatu." A variant of **Plate 109**, Vol. 1 related to *Flight 714*.

Vlucht is Dutch for "flight." A visual play on *Flight 714*.

Belgian Tintin of 1954 (*Explorers on the Moon*) meets British Dr Who of 1963, the Tardis.

"The Witch /Sorceress' Beast." A pastiche by Yves Rodier, see interview on p. 207.

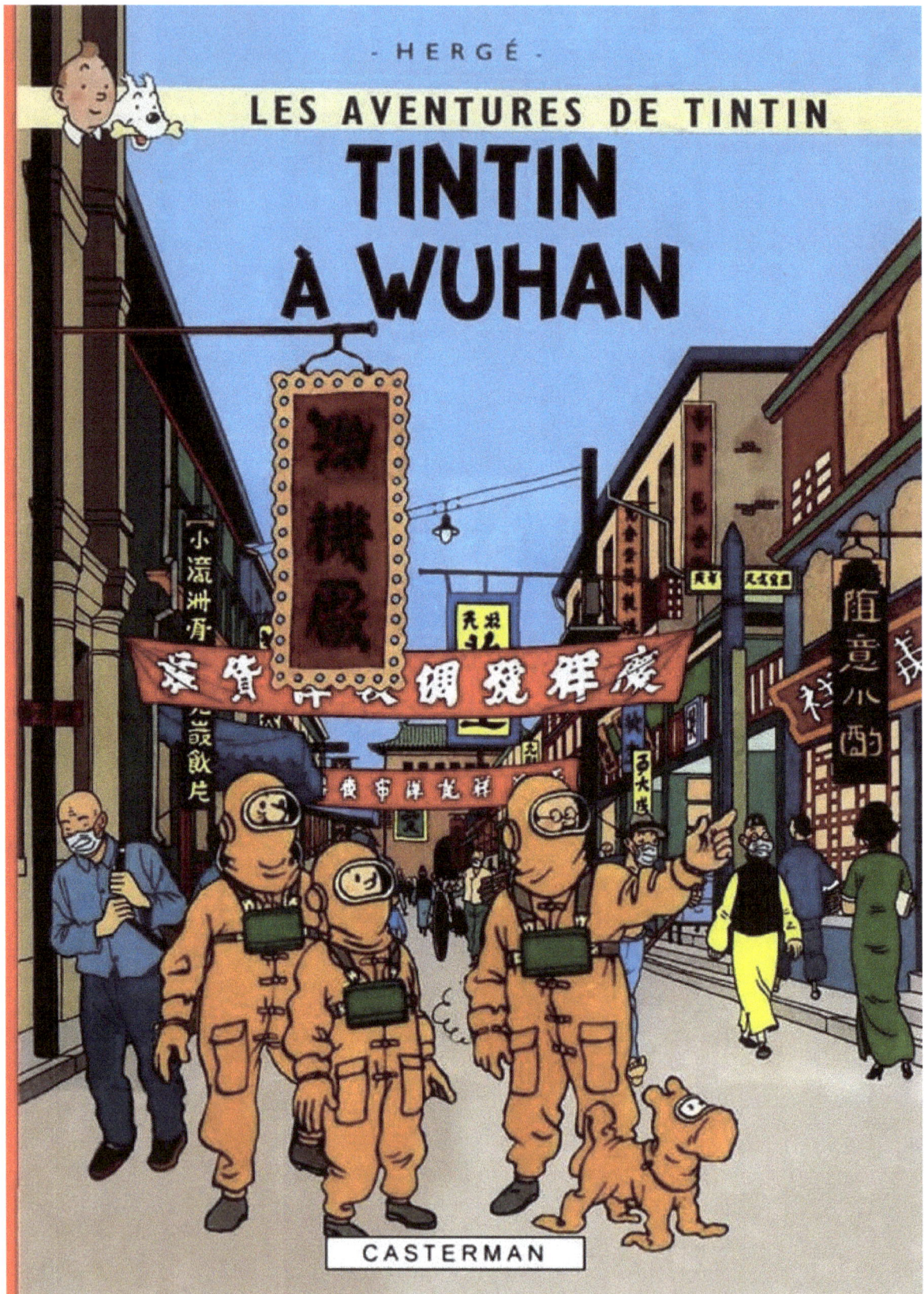

Early in 2020 as this book was being written, the coronavirus *Covid-19* began to spread across the globe and many nations closed their borders (NZ 14 March 2020). Ground zero was Wuhan, China. This pastiche appeared early in 2020 when the virus was still not a declared pandemic but was accelerating.

X-Ray irradiation of *The Red Sea Sharks*. Are the raft barrels atomic waste?

THE ADVENTURES OF DINDIN

SHOCK OF COKE

swapmeetdave.com

A variation but with "DinDin.""Coke en Stock" ("Coke in Stock") is the original French title for "The Red Sea Sharks."

"The Yellow Shadow of the Mark." A reference to Jacobs' *The Yellow 'M'*. See **Plate 152** and Section **8.A.**

The Great Dane from *Castafiore Affair* and the elephant from *Cigars of the Pharaoh*.

8. Selected Jacobs Annuals

Several of these Jacobs covers and titles are adopted and used as polyploid Tintin pastiches. Such as:

A see Plate 152
B Plate 20
I Plate 72
N Plate 262.

A

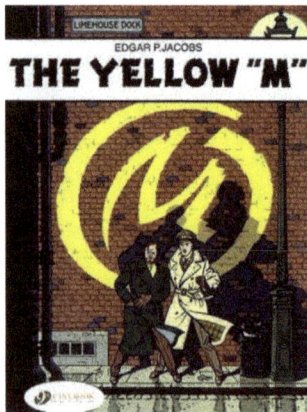

B

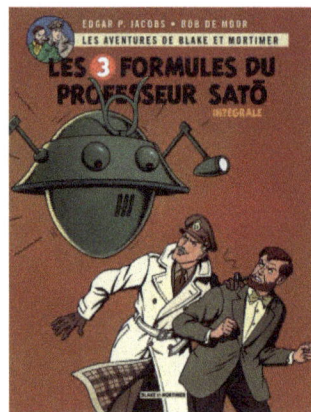

C

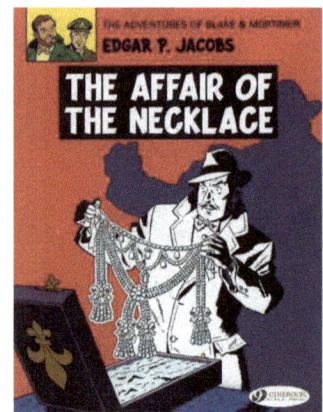

D

E

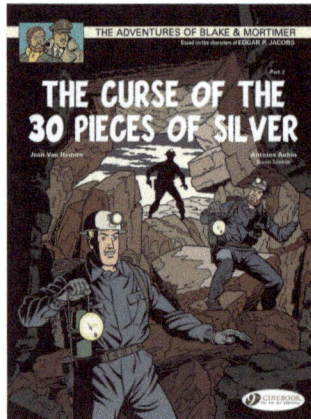

F

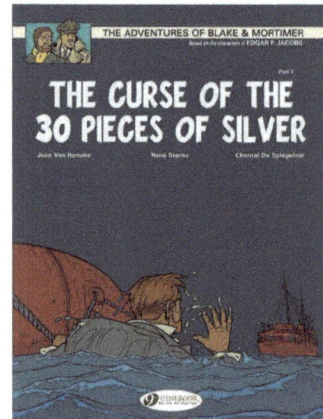

G

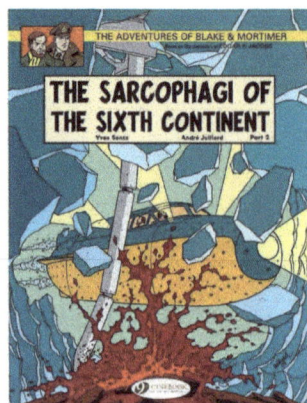

H

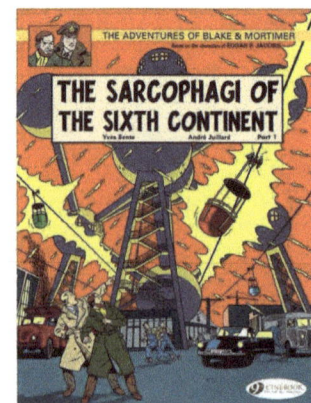

I

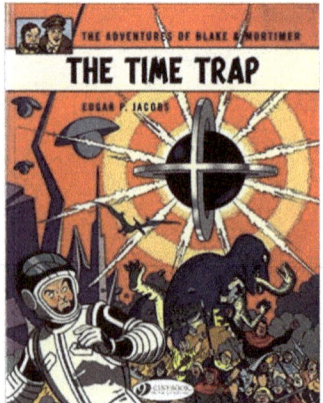

J

K

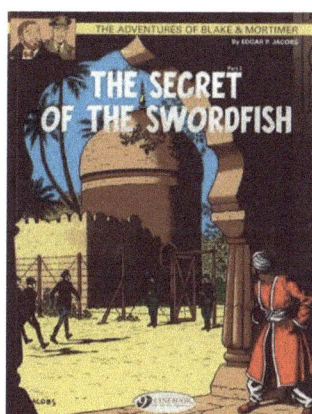

L

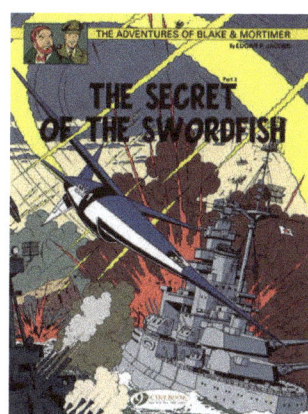

M

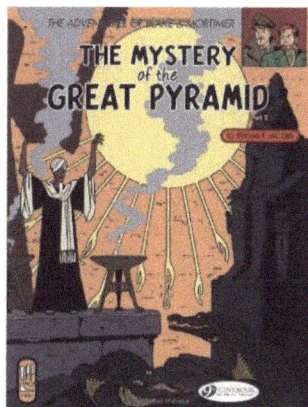

N

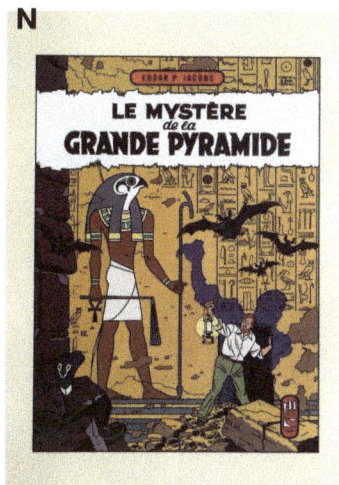

O

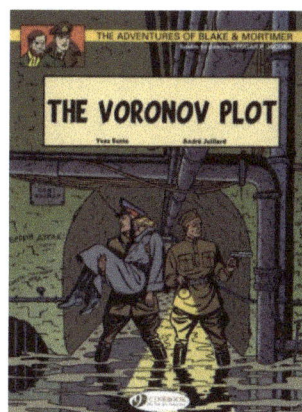

P

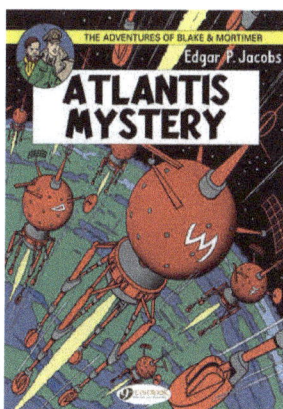

Q

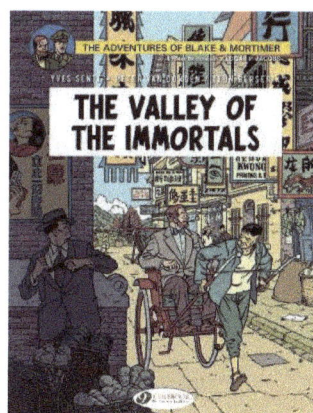

R

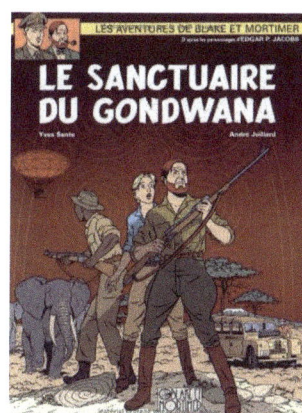

9. Index of the 222 Covers, Vol. 2.   Plate

Credits/acknowledgements: cover art and back cover layout and text, the author; back cover, details from plates 170, 234; frontispiece p. 178 © Moulinsart; Maiden New Zealand images p. 179-180, the author; images p. 181 and plates 112-333, the respective pastiche artists; the annuals and *Tintin* magazine 1949-50, p. 182 © Moulinsart; photo *Museé Hergé* unknown; Bob de Moor sketches p. 185-186, © Moulinsart; cartoon p. 198, Dubus, Belgium and *Sydney Morning Herald*; books p. 188, 190 © Moulinsart; cartoon p. 190, Nami; sketches p. 192-195, Bob de Moor or Hergé, © Moulinsart; cartoon 1976, p. 196 and 198 © *King Features*; books p. 197 *Hatchette*; *Lucky Luke* p. 200 © Morris; *Oumpah* p. 201 and Asterix as Beric p. 202, © Uderzo and Goscinny in *Valiant* magazine; cartoon p. 202, Nami; *Iznogoud* p. 203 © Jean Tabary/*Cinebook*; *Bluecoats* p. 203 *Spirou* magazine and Raoul Cauvin and Louis Salvérius/Willy Lambil; images p. 204, 205 Bob de Moor/Studios Hergé? (© Moulinsart); images p. 206, Bob de Moor and Yves Rodier (and p. 207); artwork p. 211, 212 Charles Burns; *Breaking Free* p. 213 *Attack* publications; sketches 214-216 Flinflins family; p. 218 Hergé artwork sold at auction, image in public sphere; book cover p. 220 the author; cartoon p. 221 the author; Jacobs' covers p. 449, 450 © Edgar P. Jacobs/*Cinebook*.